D0768718

HOMELAND OR HOLY LAND?

Yonatan Ratosh, 1909–1981

HOMELAND
OR
HOLY LAND?

The "Canaanite" Critique of Israel

JAMES S. DIAMOND

INDIANA UNIVERSITY PRESS
BLOOMINGTON / INDIANAPOLIS

Manufactured in the United States of America

Library of Congress Cataloging-in-Publication Data

Diamond, James S.
Homeland or Holy Land?

Bibliography: p.
Includes index.
1. Canaanites (Movement) 2. Ratosh, Yonathan, 1909–1981—Political
and social views. 3. Israel—Politics and government. 4. Jews—Israel—
Identity.
I. Title.
DS149.D563 1986   305.8'924'05694   85-45671
ISBN 0-253-13823-X

1   2   3   4   5   90   89   88   87   86

To Judy

I would like to clarify what is at stake here by two metaphors. Can Israel and its function be compared with a rocket . . . from which parts detach themselves and shoot out into the unknown toward the promised landscape . . . ? The astronauts are, to be sure, directed from the earth but they must themselves see to it that they advance; they struggle for air, have to come to terms with their gravity and weightlessness, and are at first able to use only such knowledge as they have learned on earth. But must not a gradual independence in the progress of their mission be reached? Will not a part of the rocket detach itself completely and lead its own life? Is Israel, created by the forces of the Jewish people and out of the native soil of the Diaspora, not destined to detach itself once and for all from that native soil and to lead a new life as a new nation with a new rootedness in the events of recent years? Or are we rather dealing—to counter the technological metaphor with a biological and historical one—with a whole whose parts are all mutually dependent on each other, where the isolation of one part, no matter how crucial a link or constituent, must lead to the destruction of the whole?

—Gershom Scholem,
"Israel and the Diaspora"

CONTENTS

PREFACE

> In the history of every people there are
> episodes which were uncomprehended by
> their contemporaries. Because the principal
> individuals involved were unusual or what
> they did was unusual (or both together were
> unusual), they left a deep impression. But
> since they proved to be beyond the grasp of
> their generation, they were distorted in its
> consciousness and called by colloquialisms
> which overlooked their essentials and seized
> upon their superficialities. Only after a
> generation, and sometimes after several
> generations, were these matters understood
> properly and only then was their history
> written and reconstructed in the annals of
> the nation.[1]

The author of this passage is referring to Nili, the Jewish espionage effort on behalf of Britain that took place in Palestine during the last years of the rule of the Ottoman Turks. He could just as well have been describing the "Canaanites," who appeared on the Palestinian scene some thirty years later, in those fateful last years of the British Mandate when the travail of a Jewish state and/or an Israeli nation had begun.

Why write about the "Canaanites" and "Canaanism"? Why try to comprehend them? For what purpose? For whose benefit? I was asked these questions many times in the course of preparing this volume. More often than not they were asked not so much out of simple curiosity but with incredulity and scorn. And more often than not there was a direct relationship between the questioners' generation and the intensity of their reaction. Those whose perception and understanding of "Canaanism" were formed a generation or two ago were the most negative.

The book that follows is an attempt to comprehend the "Canaanite" or "Young Hebrews" phenomenon from the vantage point of my own generation, three or four decades after the ideology originated and flourished. My substantive answers to the above questions are set forth in chapter 1. This preface is the place to record some more personal responses.

There is a straight line between this book and my earlier one on Barukh Kurzweil.[2] As I explained in the preface to it, the central question or set of questions that has fueled my humanistic study is the large one of the meaning of secularism and modernity, especially for Jewish culture. In this regard I realized at a certain point that the thought and work of Yonatan Ratosh would be no less interesting and instructive to ponder than the literary and cultural criticism of Barukh Kurzweil.

Here I must ask the reader to stop and take note of a basic presupposition upon which the present work rests. Those who know anything at all about either Kurzweil or "Canaanism" are likely to remember that it was Kurzweil's essay on the "Canaanites" that drew wide attention to them.[3] In spite of the fact that their numbers were small, he was the first one to take their ideas seriously. It is only fair to say, however, that over the years Kurzweil's assessment has not met with unanimous acceptance. There have been some who have felt, and even today feel, that just as Kurzweil misunderstood Zionism, so did he misunderstand the "Canaanites" and the challenges he saw them representing. This is not the place to debate this matter. Suffice it to say that the book that follows is predicated on the assumption that the "Canaanite" thesis is indeed deserving of careful consideration and analysis. I would, therefore, advise any reader who has already dismissed either Kurzweil's estimation of "Canaanism" or this premise about it to close this book now and go for a walk or a bicycle ride, or better, if he or she is so inclined, to use the time to study Torah.

On the surface no two individuals would seem to be more dissimilar than Barukh Kurzweil and Yonatan Ratosh. Their thinking would appear to go in completely opposite directions. Yet a closer look will show that there are some striking affinities between them. Chronologically, both are contemporaries, members of the same generation. Both are products of the same cultural situation and experience, or more precisely, as Dan Miron puts it, of the same cultural crisis.[4] Both are paragons of men who were profoundly alienated from the society around them but who nevertheless were able to function within it—and to function with arresting creativity.

But there is more to it than this. Both are, to draw on Isaiah Berlin's celebrated dichotomy, "hedgehogs" and not "foxes."[5] Both know one big thing: that the present, the Jewish present, is fundamentally disconnected from the past, the religious past. The work of both is dominated by and proceeds, however differently, from this same *idée fixe*. In response to it, both monistically set up large and impressive conceptual systems.

Now by temperament and conviction I am, for better or worse, a "fox." Problems and issues, expecially those that arise in humanistic studies, are for me *ipso facto* susceptible to multiple solutions and interpretations. Absolutes make me viscerally uneasy, for by purporting to subordinate everything to what Berlin describes as "a single, universal, organizing principle,"[6] they oversimplify multivalent reality. That is why I find congenial those modes of thought which acknowledge their relativity, time-boundedness, and contextuality and which indicate a sense of and an appreciation for the dialectical.

Perhaps that is why I like to study "hedgehogs." They challenge me. I suppose I am both fascinated by and suspicious of their monism, even as I may be a bit envious of it. Perhaps I need to satisfy myself that I am able to come to terms with it. That may well be one reason I studied Barukh Kurzweil and why I now choose to look at Yonatan Ratosh. The ideational systems they each construct not only present tempting targets to "foxes" like me; more important, when these systems are held up to the light and analyzed, when it is shown what such system-building does and does not achieve, a valuable body of insight accrues.

That is one subjective motivation for this book. There is also another, one no less existential. This one derives from my ongoing encounter with the reality and the claims of Zionism and the State of Israel. I have little doubt that the appearance of this new/old state upon the stage of human history in this century is a "root event" and fraught with significance. What I have been struggling with for over twenty years now, along with countless others, is to discover what this significance might be, what the existence and availability of a Jewish state and/or an Israeli nation might mean with respect to the totality of Jewish history and the aspirations of Jewish religion.

I feel increasingly pressed to come up with at least the rudiments of working answers, and this for three reasons. First: because the entire phenomenon of a modern, ostensibly secular nation-state that calls itself Jewish is so confusing. Every time I read or contemplate Zionist history I am struck by a conflict and contradiction that I (and many others) see lying at its heart, and every time I am in Israel I am overwhelmed by the social and political tensions that I see engendered by this contradiction as they assert themselves and are lived out daily. The conflict is between the religious and the secular. It is a matter not only of life content but of world view. Complex as it is, Israel may very well be reduced to a tale of two cities—Jerusalem and Tel Aviv—and it has not yet determined which of the two *opposing* world views each city embodies, and which of the *contradictory* values that flow from these world views determine its essence and its purpose.

Second, I need answers because Israel does not exist in a vacuum. It presumes or arrogates to itself the responsibility to speak and act for all Jews wherever they are. What Israel says and does, therefore, especially with respect to the consequences of the ideological contradiction that lies at its heart, implicates me. If I am to be implicated in these dilemmas, then I ought at least to be able to explicate them.

The third reason should be evident from what I have noted above about hedgehogs and foxes. Whatever else one can say about it, Zionism is a monism. It presents the Jew and the world with the intimidating Absolute that the only legitimate and guaranteed modality of Jewish existence is as a citizen within the borders of its nation-state. Especially after the destruction of European Jewry, Israel is the quintessential hedgehog. It claims to know "one big thing." While I cannot presume to gainsay this claim or to prejudge history before it will have happened, my understanding of Jewish history and my own self-understanding as a Jew, however imperfect, impel me to a foxlike perspective. To understand the Jewish experience on this planet is to know "many things"— many times, many places, many modalities, and many possibilities. This is why Zionism and what it has produced is a necessary and important subject for inquiry.

The reader will by now have realized that I am not neutral or apathetic about the issues that this book raises. I do not see how anyone could pretend to be. Yet in this writing I have been conscious of and tried to maintain a balance between the two elements that comprise all responsible humanistic endeavor—rigor and passion. These two have never been very compatible, and the struggle by each to gain the upper hand will be quite apparent on the pages that follow. Where rigor clearly won out, the victory is celebrated in a footnote. Where passion prevailed and argument escalated into polemic, the polemic has been dispatched to the "Excursus." But such relegation has at times proven impossible, particularly in parts of chapters 4 and 5.

This leads me to note the two different kinds of readers for whom this book is intended. One group are those who are specialists in the several fields with which the "Canaanite" phenomenon intersects. The other are the many informed nonacademic individuals who are variously curious, concerned, or perplexed about what is unfolding within Israel. The former group, who justifiably expect more rigor than passion in a scholarly study, will undoubtedly be more interested in my footnotes than in my arguments. For the latter group the reverse may be true. In any case, I do not wish to imply either that these two readerships I have in mind are mutually exclusive or, conversely, that this book stands or falls on the speculative argument of the appendix.

Finally, two technical observations: Unless otherwise indicated, every translation into English of material that was originally in Hebrew is my own. This is also true of most titles of books and articles that exist only in Hebrew and that are referred to in the notes. A transliteration of the original Hebrew title can be found in the bibliography, so that a reader who so desires can track down any Hebrew original.

ACKNOWLEDGMENTS

The research for this study was done during 1983–84, most of it in Israel. I should like to express my thanks to Aharon Amir, Boaz Evron, Professor Uzi Ornan, and Hayim Guri for the assistance they provided me in getting to source material and in understanding the many dimensions of the history and implications of the "Hebrew" idea as Ratosh developed it. My debt to them will be quite evident in this book, as will the value of the personal interviews they so generously granted me.

A number of colleagues read all or portions of the manuscript at various stages in its preparation and made available to me their time, learning, and insight: Professors Solon Beinfeld and Gerald Izenberg of Washington University, Professor Stephen Katz of Indiana University, Max Ticktin of the George Washington University, Dr. Lawrence Davidson, Dr. Sheldon Gellar, and Dr. Michel Nutkiewicz. They each gave me excellent counsel, more, I am afraid, than I took.

Several other individuals helped me in various important and meaningful ways. Each of them, therefore, will understand my thanks: Professor Henry Berger of Washington University, Dafnit Mizrahi of the National and University Library at the Hebrew University in Jerusalem, Simha Berkowitz, Laya Firestone-Seghi, and Rabbi Devorah Jacobson. I particularly wish to thank Professor Avner Cohen, now of Tel Aviv University, who in some seminal conversations helped plant in my mind the first seeds of this work.

My appreciation also goes to the B'nai B'rith Hillel Foundations for awarding me a sabbatical leave in order to pursue the research and writing of this volume, and to Indiana University Press for the sensitive and considerate manner in which they have handled all aspects of its publication.

My deepest gratitude is to my wife, Judy. Dedicating this book to her is only a small expression of what I owe to her.

HOMELAND OR HOLY LAND?

I

THE IMPORTANCE OF "CANAANISM"

I

A double subject animates this book: a man and a movement. The man is Yonatan Ratosh (1909–81), who developed a clearly defined anti-Zionist ideology that sought, but failed, to become a movement—"Canaanism." The movement is Zionism, which in 1948 crystallized itself in the State of Israel but, notwithstanding this fact, has supported an ideology, or more correctly ideologies, that are variously diffuse, contradictory, and confusing.

The perspective from which I would invite the reader to see this twofold subject is that suggested by the figure-ground relationship. For in understanding the ideological struggle against Zionism of Yonatan Ratosh and some of his followers, we will not only learn about "Canaanism" and thus encounter one of the most interesting episodes in Israel's social and cultural history; we will also gain some insight into the larger story in which the episode occurred.

In its broadest sense this study can be seen as the beginning of an inquiry into the intrinsic nature of Zionism and into some of the most perplexing and vexing questions that remain about it: What is the meaning of the State of Israel within the context of Jewish history?[1] What is the meaning of the State of Israel within the context of the Middle East? What makes Israel a Jewish state? What is the nature of Israeli identity? What is the relationship between Zionism and Judaism? Between Jewish peoplehood, Jewish nationalism, and Jewish religion? Between Israel and world Jewry?

These are huge and overwhelming questions. After nearly four decades of Jewish national sovereignty and nearly a century after the inception of "the true Copernican revolution which modern Zionism announced" in Jewish history,[2] there is much less clarity about these matters than we would expect. Or than we need. To be sure, some would argue that the very size and depth of these questions render them

1

unanswerable within a human framework and, therefore, irrelevant, meaningless, or even absurd. But the historian of ideas cannot take refuge in such a perspective. In the face of what is ultimately at stake in the Arab-Israeli conflict and in the Middle East as a whole, I think the more clarity we possess about these ultimate questions, the better off we are.

This is hardly to imply that the goal of this book is to furnish or even suggest specific answers. No—the presumption upon which this inquiry rests is somewhat more modest. This is an inquiry, a probe. The methodology here is akin to one of the ways in which a religion, for example, can profitably be studied: instead of examining its theological doctrines frontally, you study those ideas or forms of belief which that particular religion has defined as heretical, and then you know something about the intrinsic nature of that religion.[3] The ideology that Yonatan Ratosh developed in the late thirties and early forties, and which reached the peak of its influence in Palestine of the late Mandate and in Israel of the fifties, must be seen, functionally, as a heresy. The "Canaanites" were perceived, attacked, vilified, and rejected in the same terms as were, in earlier times in Jewish history, the Sadducees, the Karaites, or the Frankists.[4] But whereas those ideologies were deemed heretical with respect to the Jewish consensus that prevailed at their respective times about God and Torah, "Canaanism" is a heresy with respect to what the Jewish consensus in this century holds about "Israel" or the corporate entity known as the Jewish people.[5]

II

What was "Canaanism?" Why is it worth studying today? Briefly put, it was an attempt to construe Jewish settlement in Palestine and in the resultant State of Israel in purely nativistic terms. For the "Canaanites" what had begun to develop in western Palestine at the end of the nineteenth century and continued in Israel in the twentieth century was related not to the historical continuity of the Jewish people but rather to the formation of a new nation. The analogy is, in part, to North America or Australia: Americans, Canadians, and Australians may be descended from English, French, and other peoples, but they are members of new nations, indigenous to and defined largely, if not exclusively, by their respective territorial borders.

In the same way, the polity that exists within the new State of Israel, although it is mostly descended from Jews, is not Jewish, because "Jewish" is understood to be strictly a religious definition. The Jewish people, to the extent that there is such an entity, is not a nation but, according to "Canaanite" ideology, a faith community, a religio-ethnic group, international and extraterritorial in nature. Nor is the polity that is evolving in

Israel Zionist, because Zionism is understood to be an attempt by Diaspora Jews to solve their problems as Diaspora Jews. From the "Canaanite" perspective Zionism and Judaism are coterminous, two sides of the same coin.

The nativist, territorialist element is key here. The polity that now inhabits Israel is a part not of the Jewish people but of a new, autochthonic, *Hebrew* nation. Whereas the Jews are understood to have begun their existence as a religion in the Babylonian Exile that followed the destruction of the First Temple in 586 B.C.E., "Canaanism"'s Hebrews are the original prebiblical inhabitants of western Palestine and, in fact, of an entire region of the Middle East. The Hebrews (*'Ivriyim*) are understood as a generic nation that comprised various groups: Amorites, Moabites, Ammonites, Phoenicians, Israelites (from whom the Jews are descended), and others. All were united by a common Semitic language, Hebrew, of which they spoke different dialects, and all were united by common cultural, religious, and commercial ties. If the values they shared later came to be described by Judaism as polytheistic, that is problematical only from the religious perspective. The modern State of Israel represents the recrudescence of this geopolitical situation, with all the possibilities attendant thereto: not a Jewish state based on and perpetuating an anachronistic Jewish religious exclusivism, but a secular entity that will seek to embrace and gradually assimilate all other non-Arab minorities indigenous to the region—Maronite Christians, Copts, Kurds, Cherkassians, Druse, Alawites, Shiites, and Armenians—into a new Hebrew confederation.[6]

The architect of this vision, though by no means its originator, was not a political scientist but, as can be expected, a poet. Yonatan Ratosh is without question one of the major figures in modern Hebrew poetry. In 1944, after an intense intellectual and emotional odyssey that I shall relate in a subsequent chapter, Ratosh organized the "Committee for the Formation of Hebrew Youth" (*Hava'ad legibbush hano'ar ha'ivri*) and announced to the *Yishuv:*

> The cells have been functioning for a while now, and the work is difficult and arduous. It is a labor of proselytization. . . . For not in one day can a person liberate his mind from the stupor of the ancient Jewish poison which eats away at him day after day, year after year. . . . For this land cannot be both Hebrew and Jewish and this *Yishuv* cannot be both a nation and a limb of the eternal Jewish dispersion. And if we shall not drive out all this sick culture of immigrants and pilgrims, then this leprosy will forever infect us, and no longer will a Hebrew homeland come to pass here or a Hebrew nation expand from here, but a Holy Land consumed by corruption and hypocrisy, one more transient center of eternal Judaism.[7]

With such rhetoric began the "Young Hebrews" (*'Ivriyim hatse'irim*) movement, known more colloquially as the "Canaanite" movement.[8]

Over the next ten years or so the "Young Hebrews" under Ratosh were visibly active, with all the trappings of a mass movement. There was an insignia—the Canaanite letter *alef* (to signify a radical new beginning)— which Ratosh designed into a flag. From 1949 until 1953, twenty-three issues of a "Canaanite" periodical, *Alef,* were published. But the number of members, those who actively and officially followed Ratosh, were always minuscule, a dozen or two at the most. In speaking of the "Canaanites" today we ought to refer to them not as a movement but as a coterie.

After 1953, when *Alef* ceased publication, the "Canaanites" ceased functioning in any collective way. From time to time Ratosh would publish new manifesto-like statements and thus seek to revivify his vision, especially at times of national trauma such as the 1967 and 1973 wars, when the fundamental ideas upon which the State of Israel rests were called into question. By the time Ratosh died in 1981, those who were old enough remembered the "Canaanites" as nothing more than an eccentric historical curiosity, and those who were younger had never heard of them at all. Some would say that as a movement "Canaanism" did not die: it was moribund from the outset. Indeed, the rhetoric of the passage from "The Opening Discourse" (*Mas'a hapetihah*) cited above, as well as its timing, tells us quite clearly what problems the new movement and its leader would face. The shrill anti-Jewish tone could hardly have been expected to win friends and influence Jewish people in large numbers, especially at a time when the *Yishuv* had begun to learn the details of the death camps in Europe.[9] Yet that was Ratosh's way: there would be no compromise with any niceties, verbal or ideological.[10]

It is, therefore, quite easy to dismiss "Canaanism" and to adduce a myriad of reasons, both intrinsic and extrinsic, to explain why it failed, why it had to fail.[11] That is not the object of this study. What must be explained and discussed is why, in spite of its failure as a movement, and in spite of its inadequacy and perhaps even its absurdity as an ideology, the network of ideas and concerns that Yonatan Ratosh developed has continued over the years to preoccupy no small number of Israeli intellectuals and artists. What is there about "Canaanism" that allows Gershon Shaked, one of Israel's leading literary critics, to note that "even though the group that carried aloft the banner of Canaanism was very small, its ideological influence extended far beyond its actual political power"?[12] Or another to write of "Canaanite" ideas: "Views which a generation ago were held by a few are now accepted in wide circles. Slogans which once were privately uttered have been transformed today into actual demands"?[13] Perhaps the real question is: what is there about Israel and its society that enabled "Canaanism" to maintain such a disproportionate influence?

To ascribe this influence to the fact that "Canaanism" offered a trenchant critique of Zionism is true, but it does not say enough. There have been several critiques of Zionism both from inside Jewish life (e.g., Neterei Karta) and from outside it (e.g., Arab nationalism).[14] "Canaanism" is the first critique that arose from *within* Zionism. "The Canaanites, whose ideas were . . . formulated prior to statehood, provided the only ideological alternative to the . . . established conceptions of the Jewish state, . . . [although] they obtained no following among Jews or Arabs."[15]

Unlike Neterei Karta, for example, which sought to sever the nexus between Jewish religion and secular Zionism, "Canaanism" linked the two together and cut the tie to both of them.[16] In doing this, "despite their numerical insignificance, the 'Canaanites' have inflicted a wound on the system and in a very sensitive spot. . . ."[17] The sensitive spot, the "Achilles heel" of Zionism, is its undefinedness, its inherent lack of clarity about whether its goals are secular or religious. Its vulnerability results from the possibility that such unclarity is not accidental or casual but wholly premeditated, the fruit of Zionism's historical willingness—some would say necessity—to play fast and loose with powerful religious ideas and symbols, and to appropriate them in a wholly secular context. One aim of this study, then, is to examine both this point of vulnerability and the wound that Ratosh's ideas signify.

The following chapters are essentially conceived as an interpretation of the "Canaanite" idea. If they do to some extent constitute a history of the "Canaanite" movement, it is a revisionist history. I approach Ratosh not as a poet but as a thinker. (This is, in fact, how he saw himself.) My contention is that when apprehended in this way, Ratosh can be construed as the first post-Zionist thinker to emerge from Israeli intellectual life. Ratosh saw the tension between the secular and the religious at the heart of the Zionist enterprise, and the unclarity and the contradictions arising from it, and he sought to resolve them. He may not have been convincing or successful in this, but my thesis is that in doing so he performed a very valuable kind of deconstruction of Zionism. When its romantic archaism is stripped away, Ratosh's thought lays bare a whole range of issues, problems, and possibilities that are very much alive at this time, both in Israel and in the Diaspora. "Canaanism" is conventionally understood as a literary-cultural phenomenon, especially outside Israel. As we shall see, it was much more a political and social ideology.

I do not believe that "Canaanism" stands or falls on the power, the accuracy, or the credibility of the mythological substructure on which it rests or of its specific historiography. It is not clear to me that these were anything other than intellectual window-dressing. After all, pagan antiquity and its mythology were, their idolatrous nature aside, profoundly religious; Ratosh was profoundly secular. And so, when these mythological and historiographical elements fall away from Ratosh's thought, what is left is a coherent and substantial ideology of secular nativism. "Ca-

naanism" can thus be transmuted into something that would still stand
not as a plausible alternative but as a critique and a challenge, perhaps
even a corrective, to current and conventional thinking about what the
telos of Israel might be.

What follows is a look at "Canaanism" from the viewpoint of today's
generation. The heady early years of the Israeli experience, when "Canaanism" was at the height of its influence, are now at best a distant
memory. The passions that surrounded Ratosh and his ideas have cooled
somewhat. Many of the dissenting political groups of the seventies that
Schnall discusses have already passed from the Israeli political scene. Yet
"Canaanism," which never evolved into a political force, still exists as an
implicit challenge, an "enzyme" of ferment within the Israeli body politic.[18]

At this time, when Zionism is under attack not only from without but
from within (viz., the phenomenon of *yeridah*), when there is a widespread feeling, both within Israel and outside it, that the Zionist idea, in
all its manifestations, is not working and has played itself out, an examination of the first Israeli post-Zionist ideology is not irrelevant.

III

Much has been written over the years about the "Canaanite" movement. It is mentioned in most books about Israeli society, politics, and
culture, but always *en passant*. More problematically, it is almost always
presented in a negative, often a lurid, light. This book is the first full
discussion of it in English. As an attempt to take the ideas "Canaanism"
developed seriously, this work builds on the only two such treatments
that exist at all, both in Hebrew.

The first is the seminal essay of Barukh Kurzweil written in 1952.[19] In
it Kurzweil demonstrated that "Canaanism" was by no means a trivial or
superficial phenomenon or a random weed that had perversely sprung
up in the Zionist garden. Rather, by tracing its intellectual roots back to
the *Haskalah* (Enlightenment) and to the later development of the
Haskalah in Berditchevsky, Brenner, and Tschernihovsky, Kurzweil
showed that "Canaanism" was a logical outcome of this anti-religious
strain in Jewish national thought. This influential essay, as much as or
more than anything "Canaanism" did as a movement, served to put the
ideology on Israel's intellectual map. Indeed, more than thirty years
after its publication, Kurzweil's work, with the acuteness of analysis and
diagnosis it displays, still stands as a paradigm of intellectual history and
cultural criticism. Kurzweil, however, overestimated the potential of
"Canaanism" as an organized movement; as we shall see, it went nowhere
in this respect, surviving only as a latent force. Further, Kurzweil saw
"Canaanism" essentially as a cultural problem. He could not foresee that

it would come to manifest itself in a related and more subtle form, as an existential problem, a problem of Israeli identity.[20]

The second work that needs mention here is the more recent study of "Canaanism" by Ya'akov Shavit.[21] Shavit has approached the subject strictly from his purview as a historian. He has continued the process that Kurzweil initiated of identifying the sources and influences that underlie "Canaanism." This has enabled him to locate the roots of Ratosh's political thought in maximalist revisionism. Specifically, Shavit has shown why it is really Adolphe Gourevitch (alias Edya Gur or A. G. Horon) who is the true originator of the "Hebrew" thesis. Because it amply presents the historical and historiographical bases of Gourevitch's thought and explains how they operate in that of Ratosh, Shavit's book is as indispensable as Kurzweil's essay in establishing that the "Canaanite" ideology rests on an ideational foundation that is not altogether spurious, even as it is debatable.

Now, while I must acknowledge my indebtedness to Shavit, as some of the following chapters will indicate, I must also point out in what ways this present work differs from and goes beyond him. First is the matter of scope. Shavit is a historian and his main interest is influences. While this approach is certainly valuable, it does not give the whole story. As Boaz Evron, an important figure in the articulation of the "Canaanite" perspective, observes, "Canaanism" is more than the product of certain intellectual influences; it is first and foremost a social phenomenon, the product of a specific society facing specific cultural tensions.[22] I do not believe Shavit has paid sufficient attention to the social dimension of the subject.

This is because of the context in which he considers "Canaanism"— and here we have a second point of difference between us. Shavit wishes to develop "Canaanism" not so much as the result of secular Zionism in general, as Kurzweil would have it, but as the culmination of a specific current or *topos* that, in his view, always existed within Zionism: the idea of the "new Jew" as "Hebrew." Shavit's thesis is that "Canaanism" represents a co-opting of this "Hebraism" and a translation of it into anti-Zionism. In and of itself, this notion is probably correct.[23] But it is not quite to the point. In what precise way is "Canaanism" anti-Zionist? How did it become so and why? These are the questions that I want to discuss, and they necessitate examining "Canaanism" in the broader context of Zionism as a whole. After all, it was against Zionism in general and its inconsistencies and paradoxes in particular, that Ratosh struggled, and it is as an attempt to square the vicious circle of these contradictions that his thought and work must be seen. The trajectory that needs to be described and analyzed, therefore, is not "from Hebrew to Canaanite," as Shavit would have it, but from Jew to "Canaanite" or, more precisely, from Zionist to "Canaanite."

In taking this approach I am much more sanguine than Shavit about the constructive ideological possibilities that "Canaanism" opens up. This may be more than a matter of context; it may also be a function of a third difference between us—perspective. Shavit writes from within Israel and, as becomes progressively clear in his book, from within the general presuppositions of Zionism. I write from outside both, and this position inevitably leads to a different viewpoint. The person inside the forest cannot see it for the trees, although he will know its details well; the person outside sees the whole forest, albeit from afar. Although both are observing the same forest, they will yet see different things or, at least, give different accounts of what they see. The experience of de Tocqueville encourages me that a certain acuity does accrue to the perspective of the outsider, notwithtanding my realization that well after this book is concluded the Israeli experience will still await, even as it deserves, its de Tocqueville.

IV

That is the hermeneutic upon which this study is founded. It leads to the following itinerary: After laying out the ambiguities of Zionism as they have been variously described and understood (chapter 2), we can consider how Ratosh sought to resolve them. This will necessitate first looking at the salient details of his life, most of them probably unknown outside Israel (chapter 3). Only then will we be in a position to present the specifics of Ratosh's critique of Zionism and to see how it works (chapter 4). At that point we can examine some ways in which the "Canaanite" ideology has been and is being appropriated and the implications it holds for some of Israel's and the Israelis' most persistent problems: the nature of Israeli identity, the relationship of the secular and the religious elements in Israeli society and institutions, the posture toward non-Jews in the Israeli polity and foreign policy, and the nature of the relationship between Israel and world Jewry (chapter 5). In a separate discussion we shall try to determine what a nativist ideology might mean with respect to Israeli culture, with particular emphasis on the Israeli artistic imagination and its expression in Hebrew literature (chapter 6). This progression will allow us to speculate in the final chapter on some of the implications of the "Canaanite" critique of Zionism and Israel.

II

THE CONTRADICTIONS OF ZIONISM

PARADOX, DIALECTIC, OR SYNCRETISM?

I

It is difficult to write about Zionism. The problems are manifold and overwhelming. For one thing, there is the problem of sources: they are so extensive, uncatalogued, and multilingual that, were mastery of them deemed to be a prerequisite for discussing Zionism, many pens and tongues besides mine would be rendered immobile.[1] Then there is the problem of bias. "When there are competing internal groups in a national liberation movement, it is the internal winner who defines the situation. . . . To a large extent [the winner's] attitudes have found their way into the literature on Zionism and Israel, both popular and scholarly. . . ."[2]

Consider, for example, the way Zangwill and the territorialist movement have been summarily dismissed "without any serious historical treatment as befits any one of the currents of Zionism. Even today the consensus regarding Herzl's achievements over Zangwill's is so great that whoever disagrees with it is looked upon with hostility and is considered a provocateur and a desecrator of something sacred."[3]

If all this is true of historical scholarship within the wide orbit of Zionism, what about the problem of interpretation when dealing with the even larger questions of Jewish history and historiography? The winners win out, but when we look at Zionism in its relationship to the totality of Jewish history, who can say yet who the "winner" is? This question has particular cogency with respect to this study, and I shall return to it implicitly in both the final chapter and the "Excursus."

In the face of this situation, Vital's suggestion seems rational and workable: the scholar who wishes to treat of Zionism must "try to by-pass the consensus and open up the subject anew . . ." while recognizing and controlling his own biases and thus "avoiding a historical revisionism for its own sake."[4]

But when the subject is Zionism this is much easier said than done. After the problems of sources and bias have been addressed, if not solved, there is a further difficulty: what are we looking at? "The [Zionist] movement was, among other things, an arena where followers of many opposing viewpoints contested with each other. . . . The Zionist *idea,* from the sociological or ideological standpoint, is a subject broader, vaguer, and denser than the Zionist *movement.* . . ."[5] Zionism, as the Israeli writer Amos Oz has felicitously put it, is a family name. Labor Zionism, Revisionism, religious Zionism, cultural Zionism, political Zionism, humanistic Zionism, territorialist Zionism—what are we dealing with? A contemporary Israeli critic has observed that

> [It is] not the denunciation of Zionism in the U.N. as a "form of racism" [that] has exposed the confusion of our relationship to it, for its objectives have not been visible to us for a long time now; it does not influence our thought patterns nor does it determine our lifestyle. Many contending factions have hitched their wagons to it; [there is] the Zionism of Israel versus the Zionism of the Diaspora, the Zionism of the secularists versus the Zionism of the religious, the Zionism of the right versus the Zionism of the left.[6]

II

It is instructive to see how some of the major attempts to present Zionism holistically have reacted to this confusion. Arthur Hertzberg begins the introduction to his still-important anthology thus: "Zionism exists, and it has had important consequences, but historical theory does not know what to do with it. . . . [H]ow to place it in some larger frame is still the most debated, and least solved, problem of Jewish historiography."[7] Hertzberg identifies "the meaning and validity of [the Jewish] past" as a central issue in trying to make sense of Zionism, and he goes on to point out a tension he sees between what he terms the revolutionary "messianic" and the conservative "defensive" currents in the Zionist idea.

Now this binary or bipolar nature of Zionism that Hertzberg observes has been noticed by others too, though not always in the same terms. This has led them to posit a paradox inherent in Zionism, again with varying definitions of what the paradox is.[8] Harold Fisch, for example, begins his interpretation thus:

> The history of Zionism in the nineteenth century is rooted in paradox. On the one hand Zionism was an expression of the desire to abolish the difference sensed by the Jews between themselves and other men. . . . On the other hand the Zionist movement constituted the ultimate affirmation

of this difference, a courageous, even defiant gesture against all attempts at assimilation by Jews in exile.[9]

This enables him to advance his thesis that "Zionism is only partially the offspring of the Enlightenment. It is also, and indeed primarily, the offspring of the Jewish myth."[10]

Then there is Shlomo Avineri, who opens his intellectual history of Zionism in almost identical words but goes in a very different direction:

> At the root of Zionism lies a paradox. On the one hand, there is no doubt about the depth and intensity of the bond between the Jewish people and the land of Israel. . . . Had this tie between them been severed and had the Jews not regarded the Land of Israel as the land of both their past and their future, then Judaism would have become a mere religious community, and would have lost its ethnic and national elements. On the other hand, the fact remains that for all of its emotional, cultural and religious intensity, this link with Palestine did not change the praxis of Jewish life in the Diaspora: Jews might pray three times a day for the deliverance that would transform the world and transport them to Jerusalem, but they did not emigrate there.[11]

Such a formulation sets up Avineri's contention that the wellsprings of Zionism are essentially secular, for it was only when the religious basis for Jewish identity broke down in the face of the Emancipation at the end of the nineteenth century that the Jewish praxis with respect to Palestine began to change. In the face of the Emancipation there was available no corresponding secular collective framework. "The forces unleashed by the French Revolution were not only those of liberalism and secularization but of nationalism as well."[12] And so Zionism developed.

In truth, if we hold these various formulations up to the light and compare them, the differences between them will be seen to be more apparent than real. All of them, really, are caught, in different ways, on the horns of the same dilemma. All are struggling, in different ways, with the same core question:

> . . . the question that in my view is the most important and the most difficult of all the relevant questions, the question that is a kind of junction at which a fundamental clarification, partly methodological and partly conceptual, must take place: where does that distinctive phenomenon called Zionism fit in [to the context] of Jewish history?[13]

III

As long as we have him on the line, so to speak, we ought to hear Vital's own answer:

> It is clear, I think, that the answer to this question will depend in part on the old question of the nature of Jewish history and its structure. Specifically, the answer will depend on [whether] . . . the respondent . . . sees in Jewish history a true continuity—vertically in time and horizontally in space—[or whether he] holds that there is, or can be, at least in principle, absolute discontinuity.[14]

In other words, any attempt to come to terms with the Zionist idea will, regardless of where it starts out from, eventually engage and reduce itself to the root question: is Zionism a continuity of or a revolt against Jewish history? It is on this basis that Gershom Scholem can say:

> Zionism has never really known itself completely—whether it is a movement of continuation and continuity, or a movement of rebellion. From the very beginning of its realization, Zionism has contained two utterly contradictory trends. . . . It is clear that the conflict between continuity and rebellion is a determining factor in the destiny of Zionism.[15]

The question in itself, as Vital has noted, is not new;[16] what is new is the implication that all the paradoxes that can be stated about Zionism can be subsumed within this central quandary. Hertzberg's antinomy of "messianic" and "defensive" elements fits in here. So does the debate, familiar in Zionist thought, about whether the essence of Zionism is to "normalize" the Jewish people and make them like all other peoples or to enable them to realize their distinctive, inescapable national destiny (which is what Fisch argues for). And so, too, does the question of whether Zionism is secular or religious in nature (which is what Avineri is, in effect, addressing). The central paradox thus absorbs all others and stands at the crossroads of which Vital speaks, halting all who would go down the road to understanding Zionism and requiring them to produce their intellectual and ideological credentials.

There are a number of strategies to get around the paradox. One is to contend that it really does not exist, that Zionism is either wholly a revolt or wholly a continuity. One of the more familiar expressions of the former tendency is Haim Hazaz's "The Sermon" ("*Haderashah*").[17] Here the speaker Yudka basically reiterates what many Zionist ideologues have said: that whatever else it may or may not have done, Zionism has turned the Jews from being the objects of history into its subjects.[18] Vital, apparently, agrees. Of the three watershed events in Jewish history of the last century—the mass migration from east to west, the destruction of the Jews of Europe, and the founding of a Jewish state—it is only the latter one that he finds to have instituted a fundamental change or break in how Jews live. For, although Israel "has not brought about the miracle of a complete transformation in the situation of the Jews," still

> Israel serves as an alternative to the traditional Jewish situation. It presents painful questions to both Orthodox and freethinkers alike. It forces the Jews, at least some of them, to deal with new problems involving

political obligations and responsibilities in a Jewish context. For these reasons and others . . . it is hard to see Israel as an integral part or stage in the Jewish historical continuity. . . .[19]

Hertzberg would concur. What Vital is describing corroborates his conclusion that

> At the cutting edge of Zionism, in its most revolutionary expression, the essential dialogue is now between the Jew and the nations of the earth [and not between the Jews and God]. What marks modern Zionism as a fresh beginning in Jewish history is that its ultimate values derive from the general milieu. The Messiah is now identified with the dream of an age of individual liberty, national freedom, and economic and social justice. . . . This is the true Copernican revolution which modern Zionism announced—and it patently represents a fundamental change not merely in the concept of the means to the Redemption but in end values.[20]

Opposing this view are those who maintain that in spite of outward differences in form and in political structure, Zionism is essentially a continuity of the terms of Jewish existence. Unlike America, for example, which began *de novo,* the Zionist enterprise is a return to the past; since it takes place on the site of the ancestral homeland, it is a true continuity.[21] Those who operate from out of a religious Zionist perspective have a comparatively easy task in making this argument, especially when they fuse the concept of *mitsvah* (commandment) in traditional Judaism with the Zionist praxis of which Avineri likes to speak.[22]

Another approach is to affirm the paradox but to hold that it is not necessarily problematical. The "continuity/rebellion" issue may be an intellectual construct that is, in reality, a trap, a trick question. After all, "the idea of history carries within it both continuity and transformation, and there are those who emphasize 'change' and others who focus on 'continuity.' "[23] Zionism's relationship to the past is, therefore, *dialectical.* The notions of "continuity" and "change" are not mutually exclusive, as we might have assumed, but rather mutually inclusive. It is a question not of "either/or" but of "both/and." Zionism properly understood is rooted not so much in a paradox as in a dialectic. Eliezer Schweid describes Zionism as

> a paradoxical effort to perpetuate Judaism outside the circle of its traditional values, in the form of a dialectical continuation of those values. . . . Zionism appeared as a movement of revolt against the orientation of an ancient tradition—in order to save that very tradition.[24]

Indeed, dialectic is inherent in any revolution. In throwing off the intolerable conditions that immediately breed it, a revolution creates a brand new situation; but that new situation is, in effect, a return to and the restoration of an earlier, tolerable and desired situation.[25] This is why it is technically correct to speak of Zionism as a revolution, although

I am certain that many who do so have in mind only one element of its dialectic.

IV

Let us take a closer look at just what this dialectic is, how it came into being, and how it functions. The volume of literature here is not commensurate with the vastness of the subject. As Shemu'el Almog observes: "in spite of the importance of Zionism's relationship to the past, a systematic study has not been done."[26] I shall note briefly some of the main insights derived from two recent works that have a bearing on this subject: Almog's study of the critical decade 1896–1906 (i.e., from Herzl's *Judenstaat* to the conference of Russian Zionists in Helsingfors) and David Kena'ani's exploration of the Second *Aliyah* and its relationship to Jewish religious tradition. The congruence of implication of both these works will serve us well later.

According to Almog, Zionism differs from other nationalisms in one important way. Instead of beginning with a defined sense of nationhood, it had to "prove the existence of a Jewish people from which the national movement [could] spring."[27] This necessitated the construction of a whole new historiography, one quite different from Orthodox theology and from the interpretation of Jewish historical experience afforded by anyone who unreservedly accepted the Emancipation. Now the past was returned to, but in a very new way: "Jewish history in all periods is a national history and anything pertaining to religion is nothing but a religious cloak over a national entity."[28] The past was seen as a glorious national continuity, and yet the religious underpinning of the Diaspora experience was rejected. There was a clear desire to break away from it. The early Zionists saw themselves both as makers of a new Jewish history and as a part of it. The two perceptions seem opposed and yet they are dialectically intertwined.

Now on top of this ambiguity, the Zionist movement, from its inception, carried within it a debate—what was to be Zionism's agenda: to save the Jews or to save Judaism? This is, of course, the well-known debate between Herzl and Ahad Ha'am. Ahad Ha'am took seriously the notion that in the new national movement, religion was subsumed as only a part of the whole fabric of Jewish national culture; it did not comprise the totality of Jewish experience. Moreover, the absolute claims of the tradition were for him implicitly historicized, and therefore relativized. The first task of Zionism for Ahad Ha'am and his erstwhile disciples in the *Demokratische Fraktion* was to continue the work of the Emancipation within a national framework and thus to forge a new Jewish cultural synthesis. The past (i.e., the religious tradition) would be utilized in this endeavor, but what would result would be a modern, secularized alternative to the Orthodoxy of the ghetto.

This was not the journey such Herzlians as Nordau and M. L. Lilienblum had signed up for. For them Zionism's sole agenda was to effect a change in the external conditions of the Jews; that it could be anything else was inconceivable to them. The linchpin of the official (i.e., Herzlian) Zionist leadership's thinking was that all Jews, both religious and secular, share in the national idea. The guiding principle was pragmatism: nothing should be done in the name of Zionism that would alienate the religious, who were justifiably threatened by the cultural Zionists.[29] Herzl even encouraged his Orthodox followers to set up their own faction within the Zionist Congress.

We must see these matters in perspective. The lines were not as clearly drawn as this description would suggest. Zionism then was a weak movement and the pragmatism of its leadership cannot necessarily be construed as a repression of ideological clarity or consistency, although it certainly amounted to that. The Second Zionist Congress had, after all, determined that Zionism had nothing to do with religion. The cultural Zionists were never purged from the movement (though some did drop out) and the genuinely dialectical relationship with the religious tradition, exemplified in the approach of Ahad Ha'am, whereby the Orthodox tradition was rejected in order for Judaism to be saved, coexisted with both the pragmatic and ambiguous relationship the Zionist leadership had with Orthodox Zionists and with the fideism of the Orthodox themselves. Indeed, the seeds of the incipient *Kulturkampf* that has threatened the State of Israel, to which I shall return in a later chapter, can be seen to have germinated in the years encompassed by Almog's study.

Zionism, then, was a melange of conflicting tendencies from the outset. Consider the following anomalies: Herzl, an assimilated West European Jew, could say to the delegates in his opening speech at the First Zionist Congress in 1897: "Zionism is a return to Judaism even before it is a return to the land of the Jews." Ahad Ha'am, an East European Jew who had far deeper roots in Judaic sources and values, could only laugh at this statement as pure rhetoric.[30] Yet it was Herzlian Zionism that demanded a state; cultural Zionism did not require one for its vision to be concretized. But in the debate over East Africa it was the cultural Zionists who, for historical reasons, insisted on Palestine, and not the Herzlians. Even more ironically, Reines and the Mizrachi faction favored East Africa (as a valid, practical achievement for Zionism); Palestine and Jerusalem could remain for them a dream unaffected by this adventure in territorialism. Almog's analysis of the sources shows that in the East Africa debate a Jewish state could be favored or opposed both in the name of historical continuity and in the name of radical change, as could the location of that state, whether it was East Africa or Palestine. Another student of the debate concludes that "the dialectical nature of Zionism, as a yearning for total revolution on the one hand, and as an aspiration for the revival of the past on the other, has never been so clearly illuminated as in the dispute over Uganda."[31] But Almog sees this as only a partially true interpretation. The whole "Uganda" episode was as much a question of pragmatic strategy as it was a question of a principled relationship to the past.[32]

The walk-out (banishment?) of the territorialists at the Seventh Zionist Congress in 1905 had the effect of siphoning off that element in the movement which had a modicum of clarity about Zionism's ends and means. Herzl's death in the previous year worked a similar consequence. Thus it was that after what Vital calls "perhaps the greatest of the movement's debates,"[33] Zionism found itself ideologically at its most diffuse. What had been a tendency was now hardening into a characteristic. "Consciousness of the past served many functions in Zionism, each one with its own features, yet all of them blurred together."[34]

The Second *Aliyah* (1904–14) comes into view now as a crucial expression of the Jewish national movement after it had resoundingly declared for Palestine and not for East Africa. It is crucial for several reasons and on several levels. For one thing it was crucial for Zionism: it served to concretize the Zionist idea for the first time since the establishment of the Zionist Congress, even though, as Kena'ani points out, it was not connected in any way to that Congress and was, in essence, not an organized movement but "an immigration of individuals."[35] The short-lived First *Aliyah* had proved itself a stillbirth. Zionism as an ideology existed only in speeches and on paper; in the wake of the debate on East Africa and Herzl's death it gave every sign of having been dissipated. The phenomenon that was the Second *Aliyah* gave the lie to this. What now was to be played out was Zionism in its specificity, actual individuals making a new life in the ancestral homeland. The Second *Aliyah* is important because in many ways it was the seed-bed of Zionism as it would develop in this century and, because of some of the individuals involved, of the State of Israel.[36] The Second *Aliyah* is therefore crucial within the framework of this discussion. It shows us how the dialectical approach to the Jewish past was lived out in actuality.

The central feature of the Second *Aliyah*, when we look at its protagonists, is secularity. True, their return was to Palestine, not East Africa. But their inner destination was away from the past as it had been understood and experienced.[37] These were individuals who had, for the most part, grown up in Orthodox homes, were familiar with the sources and observances of the religious tradition, but who no longer believed in the transcendent basis and claims of that tradition.[38] The paradigm here is Feierberg, although he did not live to see and perhaps even participate in the Second *Aliyah*. His fundamental question, "Whither?" is answered in his novella of that name in geographical terms—"eastward"—but he does not spell out his answer in any conceptual terms. What happened during the Second *Aliyah* was that religious values which [Jewish] young people had acquired at home and in the traditional school underwent, as they grew up, a rationalization into secular terms. To be sure, this was not the *novum* of the Second *Aliyah*. It had been developed by legions of writers and thinkers who preceded it [the Second *Aliyah*], especially Ahad Ha'am, and who had already labored to place Judaism on a secular foundation, each in his own way. The *novum* [of the Second *Aliyah*] . . . was its zealousness for those parts of the historical tradition which it retained, which it translated into concrete, practical terms.[39]

In other words, for secularized young Jews of the Russian Pale of Settlement to reject Jewish religion per se was *de rigueur;* Bundists and Zionists alike did that. Where the young Zionists who formed the Second *Aliyah* differed from the Bundists was in their acceptance of a historical tradition, their rejection of transcendental religion notwithstanding. The past did not obligate them to perform *mitsvot* (religious command-ments), but they still felt and could speak of a "historical connection" to it.[40] And so a secular reinterpretation could proceed. "Everyone focussed on the national function" of the tradition and the historical past.[41] The "Holy Land" became the "Land of Israel"; the "Holy Tongue" became *'Ivrit*, a secular vernacular; the "Holy Scriptures" be-came the *Tanakh*. The Hebrew calendar was retained but its holidays and celebrations were secularized. Everything was under the sign of a prag-matic positivism. "The tendency visible from several treatments of that period is that the content . . . [of the tradition] is transformed into a means. . . ."[42] This is the context of Ahad Ha'am's oft-quoted remark that "more than Israel has kept the Sabbath, the Sabbath has kept Israel." Where a component of the tradition was not susceptible to a nationalistic interpretation (e.g., Rosh Hashanah), it was ignored, sometimes with equanimity, sometimes uneasily.[43]

Thus was the old wine placed into new bottles. The past was both rejected and retained, *used* selectively and rationalized.

> Zionism seeks, then, to turn Judaism from a religious into a national concept and to *process anew* the historical tradition. . . . Zionism blends the aspiration to national liberation with the tendency to *national reconstruction,* and it needed the legitimation from history. The absence of a nation in the accepted sense forced it not to settle for giving a national interpretation to older traditions but to *create something new* from the old material.[44]

The flag designed by the Zionist movement and later adopted by the State of Israel can thus be seen to embody perfectly this dialectical relationship to the past: the Star of David is framed by the blue and white of the *tallit* containing the *tsitsit* (ritual fringes), the mnemonic device for the heavenly sphere; the ancient prayer-shawl is appropriated, trans-muted into the flag of a modern, secular nation-state.[45]

V

Even so there were during the Second *Aliyah* individuals who did not accept this dialectic, who raised questions about the rationalization process or drew conclusions from it that were at variance with the consensus about it.

The most important of these figures is Yosef Hayim Brenner. In November 1910, under the pseudonym Yosef Haver, Brenner wrote a long article in *Hapo'el hatsa'ir* in which his stated objective was to survey the Jewish condition as reflected in the Jewish press of the previous year.[46] In passing he refers to the increasing incidence of apostasy among Jews and the furor created by it, a furor he professes not to understand or to sanction, since he claims that the entire phenomenon of Jewish apostasy is of no concern to him. After all, he argues, why should we worry about the loss of such Jews? They were never a real part of the Jewish polity anyway, even before their apostasy. Religious commitment alone is of no consequence, since religion in general, whether Jewish or Christian, is a human product that has no relation to ethical behavior.

> The key question of our life as Jews is not that of Jewish religion [or of Jewish] survival. . . . The confusion between these two is to be nipped in the bud. Ahad Ha'am made this mistake and regretted it. But we, his free Jewish colleagues, we have nothing at all to do with Judaism. Yet we are a part of the [Jewish] whole not one whit less than those who put on *tefillin* [phylacteries] and . . . *tsitsit* [ritual fringes]. We say that the key question of our life is the question of a productive place for us as Jews who live everywhere oppressed, landless, without a language. . . . The environment of the [non-Jewish] majority [in the Diaspora] befuddles us, consumes us, blurs our image. . . . We, the living Jews, whether we fast or eat milk and meat together on Yom Kippur, we shall not cease to feel ourselves as Jews . . . and to fight for our survival.[47]

What we have here is a resounding affirmation of the essential secularity of Zionism and an attempt to break apart the synthesis Brenner saw developing between Jewish nationalism and Jewish religion. If Jewishness is now being founded on a national basis, then for Brenner it really makes no difference what the religious modifier of the Jews in the national movement is, be it Jewish, Christian, or whatever. In truth, religion to Brenner is irrelevant and possibly even harmful to Zionism's attempt to re-create the Jew in a new mold. He holds himself up as one such new Jew, a "free Hebrew," who is already living beyond Judaism. "From the hypnotic spell of the twenty-four books of the Bible I have been liberated for some time now."[48]

One begins to hear in Brenner and in other luminaries of the period such as Yosef Aharonovits and Alexander Cheshin the first strains of secular nativism. Religion is opposed not only because it is irrelevant and spurious but because it is the staple of Jewish life in the *galut* (exile). As such it is the main symptom of the Jewish people's sickness there. Those Zionist ideologues in the Diaspora who clamor for utilizing the religious tradition as a national preservative are "hypocritical" and "superficial."

> Certainly there was a time when the religion was a shield against the punishment that came upon [the Jewish] nation . . . but the historical truth is that it was not the religion which gave birth to nationhood but vice versa. . . . To the extent that nationalism will continue to free itself from the yoke of strangers and stand on its own, to the extent that it will begin to create its own original values, to that extent will it remove from itself the religious modality. . . . It needs no outside help or reinforcement.[49]

Now this secular sensibility was not confined solely to the workers of the Second *Aliyah*.[50] It has to be seen not just as a rebellion against the past but as an expression of a vitalistic consciousness pervading several elements of the populace that what was taking shape in Palestine was new and secular and qualitatively different from the past, from the religious tradition and from the Diaspora. In this sensibility, which I call nativism, the past, the tradition, and the Diaspora are all covalent. There is a palpable resistance to Zionist ideologues of the Diaspora who call for a link to the past. These critiques of the Zionist consensus in the Second *Aliyah* regarding the secular reinterpretation of the religious past, the dialectic I have been describing, anticipate that of Ratosh a generation later.

VI

But these critiques are the exception, not the rule. The consensus of the Second *Aliyah* was to affirm the dialectic of Zionism's relationship to and use of the past. The representative figure of this consensus, in contradistinction to Brenner, is Berl Katznelson.[51] In fact, the consensus holds among all who would affirm Zionism from the days of the Second *Aliyah* down to the present. The dialectic is not only defended as unproblematical and consistent but is celebrated as a source of strength. Almog, for example, is clear that "in spite of the importance of the historical link [to the past] Zionism does not stand on this alone. . . . In spite of the abandoned struggle between various motifs, Zionism achieved a high degree of integration among them." This is because it became a living, all-encompassing national movement.[52] Because it was able to meet various needs of various kinds of Jews, Zionism, in spite of the ambiguity that lies at its heart, was able to unite them under its "old-new" banner.[53]

Gershom Scholem argues in similar terms. To him Zionism is a "living thing with a dialectic of its own." Although he is aware that this dialectic has "determined all the troubles we are confronted with today," and that "for the time being there is no synthesis between [the] . . . contradictory trends within Zionism," still these trends are a source of dynamic creativity "and not merely a power of endurance. . . . Innovation cannot be defined in advance. Because innovation arises, not from denying one's tradition, but from a dialectic, a metamorphosis of tradition. And these two trends have not yet run their course."[54]

Sometimes the contradictions of Zionism are upheld in philosophical or even theological terms. A good example of this approach is Harold Fisch's interpretation of the Zionist experience. Fisch sees very clearly the conflicting tendencies I have been describing, but he views them with equanimity. "[They] are not so much a conflict between groups . . . as an ambiguity within the movement as a whole . . . so much so that it is almost possible to say that what unites the Zionist movement as a whole is precisely an unwritten consent to harbor this ambiguity!"[55] He offers a close reading of the State of Israel's Declaration of Independence to demonstrate this point. In that document, which he perceptively notes "is all that Israel has in the way of a written constitution"[56] (a point to which I shall return in a later chapter), overtly religious language is employed: terms like "the Rock of Israel," "the soil of the Homeland," "the Eve of the Sabbath." But always there is a vagueness about these concepts, and they are susceptible to interpretation and acceptance by secular and religious Zionists alike. Moreover, in regard to the dating of the document,

> equivocation ends and gives way to two clear, parallel and separate mea-
> surements of time: "5th Iyar 5708" and "14th May 1948." . . . To bring
> these two notions of time together and to endure their contradiction is a
> work of paradox and pain; and this is what the signatories to the Declara-
> tion of Independence took upon themselves to suffer.[57]

We have already seen that this tendency to overlook and perhaps even deliberately foster this ambiguity was characteristic of Zionism from Herzl's day. There were probably a number of reasons for this. We can say, for instance, that they were pragmatic—to keep a weak movement together—and in truth, at every point the secular leaders of Zionism indulged the needs and claims of the Orthodox.[58] Or we can say that the impetus to tolerate ambiguity was not due to any ratiocinative process. Walter Laqueur has put this well: "Zionism was not so much a logical conclusion as an emotional necessity."[59]

What Fisch does is to impute to the entire Zionist enterprise a latent motivation, an unarticulated and invisible *telos*. Zionism is a working out of the inexorable destiny of the Jewish people, a destiny Fisch under-stands as expressed in what he sees as the fundamental theological myth of Judaism—the concept of the *berit* (covenant) between the Jewish people and God.[60] For Fisch the dialectic of Zionism is sustained, justified, and encouraged because more than one hermeneutic of history and reality are at work within it. What is *manifestly* secular is *intrinsically* sacred. This is the argument on which all religious Zionism ultimately rests and which was developed perhaps in its fullest form in the thought of Rav Kook.[61]

Less mystically inclined Zionist apologists do not, of course, go that far. The most intellectually honest of them eschew all triumphalism and openly own up to the problem of internal contradiction. Eliezer Schweid sums up the entire matter lucidly. If "Zionism was no more than an experiment in the paradoxical business of living as a Jew—outside of Judaism,"[62] then

> Zionism ended up caught inextricably between its conflicting drives. It shot back and forth between the denial which held an affirmation and the affirmation which contained a denial. The only possibility of working to save what could be rescued of the tradition without foregoing the revolt was to put off a frontal conflict with the tradition and its culture. . . . But postponing the confrontation did not always lead to a cancellation of the reality of the problem. Sometimes it worsened it many times over.[63]

Nevertheless, the assumption of such rationalistic approaches to the matter is that the strategy of postponement is justified and does not foreclose a future rapprochement between Zionism and Judaism.

VII

On the other hand, there have been those who are not so sure about this assumption. It is not simply that they are unwilling to grant Zionism and its fruits the ontological status that we see accorded it by Fisch and others who are less unabashedly theological in their outlook. Rather it is that they are unable to accept the whole dialectical framework I have been describing. They are unwilling to fit the paradoxes of Zionism into it. In short, they are put off and troubled by the very paradoxes themselves. For them Zionism is problematic because it is a syncretism.

Who are the demurrers? Considering all the foregoing, they are not difficult to identify. If the central paradox of Zionism devolves from the way in which it relates to and handles the past, those who will be troubled by it are those who come with a preconceived notion of what the Jewish past contains and entails, and of how it is to be handled.

I use the term syncretism advisedly because it points up the issues of perspective and prior assumptions that are so important in understanding and assessing conflicting opinions in matters of this kind. To call something a syncretism or syncretistic is not ipso facto to critique it or to judge it negatively. Webster's Third International Dictionary defines syncretism in different ways. Syncretism is "**1:** the reconciliation or union of conflicting (as religious) beliefs or an effort intending such **2:** a flagrant compromise in religion or philosophy, eclecticism that is illogical or leads to inconsistency, uncritical acceptance of conflicting or divergent beliefs or principles."[64] In the first sense syncretism is not a pejorative term. One can call Zionism a syncretism in this sense and thereby not be passing a negative judgement upon it; on the contrary, one can mean something very positive. Those who reject Zionism as syncretistic use the word in its second sense.

The most obvious example of the latter are those ultra-Orthodox Jews for whom the past as past really does not exist. It does not exist because it is eternal, and so it extends into the present and the future. For these Jews Zionism is unacceptable because, in fashioning the alloy of sacred past and secular present, it represents an unacceptable syncretism. This is the nub of the anti-Zionist outlook of such groups as Neturei Karta and some elements of Agudat Yisra'el even though their rejection of Zionism is usually couched in less abstract terms—as a "false messianism" or a national sell-out to the assimilationist principles of Emancipation and Enlightenment.

One clear instance of this kind of critique of Zionism is found in the thought of Barukh Kurzweil. Kurzweil, while he was not identified with ultra-Orthodoxy, nevertheless was deeply influenced by its world view, especially in regard to Zionism.[65] Although he never used the term "syncretism," that quality (in the second sense given above) is really the difficulty Kurzweil found with Zionism and Israel and, of course, the culture that flowed from them. What for Rav Kook was a mystical holy integration of the old and the new in the Zionist movement was to Kurzweil, the severe rationalist, a gross intermingling of the sacred and the profane. "Double-entry bookkeeping" in the spiritual sense was how he described Zionism's dialectical relationship to the past.

> On one hand we are the people of the Book, the descendants of the prophets and their spiritual heirs, so to speak, and we appear in the name of some spiritual or moral purpose. But in actuality our communal and private lives are totally secular, an estrangement from all the sublime words we use so facilely when it is appropriate and [even] when inappropriate.[66]

Zionism's use of the past, which I have termed a "reinterpretation" or an "appropriation," Kurzweil saw as "expropriation." To him you could not detach words, ideas, symbols, or ceremonies that existed in a sacral sphere and mechanistically insert them into a secular sphere without doing violence to both the sacred and the secular.

It would be a mistake to see Kurzweil's critique of Zionism strictly as a theoretical one, a kind of intellectual setting of accounts. On the contrary, what energizes the critique is a deep concern for the practical realities of Jewish statehood. Kurzweil understood very well the historical situation that necessitated the process of which he is so critical; he was simply fearful of the price it would exact and the spiritual dilemmas that would arise out of the solution to pressing physical problems. Since Zionism is to him essentially a syncretism, its state is founded on "a flagrant compromise." Its national life will be "illogical" and will "lead to inconsistency in matters of public policy."[67]

But such a judgment will be reached not only by those who relate to the past in the metahistorical terms that Kurzweil does. Those who begin from antipodal premises—for whom the past has no determinative claim, for whom the Jewish past is irretrievable—will arrive at the same conclusion. For if Zionism's embrace of modernity poses problems for religionist Jews, its dialectical embrace of the religious past makes the Jewish secularist equally uncomfortable. Such a one is in "what the distinguished Biblical historian Yehezkel Kaufmann has called a tragic situation, for it is 'hard to reconcile ourselves to the idea that our nationalism derives from a faith that no longer exists in our hearts.' "[68] Those secularists who are unwilling or unable to effect this reconciliation will also see Zionism's reinterpretation of the tradition as syncretistic.[69] They too, if they are so inclined, can furnish a critique of Zionism's contradictions and the resultant inadequacies and confusions of Israeli polity and policy. Though it starts from opposing premises, this critique leads to conclusions startlingly similar to Kurzweil's.

One who was so inclined was Yonatan Ratosh.[70] Ratosh was alive to all the issues touched upon in this chapter.

> If we wish to sum up faithfully the common denominator of Zionism from its inception, with all its currents, parties and conceptions, which quite often discredited each other's Zionism, it seems to me that we will arrive at a somewhat paradoxical formulation: Zionism is essentially an attempt to provide an undefined answer (from a "spiritual center" to an empire) to an undefined problem (the Jewish question, all depending on the various attitudes towards the question of what Judaism is) of an undefined human grouping (all the Jews, according to the various conceptions of "Who is a Jew?"—or portions thereof) in an undefined territory (from Western Palestine, or a portion thereof—to the borders of Egypt and the Euphrates).[71]

Yonatan Ratosh could not tolerate this undefinedness. Dialectical reality was insufferable to him. Why this was, and how he proposed to undo the dialectic of Zionism and thus reconstruct Israeli reality, are the subjects of the next two chapters. What is gained from this reconstruction is the subject of those that follow.

III

YONATAN RATOSH

THE TRANSFORMATION OF URIEL HALPERN

To discuss Yonatan Ratosh as anything other than a poet requires some explanation. It is not to suggest that the nonpoetic elements of his life's work—the voluminous geopolitical and ideological writings he left—are "better" or more important than the poetry. Nor is there the implication that an understanding of this side of Ratosh is a necessary condition for an understanding of his poetry and its wellsprings (although that is certainly a possibility).[1] Indeed, the problem of the relationship between Ratosh's prose and his poetry is one of the staples of Ratosh criticism.[2] The debate over whether the interpretation of the poetry is best served by linking it to the poet's ideology or by separating the two, while it presents interesting and important methodological and esthetic questions, is not the focus of this chapter or the next.

My purpose is, literally and figuratively, more prosaic. I want to present the rudiments of Ratosh's life and thought and then to identify and analyze those strands within them that constitute and set them up as a critique of Zionism.[3]

There is no question that Ratosh deserves to be treated as a thinker. Although he had no formal training or advanced degree in political or social theory and was, in many respects, an autodidact, Ratosh wrote prolifically in these areas. This was a matter of something more than presumptuousness on his part. The immensity and intensity of the intellectual effort put forth in these writings are testimony to a mind engaged deeply with the larger issues of the society from which it sprang and which nourished it. In one of the many interviews Ratosh gave, he observes that

> poetry is [only] one of my areas of interest, as are language and criticism, except that it is, of course, more personal. But without any doubt it is not the main area. In actuality, what preoccupies me most of the time are the fundamental questions of our reality, of our existence, of our identity, our future, and, if you wish, of our world. For me the publication of an issue

of *Alef* always takes precedence over [the publication] of a volume of poems. . . . I am saying essentially the same things in all areas.[4]

My use of the word "mind" just now to describe Ratosh was not coincidental. Subjectively, he understood himself to be primarily a scholar, a student, an inquirer into the past and present.[5] Objectively, this self-perception is accurate: the primary modality in which he operated was that of intellect and *ratio*. This was true in person as well as on the printed page. Those who knew him well and conversed with him at length describe the "Socratic" nature of his attempts to search out the flaws in his interlocutors' arguments and positions.[6] Even his poetry, its "Dionysian" surface and details notwithstanding, is the fruit of a cerebral, "Apollonian" effort to work things out carefully and clearly, from the metricality of the lines to the geometricality of the formal structure.[7] An erstwhile disciple could say, "Indeed, as much as poets are depicted as 'energized by feeling' and lacking in intellectual solidity or ability to think abstractly—Ratosh is one of the most intellectual and logical men I have ever met. . . ."[8]

When we add to all this the fact that the nonpoetic writings of Yonatan Ratosh are substantial not only in quantity but also in influence and in the provocativeness of their implication, it becomes clear that they unquestionably deserve presentation and interpretation no less than his poetry. In truth, they deserve monographic treatment, considered in conjunction with Ratosh's total output.

What follows in this chapter and the next does not purport to do that or to be that. As I hope is now clear, my objective is relatively more modest and limited: to present the critique of Zionism that Ratosh developed and to assess that critique. But it is difficult, if not impossible, to do this in an ideational vacuum. More than with most thinkers, Ratosh's thought cannot be grasped in antiseptic isolation from the details of his life and intellectual development. He came to the position he held not through detached reflection but through a passionate engagement with some of the major events and personalities of Mandate Palestine and because of certain specific experiences and encounters. These need to be noted before his critique of Zionism is examined; they are an essential part of the critique.

Nevertheless, just as the total treatment of Ratosh in these two chapters fall short of being a monograph, this survey of his life makes no claim to being a definitive biography, chronological or intellectual, of him, or for that matter, a complete history of the "Canaanite" movement. I want simply to tell the story of a life with an eye toward delineating the growth to consciousness of its protagonist as, alternately, a non-Zionist, an anti-Zionist, or a "Hebrew."[9] The story is in itself fascinating and unfamiliar, and it illuminates aspects and persons in the history of the State of Israel who have hitherto existed in the shadows.

I

Yonatan Ratosh was born in Warsaw in 1909, as Uriel Halpern.[10] Although this place of birth technically stamped him as having been born in the Diaspora, he might just as well have been born in Palestine, for the only language that was ever spoken in the Halpern home was Hebrew. The father, Yehiel Halpern, was an educator involved in the establishment and operation (including the training of teachers) of Hebrew kindergartens for Jewish children in Warsaw and, after 1914, in Odessa. For him the Hebrew language was an end in itself and his goal of all-Hebrew kindergartens (*'ivrit be'ivrit*), pursued in the face of many who told him that it was unrealistic, became a crusade. Ratosh thus grew up with a father

> who saw strange dreams while awake without grounding him in real-
> ity. . . . He transgressed the most elementary principles of education by
> presuming to teach young children a strange language, a dead language,
> by imbuing their tender souls with a yearning for vain dreams of a far-off
> land, by a total lack of concreteness in his work.[11]

Small wonder that later on the son would also regard the quixotic as normative and continue the father's mission in a similar way and in similar terms.[12]

The home was secular and Zionist, which meant that Ratosh received a thorough background in Bible, medieval and modern Hebrew literature, and perhaps also rabbinic literature; but there was no religious observance or involvement in the synagogue, liturgy, or ritual.[13] In 1919 or 1920, in the wake of the Russian Revolution, the family emigrated to Palestine. Ratosh attended the Hebrew Gymnasia in Jerusalem and, later, the Herzliah Gymnasia in Tel Aviv. But this relocation to a Hebrew-speaking society did not, apparently, satisfy Ratosh emotionally. At some point after the move, whether earlier or later, a sense of estrangement began to set in. Everything in the *Yishuv* as he saw it developing seemed as foreign to him as what he might have remembered from Warsaw or Odessa. "Above all I had a sense of being a total outsider to everything, to—how shall I say it—to all of Zionism. I had a sense of estrangement from the whole way of life, the whole establishment, the entire dominant ideology, to all these things."[14] It is unclear to me what the source for this sensibility was—whether we can ascribe it to an emerging poetic ego that needed to differentiate itself from the world in order to establish its voice, or whether there were other subjective and objective factors operating in the way Ratosh met the world, about which we can only speculate. Ratosh himself always regarded the distinctive linguistic basis on which his early life rested as decisive.

> I think that among my contemporaries there is no one, or there was no one, whose sole mother-tongue and whose language of learning and education was Hebrew and only Hebrew. This relates to the perception of everything. That is, I have a completely different approach to all the root problems which confront me, or more precisely, [which confront] us, to how reality is construed.[15]

The core problem that preoccupied Ratosh was essentially one of identity, "Who am I?" In an inchoate way Ratosh was bumping into the incongruities of being a secular Jew.

> One Sabbath morning I was sitting with two boys my age on a bench on Allenby Street smoking. A Jewish fellow came over to us, I don't re-member if he was from the ultra-Orthodox or simply a traditionalist, and he reminded us about [the prohibition of] smoking on the Sabbath. My friends extinguished their cigarettes. I refused saying, "But I am not a Jew." The man didn't know what to make of what I said. Perhaps it was unclear even to me. I only know that I wasn't at all religious.[16]

This event occurred during his teens, after he had graduated from the Gymnasia and was studying at the newly founded Hebrew University. Ratosh began to understand that the question he was asking about the oxymoronic nature of his existence as a secular Jew was applicable on a wider scale to the whole collective enterprise that was unfolding in Palestine after the Balfour Declaration in the early years of the British Mandate. Actually, the question of identity was the root issue for Ratosh all his life. It is the one with which he opens the short memoir he wrote in 1980, a year before his death:

> The basic, fundamental question, "the question" in regard to the Hebrew *Yishuv* in Palestine, whether stated explicitly by thinkers such as Klatzkin for example, or as a general sensibility vaguely felt by residents of this land, regardless of whether they were born or grew up here, has been, since the end of the nineteenth century . . . the question of identity; or, in other words, that of self-definition; how does one define himself, his identity, or in less blatant language, his distinctiveness, his essential . . . separateness from world Jewry, from Judaism wherever it may be.[17]

Implicitly Ratosh is really asking after the nature of Zionism. What is important about his question is his tacit realization that he would find the answer on a personal level only when he would find it in the collective sense. "Who am I?" is for Ratosh coterminous with "Who are we here?"

Now within this large question Ratosh, in his later years, identified in his systematic manner three other, related questions or problems that were of concern to him: the British, the Arabs, and the Jews. Who were these three entities? What were they doing in Palestine? How did they relate to his life there? Ratosh attacked these problems *seriatim*. He began in the twenties with the British issue; he was able to address the Arab and Jewish issues only later, in the late thirties, after undergoing a formative experience that I shall describe below. We can, however, note now that if in retrospect Ratosh saw the British, Arab, and Jewish questions as three discrete problems, he came to solve them all in the same way. Ultimately they became for him not three different issues but one interrelated problem or three manifestations of the same problem.

Thus, whereas his parents' and teachers' generation, not to mention the official Zionist leadership, perceived Britain as "the enlightened, liberal empire of Europe, the lover of freedom and the Jews, in my eyes she appeared as an oppressive monarchy to whose 'colonial office' we were tied. . . . For me, from my childhood on, she was simply a foreign ruler."[18] The fact is that Ratosh was having growing doubts about the whole Labor Zionist approach that was active and visible on the political horizon of Palestine of the mid-twenties:

> I never saw any difference between the *halukah* [philanthropic] admin-
> istration of the old *Yishuv* and the fiscal control of the Zionist Congress
> and the Jewish Agency after it, between the *Rabbi Meir Ba'al Haness* Fund
> and the Jewish National Fund; I never saw the logic of including Commu-
> nists, [who were] partners in Arab insurgency, within the Histadrut [La-
> bor Federation], even if they were workers; and above all I didn't believe
> that the country would be redeemed by the Jewish National Fund, by
> money, by [the policy of] dunam after dunam, not that I opposed settle-
> ment or buying land. I just didn't believe that this was the royal road to
> . . . independence. . . . In time I began to have second thoughts about all
> the basic assumptions of Zionist policy. . . .[19]

We see Ratosh, then, until 1929 as an *isolado*, disaffected and unwilling, perhaps unable, to be part of any existing political group.

This situation changed in 1929, when he met Abba Ahime'ir. Ahime'ir was an intellectual who had written his doctoral dissertation on Spengler at the University of Vienna in 1924. He had subsequently come to Palestine with the Tse'irei Tsiyon, the right wing of the socialist Po'alei Tsiyon. In 1928 he defected to the Revisionist Workers party (the left wing of the Zionist right), principally because he was unhappy with the Marxist opposition to nationalism.[20] For Ahime'ir the enemy was not the Arabs but the British; like Ratosh he saw them as a foreign occupying power. Moreover, his world view was remarkably similar to that of Ratosh.

> How shall we realize the Zionist dream? Said A. D. Gordon: with a hoe;
> let us plant tomatoes! Said the ultra-Orthodox: with prayer—and they
> were more realistic than all the other Zionists. But they forgot one thing:
> in all of human history—and this is a most pessimistic matter—no state
> was established, no human society was ever founded other than through

that sticky substance that has a red color. . . . In all of human history no
state ever arose through people saying "let us go to a desolate place, begin
to work and set up there a society of righteousness and integrity and
pacifism. . . ." States have arisen through tragedy, wars, calamities, hatred,
conflict and many problems.[21]

This kind of thinking was attractive to Ratosh, as was the guerilla-
theater type of anti-British activism that Ahime'ir initiated through the
group he organized, the Berit Habiryonim. That there was influence
here is clear, but its extent and its exact nature are not. Of the Berit
Habiryonim, Ratosh notes:

> What appealed to me was, of course, their anti-Britishism. What spoke to
> me less was their whole ideology, which, in my view, was very confused
> and ineffectual, a kind of quixotic war against all the windmills of the
> world at one time: against the British, anti-Semitism, Marxism . . . Mapai,
> without any focus. Essentially I saw them as a kind of educational youth
> group, not a real political movement.[22]

There is no indication that Ratosh was involved in any active way with the
Berit Habiryonim.

There are a number of other elements in Ahime'ir's thought and style
that seem more obviously to have affected Ratosh. One was the way in
which language was used with reference to the Zionist establishment. In
the columns of *Hazit ha'am*, the official organ of the Palestine Revisionist
party, Ahime'ir had no hesitation about describing the institutions of the
Yishuv in the most intemperate terms. Mapai leaders were called "the
Judenrat" and "Sanballats," the Histadrut was "the Kremlin," its flag "the
red rag."[23] The precedent for this style had been set by another recent
defector from the left, Uri Tsvi Greenberg.[24] Later on, as we shall see,
Ratosh would appropriate this rhetorical diminution of normative
Zionism and its leaders for his own purposes.

Second was the way in which the younger generation was conceived as
the vanguard of the new order. In an interview with Ahime'ir in February 1933, when he was probably at the height of his public career, we
find the following:

> Q: What is the role of the youth at this time? A: To cleanse its soul of
> foreign worship ['*avodah zarah*], to create brigades to fight anti-Semitism.
> And the main thing: every young person should remember that transcen-
> dent Providence has placed upon his generation [the task] to participate in
> the establishment of Jewish sovereignty [*malkhut yisra'el*].[25]

A decade later Ratosh would write an "Open Letter to the Hebrew
Youth" that would make a similar appeal but in different terms.

The third and perhaps most important facet of Ahime'ir's thought for
Ratosh was the concept just cited: *malkhut yisra'el*. This was not a locution

original with Ahime'ir or one on which he had a monopoly. Rather it was a concept or vision central to the entire Revisionist movement.

> First given currency in the 1920's by the nationalist poet Uri Tsvi Green-berg, *malkhut yisra'el* had tremendous resonance. . . . While vague as to its nature, [it] implied restoration of former glory and that meant restoration of Jewish sovereignty not over the ancient territory in its most confined shape but over the ancient land at the peak of ethnic Jewish settlement.[26]

In other words, we may say that Ratosh finally found in Ahime'ir an ideological and political framework in which he could function and develop. Precisely defined, this was not the Berit Habiryonim per se but rather the maximalist wing of Zev Jabotinsky's Revisionist party, of which wing Ahime'ir was the leader.[27] Ratosh saw this, at least initially, as the best arena in which to realize his anti-British aspirations, although he did not officially join the party. His understanding—perhaps it was a hope— was that the real agenda of Revisionism was embodied in the people around Ahime'ir and that Jabotinsky and his followers represented merely the official, external, proper face of the party, its diplomatic corps.[28]

This assumption was to prove false. In April 1934 Ratosh was invited to join the editorial staff of the new Revisionist newspaper *Hayarden*. Thus began a four-year experience in which Ratosh from the purview of a party organ would gradually come to the realization that, in spite of the militant "integral" nationalism it declared as its basis, Revisionism under Jabotinsky was no less committed to the legal channels of negotiation and political niceties than were Labor Zionism under Ben Gurion and General Zionism under Weizmann. It became apparent to him that Jabotinsky's support of and commitment to Ahime'ir was at best ambivalent.[29] Most distressingly, it became clear that Jabotinsky's Ten-Year Plan, whereby the Balfour Declaration would finally be concretized by settling a million and a half European Jews in Palestine over a decade, thus to make them a majority and achieve Jewish sovereignty—it became clear to Ratosh that such a program, even if workable, was intolerable.[30] It would only prolong the occupation of the British and the non-sovereign status of the Jews of Palestine. Ratosh's original suspicion of the entire Zionist enterprise now intensified: Revisionism, too, was part of what he saw as a collusion of European Diaspora Jews with European non-Jews to decide the fate of Palestinian Jews.

This kind of thinking deflected Ratosh from the political arena toward the paramilitary structure that had begun to form in the wake of the Arab uprisings of 1929. Haganah "B" (officially known as the *Haganah Le'umit* [National Defense]) had come into existence as an alternative to the moderate defense corps of the *Yishuv*, the Haganah. Ratosh joined it

in 1930, even undergoing an officers' training course with its first com-
mander, Avraham Tehomi (Gid'on). But in 1936 the Ten-Year Plan for
Palestine was officially adopted by Jabotinsky's New Zionist Party and
Ratosh was zealous to ensure that Haganah "B," although it was not
formally a part of the party, would dissociate itself from it. There was,
moreover, in that year an additional development that fueled Ratosh's
involvement in Haganah "B": the Arab hostilities and Jabotinsky's initial
directive that Haganah "B" practice restraint (*havlagah*) and not engage
in counteractions.

At the urging of Tehomi's *aide de camp*, a young firebrand named
Abraham Stern, Ratosh began to articulate his political views to Tehomi.
Ratosh had known Stern since 1928, when both were students at the
Hebrew University, but only casually. Now there was a shared concern
between them: to get the British out of Palestine. When Tehomi in 1937
chose to return to the Haganah, and Stern became a senior officer in
Haganah "B" (now called the *Irgun Tsva'i Le'umi* [National Military Or-
ganization]), the two worked in close cooperation. Ratosh began to edit
the clandestine publication of the Irgun, which he had named *Baherev*
(With the sword), just as in 1936 he had edited *Ha'ekdah* (The pistol), a
training manual Stern and David Razi'el had written. Stern, who had an
active poetic muse, looked upon Ratosh as his advisor in this area. For his
part, Ratosh saw in Stern and the Irgun the best hope of ridding
Palestine of foreign influence; he was impressed with Stern's independence of mind and with the fact that he was not really controlled by
Jabotinsky.[31]

In July 1937 the Palestine Royal Commission published its report,
conventionally known as the Peel Report. It recommended the partition
of Palestine into three entities: a small Jewish state, a larger Arab state,
and a British enclave under permanent mandate. At about this time the
editor-in-chief of *Hayarden,* Dr. Binyamin Lubotsky-Eliav, who had kept
the publication firmly within the Jabotinsky orbit, was jailed by the
British.[32] These two events enabled Ratosh (Halpern) to turn *Hayarden*
into a veritable forum for his views. Throughout that autumn he published five articles in reaction to the Peel Report. These were written in
order to shape opinion within the Palestine Revisionist Council, which
would, at the end of January 1938, travel to Prague for the congress of
the full New Zionist Party and a debate on the Peel Report. In December
1937 Ratosh even appeared before the council to argue in person what
he had been arguing in print. These articles, as well as the speech he
gave to the council, are worth looking at, for they constitute a kind of
summary of Ratosh's political development up to that point.[33]

Specifically, they show a Januslike Ratosh looking backward and forward at the same time. The essential thrust of all these utterances is that
of maximalist Revisionism: Jewish sovereignty should precede Jewish

settlement. Sovereignty is a prerequisite for settlement and not the other way around, as Labor Zionism would have it. Therefore Ratosh urges the Revisionists to abandon Jabotinsky's Ten-Year Plan and instead respond to the Peel Report with a demand for immediate Jewish sovereignty. Such a demand he feels is "the cornerstone of Herzl's teaching and the quintessence of political Zionism [i.e., Revisionism]. . . . This demand takes precedence over all settlement activity and is not in any way conditioned by the status, class, or absolute or relative number of Jews in Palestine."[34] After all, he notes, the Arabs have asked for the maximum; why should the Jews demand any less? Ratosh speaks here repeatedly of *malkhut yisra'el,* as we would expect of a good Revisionist. But he does so in the context of a larger vision of Zionism that is at once revealing and crucial to any understanding of why he would eventually come to break with it:

> In the eyes of a practical Zionist [i.e., Labor Zionist] there is a place for the existence of Jewish communities in the Diaspora. Repatriation, the return to Zion—these are for the Messianic era; until then [this] practical Zionism can continue both here and there, even if it is more secure here. It can be done on a large scale or on a small scale, since it is an end unto itself both in Palestine and in other countries. But as far as political Zionism [i.e., Revisionism] goes, the end and the operative question together are to turn Palestine into *malkhut yisra'el.* The Diaspora is the locus of abandoned and despised positions. Zionism is not an evolutionary process, a gradual transition of the Jewish center of gravity to a new geographic area. It is not like other Jewish emigration patterns which transposed the center of Judaism from country to country—from Spain in the middle ages to Russia and, later, to America. The Jewish concern in Palestine is intrinsically different from any other country. Zionism is a revolution. It means a revolt against a life of dependence on the masters of the land, an end to living only within the economic sphere. Zionism came to restore to the Jewish people its own political sovereignty over its territory.[35]

Ratosh here is clearly (still) within the orbit of Zionism, albeit at the outside edge. He accepts the idea of a Jewish people and is operating within its framework.

But there are elements here that presage things to come. He is not predisposed to construe Zionism in its connection to the past; there is only newness, revolution, and the future. What fuels everything is the vision of sovereignty. Ratosh in these articles already exhibits a deep trust in the power of an idea to energize and activate the masses. "The end determines the means. Its formulation determines the line of battle. The flag summons the battalions and the idea arouses the forces fighting for its realization."[36] There is a mystical, yet pragmatic, faith in the future and in the people. If Zionism is utopian, it is "much less utopian than [positing] the continuity of Jewish existence in the Diaspora."[37] It is the youth who will bring about the Zionist revolution because they are the most rebellious.

> The main question is why political Zionism [i.e., Revisionism] has not succeeded in gathering to its flag all that is active, aggressive, thoughtful, and explosive within the Hebrew youth, [among whom] there is now great ferment. . . . For such youth to find fulfillment in the context of this [Revisionist] front it is necessary that the [leaders of the] front take the youth and the potential power hidden within it into account. And this youth is growing up rapidly.[38]

At this point Ratosh probably had the Irgun in mind as the primary agent of the Zionist revolution he envisioned; later on he would look beyond it.[39]

How was Ratosh-Halpern's proposal received? It is not hard to guess. His anti-British argument carried the clear implication that the Mandate was illegal. At a time when Jabotinsky was interested in a cooperative relationship with England, this was an undesirable point to make. Ratosh was relieved of his responsibilities at *Hayarden*. Yet so zealous was he to prosecute his case that, by his own admission, he "joined for the first and last time in my life a party (in which I did not believe)" in order to be able to argue it to the congress in Prague in early 1938. His hope was that the adoption of his idea would expedite the formation of a political and military underground to resist the British in Palestine.[40] But at the congress he fared no better. Jabotinsky dispatched a directive to Ratosh to drop his proposal. When this attempt had no results, Jabotinsky himself summoned him for a short walk in the corridors.[41] But Ratosh, with characteristic obduracy, did not relent. Instead he presented his case to the Political Executive for consideration as an agenda item. The motion was defeated, with only two voting in favor—Ratosh and Menahem Begin. Finally, when Ratosh spoke for his proposal in the plenary session, it was resoundingly removed from the agenda. "My words were as a voice calling in the wilderness. The overwhelming majority simply did not understand me. I, of course, spoke Hebrew, my only language, and they simply didn't know it."[42]

Ratosh was understandably crushed. He attributes his disappointment to the "lack of any response and practical results from the camp of Jabotinsky's movement."[43] But there was a deeper reason for it: the fiasco at Prague reinforced his perception that Zionism was as foreign an entity as the British.[44] Stifled and frustrated by the whole experience, Ratosh at this point felt the need to "gather my thoughts and try to find the flaw that foiled a mode of thought as clear and as simple as the one I had raised."[45] He repaired to Paris.[46] He had spent a year or so studying there in 1929–30. That visit had apparently challenged his sense of identity even more than some of his boyhood experiences in Palestine.[47] This one was to transform it.

II

In Paris Ratosh began to immerse himself in the study of Jewish history. Evidently he wanted now to get to the bottom of the "British problem" that had been bothering him for so long, to understand what the problem was. Shavit's excellent research and discussion of this little-known phase of Ratosh's development make it clear that Ratosh was concentrating not so much on studying as on writing a history of the Jewish people, one that would provide an empirical underpinning for his maximalist demands that had been treated so shabbily at Prague. To this end he began to write in the spring of 1938 a series of articles on Jewish history. These appeared in the newspaper *Haboker* under the *nom de plume* A. L. Haran.[48]

It was at this time that Ratosh met Adolphe (Edya) Gourevitch. Almost immediately the writing came to a stop. Gourevitch (he later also Hebraized his name to Gur and to A. G. Horon) was a Semitics scholar and a close friend of Zev Jabotinsky's son Eri.[49] In 1929–32 he had published in the Revisionist periodical *Rassvet* a series of nine articles, written in Russian, on the origins and history of the Jews. In these he had argued not only that ancient Carthage was a Hebrew settlement (in Aramaic: *Karta hadata,* "new city") and that Hannibal and the Carthaginians were Hebrews, but, more important, that there was a distinction between Jews and Hebrews. The Jews, he maintained, were an outgrowth of the latter. Now, in the spring of 1938, Gourevitch-Horon was updating his picture of the Semitic past in a series of ten lectures in Paris, which he soon condensed into a pamphlet entitled "Canaan et les Hébreux."[50] Ratosh read this pamphlet and evidently held many long conversations with its author. He described the effect of this encounter as "a liberating shock."[51] Here was the very history he had wanted to write, except its author had the tools he was lacking—a thorough grounding in biblical criticism, Semitic philology, ancient history, and the history of religion. Here was a systematic treatment of the past that he had not found in Ahime'ir, one that spoke directly to the "Jewish problem" that had preoccupied him and, what was more, related it to the "Arab problem."[52]

The nub of Horon's approach was to look at the ancient Near East holistically, in line with the biblical scholarship that had flourished among Protestants in Europe since Wellhausen. In this perspective the human entity that inhabited western Palestine in antiquity, the Hebrews (of which the Phoenicians or Sidonites were a northern subgroup) were in essence a part of a larger entity and region that comprised various other groups—Ammonites, Edomites, Amorites, Moabites, Israelites, Canaanites. Originally all were united linguistically (they all spoke various dialects of Hebrew), culturally (they all worshipped pagan deities), and politically (they were all federated into a regional covenant). The

Ugaritic findings at Ras Shamra appeared to bear all this out. That there came about a group that saw itself as different and monotheistic was due to certain specific historical developments that took place much later, in the wake of the Babylonian Exile of the Israelites after 586 b.c.e. It was then, argued Horon, under the new monotheistic ideas of Ezra, that the Israelite element of the pagan Hebrews was transformed into a religious group later called "Jews." At that point was a new myth of the meaning and purpose of their existence as a separate entity propounded. The "Return to Zion" was mandated on the basis of reinterpretation of earlier material into stories about Patriarchs and an Exodus from Egypt.[53]

It is not my intention here to sustain or refute these arguments but rather to note their implications or, more precisely, to note some of the inferences Ratosh drew from them. For our purposes the main one was to debunk the notion of a Jewish people, which is, of course, the central notion on which Zionism rests. In this construction of history the Jews are a religious entity and not a polity. The true polity was the Hebrews, who were rooted in a land and tied together by a language; the Israelites, from whom the Jews are descended, evolved in the Babylonian Exile into an aterritorial or extraterritorial faith community that later on came to speak many languages. Biblical and all subsequent Jewish historiography is thus a willful construct, historically false and serving the needs of the faith community. The historiography that this new reading of the past suggests is thus seen as "scientific" and therefore "true" and "natural."

It is at this point relevant to note that Horon, too, had been a Revisionist, except that he had been much closer to Jabotinsky than Ratosh was. And like Ratosh he had broken with the party and its leader, only three years earlier than Ratosh. In 1935 Jabotinsky called a congress of the Revisionist movement in Vienna, at which the New Zionist Organization was formed. During the deliberations Jabotinsky

> decided to introduce a quasi-religious plank into the revisionist constitution. He had rediscovered, as it were, the sacred treasures of Jewish tradition. Indifferent tolerance was no longer enough; he even mentioned the necessity of a synthesis between nationalism and religion. His explanations for this sudden turnabout are unconvincing; this was not a case of sudden conversion. However vehemently he denied it, Jabotinsky's real intention was to gain the support of orthodox-religious circles in eastern Europe. Perhaps the stand taken by Rabbi Kook . . . in defence of the Biryonim, under attack at the time of the Arlosoroff crisis, influenced him. Perhaps . . . Jabotinsky felt that secular impulses were insufficient to generate and maintain moral integrity in a nation. Be that as it may, basically it was a tactical move lacking inner conviction.[54]

During the constitutional debate only two individuals spoke against the religious plank. One was Horon.

For him Zionism was not the realization of the Jewish vision but an
absolute rebellion against *galut* [exile] and all that it entailed. More correctly, even then he scorned Zionism and wanted something else in its
place. Zionism was androgynous, illogical, an attempt to establish in the
name of the religious tradition something that, should it ever succeed,
would have to deliver the death-blow to the tradition and to the very
existence of Judaism. For him the word "Jew" was linked to two thousand
years of *galut* and only to this.[55]

Horon was wont to say that "the event of the birth of a new nation should
not be hidden behind a Jewish veil, as part of an attempt to convince the
whole world that finally something Jewish was happening in Palestine at
a time when . . . something Hebrew was occurring in Canaan."[56]

We can see that for Horon, Zionism was intrinsically secular, an unam-
biguous break with the Jewish past. When the Revisionists adopted in
their constitution the religious plank that Jabotinsky wanted and thus
officially came around to the same dialectical relationship to the past that
their Labor Zionist cohorts had been holding for three decades, Horon
broke with them. In 1938 in Paris a similar development was now taking
place in Ratosh. We have already seen that he too originally saw Zionism
strictly as a secular revolution and a break with the past. But now, under
the tutelage of Horon, he began to understand the nature of the revolution and that past more sharply.

Judaism from its inception was not a continuity, however distorted, of the
Hebrew world but a human group that arose on the ruins of the ancient
Hebrew world after its destruction. . . . And since Judaism was never a
nation, so Zionism from its beginnings and in its essence was never and is
not a national movement, including not only Weizmann but also Jabotinsky.[57]

Now he knew why Zionism and its adherents were so foreign to him:
they were Diaspora Jews seeking, under Jabotinsky as under Herzl, to
solve their problems as Jews in the twentieth century in the same terms
as the Babylonian exiles, under Ezra, sought to solve theirs: by returning
to a Jewish construct called "Zion." The national enterprise that was
taking place in Palestine had betrayed its mission when it made an
alliance with the Jewish past, with the Jewish religion, and, in its obsequious attitude to the British, with the Jewish spirit. For Ratosh as for
Horon, Zionism was to be rejected as a Diaspora phenomenon—foreign,
religious, and, therefore, "unnatural." The national enterprise that was
developing in Palestine was a Hebrew one, rooted solely in that territory
and that language. If there was any past that would be returned to or
appropriated, it was the pre-Jewish Hebrew past. As Shavit felicitously
puts it, "the Hebrew did not return to his land in order to be a Jew."[58]

Thus did the vision of a Hebrew nation begin to take shape in Ratosh's mind. Thus did he begin to understand the nature of the sovereignty he had wanted recognized and granted forthwith, and for which he had so passionately argued: not a state for the Jews but the legitimation through statehood of the indigenous Hebrew nation that was beginning its life anew in Palestine. Thus did the concept of *malkhut yisra'el*, which he had espoused as a maximalist Revisionist, now become transmuted into the notion of *Erets Haperat* (the Land of the Euphrates) or *Erets Hakedem* (the Land of the East).[59] Borders that had been mandated by the Bible were now mandated by the historical, archeological, and linguistic record of the ancient Near East.

And thus did Ratosh, under Horon, begin to attain clarity about the three problems that had vexed him since his youth. The "British problem" was that of foreigners occupying a land that did not really belong to them. The "Jewish Problem," we can now see, was the same: Zionism represented a usurpation of "the Land of the Euphrates" by an agency every bit as foreign and as pernicious as the British. Likewise the "Arab problem," for another implication of Horon's thought (or method) was that just as there is no Jewish people, so is there no Arab people. There are large numbers of individuals in that region bound up in the faith community of Islam, just as there are individuals bound up in the faith community of Judaism. But the polity is Hebrew. Ratosh thus began to understand the "Arab problem" as that of Pan-Arabism, which in this perspective was no less a threat to the incipient Hebrew nation than Zionism or the British mandate. This is why in time Ratosh would argue that the natural allies of the new Hebrew nation were those non-Moslem entities such as the Copts, Maronites, Cherkassians, Kurds, Armenians, and Druse, who were not a part of the Pan-Arab constellation and would want to resist it. And with regard to those who call themselves Arabs, the task of the Hebrew national movement would have to be the same one as with the Jews: to bring them back to their Hebrew sources and identity.[60]

By his own admission Ratosh did not come to these conclusions quickly or accept Horon's ideas easily. In spite of his thoroughly secular background, he describes himself as having been

> still in the grip of the traditional Jewish trap of the Hebrew-Jewish-Israeli identity. . . . Anyone educated as I and my contemporaries and those younger than we were, in the lap of Bible stories and Zionism from childhood, would have difficulty in coming to a position in which it would be possible to see things in this way. . . . It [this background] was ideological propaganda, in plain language: brainwashing.[61]

But gradually Ratosh transformed his consciousness and his identity. He remained in Paris from early 1938 until the outbreak of World War II in September 1939. It was during this time that Uriel Halpern formally became Yonatan Ratosh.[62] If we say that the "Canaanite" movement has its origins at this time and place, two facts need to be noted.

First is the irony that Shavit has observed: that a mode of thought and a movement that are nativistic and Hebrew in nature were spawned not in Tel Aviv but in Paris.[63] Second, this brief account of the fateful meeting of Ratosh with Horon suggests that the true origins of "Canaanism" are in Horon, not in Ratosh. There are those who believe that a careful reading of Ratosh indicates that he was already moving toward "Canaanism" in 1937 and had he never met Horon he would still have arrived there.[64] But by his own admission Ratosh says that his encounter with Horon was formative. Ratosh's prime disciple, Aharon Amir, describes Ratosh's experience in Paris as something like what happened to Paul of Tarsus on the road to Damascus.[65] To the extent that Horon gave Ratosh the intellectual tools and, what is more important for our purposes, enabled him to perform the conceptual move of linking Zionism and Judaism so that in transcending or rejecting one, he would transcend or reject the other—to that extent is Horon without question the founder of the "Canaanite" idea as a mode of thought, as a heresy. Ratosh, however, is clearly the initiator of the attempt to translate the "Canaanite" idea into a movement.[66]

III

With the outbreak of World War II Ratosh returned to Tel Aviv. He apparently would have been content to remain in Paris for an additional year, since he was deeply engrossed in consolidating everything he had absorbed during the previous year and was in the process of summarizing it in writing. But in September 1939 he chose to return to Palestine.[67] The summary he had written was inadvertently left behind in Paris but the ideas were still fresh in his mind. Moreover, just prior to his departure from Paris, in response to the British White Paper, he had drafted an outline of the steps he thought necessary for the formation of a Hebrew liberation movement. Accordingly, when he arrived back in Tel Aviv he was quite clear about his goals.

The obvious focus of his political and ideological energies now was the Irgun. The idea of that body as the primary catalyst of Hebrew liberation had long been with him. Now its potential to assume this role was even clearer, for it was at this time that Stern was leading a faction out of the Irgun to form a new underground paramilitary organization. Jabotinsky had instructed that as long as Germany was to be resisted the Irgun was to cooperate with Britain in the fight; Stern, however, was adamant that the primary struggle was to achieve *malkhut yisra'el,* and therefore the British were the real enemy. With this open break with Jabotinsky, Ratosh saw a real chance to realize with Stern what had evolved in his mind in Paris.[68] Although Stern was two years older than he, Ratosh fancied himself as something of a mentor to him and, as we have seen, the two had worked together in the Irgun in the mid-thirties. There was also a philosophical congruence between them about the means that the struggle for liberation would have to employ—both were clear that the British would be dislodged only by bullets and bombs and that a nation is born not through diplomacy but in blood and death. They were in similar agreement about ends as well, at least so Ratosh thought.

He was wrong. As with the Revisionist party in 1938, so now in 1940 was Ratosh to be disappointed with Stern. There were some things about him that Ratosh either had overlooked or of which he was simply unaware. For Stern the words "Hebrew" and "Jew" were not antithetical as they were for Ratosh, but complementary. As close as he may have been with Ratosh, Stern's maximalist roots lay elsewhere—in the messianic, "theological" Revisionism of Uri Tsvi Greenberg and Israel Scheib (Eldad). Stern's attitude and relationship to Jewish religion and tradition were entirely different from Ratosh's[69] After all, he had not undergone the conversion experience Ratosh had just had in Paris, nor is there any reason to suppose that he was or would be interested in or susceptible to such an experience. And so when Stern came out in the autumn of 1940 with the eighteen-point manifesto of his new group, the '*Ikarei hatehiyah* (The principles of revival), Ratosh would not find therein precisely the program he had in mind. True, the document talked of Hebrew liberation, but a different spirit animated it.

> The Hebrew, anti-Zionist "Canaanism" of Ratosh and the Jewish-Hebrew national messianism of [Stern] drew from the same source, but developed in different and opposing directions. Both views sought to revive the sovereign-territorial element in the history of the Jewish people, but emphasized the formative role of "the physical homeland," both were sharply critical of the Zionist political establishment, both advocated military activism, and the map of territorial sovereignty of both was large— but their relationship to Jewish history and their vision of national culture were completely different. The emphasis on *erets yisra'el* and similar terminologies are what blur the qualitative difference between the two.[70]

At this point Ratosh broke with Stern. But a little over a year later, in February 1942, Stern was killed by the British. In the aftermath his group began to undergo a reorganization, changing its name to *Lohamei Herut Yisra'el* or Lehi (Fighters for the Freedom of Israel) and, more importantly, engaging in a new struggle for ideological clarity.[71] Ratosh, who we can see was tirelessly persistent, now saw another chance. The young men gravitating toward the new Lehi represented to him the best of the younger generation. They were the best because they were channeling their capacity for rebellion, a capacity with which Ratosh could identify, in a way very close to what he had in mind: not only were they anti-British but many of them (not all) were antireligious and anti-Zionist.[72]

It was at about this time, in late 1942 or early 1943, in the absence of any firm ideological institution that might have appeared suitable as a base on which to build, that Ratosh organized his own group, the *Va'ad Legibbush Hano'ar Ha'ivri* (Committee for the Formation of Hebrew Youth). This group consisted at first of perhaps ten or twelve young intellectual or artistic types, some of whom were active in the underground. Included in the core group were Aharon Amir, Binyamin Tammuz, Moshe Giora-Elimelekh, Uzi Ornan (Ratosh's brother), and Avraham Rimmon.[73] Functionally the group resembled nothing so much as a Hasidic Rebbe and his disciples: Ratosh would expound the "Canaanite" Torah and the disciples would listen and learn. In 1943 the committee issued its first public utterance—the "Ketav el hano'ar ha'ivri" (Open letter to the Hebrew youth). Written by Ratosh, it is at once a proclamation of the existence of Hebrew nationhood and a call to its banner. If we regard Ratosh's conception of the situation of Jewish youth in Palestine microcosmically, it becomes immediately clear that this ringing document is really nothing other than a projection of this conception into and onto the macrocosm.

> The Committee for the Formation of Hebrew Youth summons you to reflect on the depth of the chasm and alienation that separates you, the Hebrew youth, from all those Jews in the Diaspora. . . . The Committee for the Formation of Hebrew Youth turns to you because you are the strength of tomorrow in this land. . . . The Committee for the Formation of Hebrew Youth is not afraid for you because of the scorn and admonishment that will be poured out upon you . . . but . . . is in fear . . . that you will become accustomed to the manners of the Jewish Diaspora, lest your heart go astray after its outlook and criteria, . . . lest you learn its ways and . . . forget who you are, a part of a normal nation, a part of the ascendant Hebrew nation. . . . And we do not promise you pleasure, neither personal nor social. We promise all who follow us the full misunderstanding of the public at large. . . . We promise the full force of the clash with Zionism, from its deepest roots to . . . its fullest power and corruption, and we promise the fullness of the blind, avaricious and vicious hatred from all the various bureaucracies—to the bitter end. . . . But we know the power of the illumination of Hebrew consciousness. This consciousness, when it will come upon you, will totally purify [you] of the vestiges of your reprehensible education. . . . The tie that binds the generations of Judaism cannot be loosened; it can only be severed. And you, child of the native land, can cut it. . . . And when all this is removed from off you, you will come to inner wholeness, to that simple and natural harmony between thought and feeling. All the hidden strengths, strangled by the chains of the Jewish dispersion and Zionist cleverness, will rouse themselves. . . . Zionism in all its wings and divisions has always known slogans—don't be misled by them. Jewish cleverness has a vague idea of what is bothering you and it will compromise with you a bit and will open to you here and there avenues of activity that will claim to fill

your needs. Stand on guard. . . . Let your eyes be opened. . . . We are few in number today and are not found everywhere. But we will get to you, and we shall meet.[74]

Ratosh realized, or was made to realize, that a coterie with ideological purity and clarity, important as it was, would not suffice to bring about the Hebrew revolution he envisioned. The base had to be broadened. One of the inner circle, Moshe Giora-Elimelekh, says he "convinced Ratosh that . . . he needed to approach a wider audience, both on the left and on the right, with things that could serve as a true common ground."[75] This led to the committee's second publication, the "Igeret 'el Lohamei Herut Yisra'el" (Epistle to the fighters for the freedom of Israel.)[76] This is a longer document and much less shrill than the breathless "Open Letter to the Hebrew Youth" (which leads me to wonder if it is not the work of a hand other than Ratosh's). Essentially it is a carefully written appeal to the Lehi, at the time of its organizational redefinition, to address itself to the nature of its ideological basis and its goals. There is an attempt to wean the Lehi away from Uri Tsvi Greenberg's "confusion of the Jewish religion with the Hebrew nation" and a fairly low-key invitation to undo this linkage. Over and over the "Epistle" makes the point that acts of terror alone are not enough; a revolution in consciousness also needs to take place.

Natan Yellin-Mor, who, after the daring escape from the Latrun detention camp in November 1943, became a part of the Lehi's leadership triumvirate (along with Yisra'el Eldad and Yitshak Shamir), tells of Ratosh's efforts to conscript the Lehi in his committee's campaign:

> The objective of his meeting with me was to find out if there was any possibility of the two organizations uniting into one body that would fight for his ideas. I listened with great interest to Shelah's ideas, which excelled in their persuasive powers. At the end I asked him what had to be done, in his opinion, at this time. He proposed crystallizing the Hebrew youth, educating it towards Hebrew consciousness. I asked him again: and what will be after you have [done all that]? . . A broad smile crossed Shelah's face: then everything will be all right, all the other problems will be easily solved.

Yellin-Mor was obviously sceptical. His knowledge of Jewish youth in Poland convinced him that they were no less tied and committed to a Hebrew sensibility than those born in Palestine, and he was not so ready to write them off. And so

> the conversation did not lead to any practical results. Nevertheless I was certain that among those who had collected themselves in the "Committee," many would find their way to the Lehi. One of the young men who joined the Lehi when he was imbued with the ideas of the "Committee for the Formation of Hebrew Youth" was—Eliahu Bet-Tsuri.[77]

Possibly because its few members were involved in various aspects of the underground, the committee at this time took on the character of a clandestine group. There was probably a measure of reason for this: the British would not appreciate the difference between revolutionary ideas and revolutionary deeds. The main focus now was to continue developing a platform and formulating it in terms intelligible to the general public. Money was becoming a factor, for the group was small and the cost of printing was large. But somehow the effort succeeded. In 1944 the committee published its *Mas'a hapetihah* (The opening discourse), a small book on the cover of which was engraved the royal blue and purple flag of the "Hebrew nation" that Ratosh had designed. The subtitle of this extended piece indicates the underground nature of the group: "In Executive Session with the Agents of the Cells (First Meeting)." So, too, does the opening sentence: "The cells have been doing their work for a while now and the labor is difficult and arduous."

Written largely, if not completely, by Ratosh, *The Opening Discourse* is unquestionably a major document of "Canaanism" and the fullest exposition of its ideas in the prestate period. Although various ideas and phrases are taken almost verbatim from the "Open Letter to the Hebrew Youth," they are reworked and developed into a sustained argument. Because *The Opening Discourse* is such an important source for understanding Ratosh's critique of Zionism, because it presents a rich array of ideas and insights, I shall reserve discussion of it for the next chapter. Suffice it to note here that it was not without its effects and results. Uri Avneri notes that

> The very notion that there was being born in Palestine a new nation separate from the Jews and which does not find its expression in Zionism, made a strong impression upon young people like me in the early forties. . . . The Zionist leadership looked miserable, a sad appendage of the British. The heart of the young [generation] was thirsty for a new message.[78]

Ratosh gave it to them by addressing both their political energies and their sense of self-identity. For many, joining the Lehi was an act of self-expression; "the involvement in politics translated itself into a cultural matter."[79] Such young men were quickly identified by their peers, and very soon a meeting with Ratosh would be arranged for them. A Socratic conversation of many hours would usually ensue, during which the novice would be put through his ideological paces. The result was sometimes a convert to the "Committee for the Formation of Hebrew Youth," more often a confirmed Lehi or Palmah member who looked upon Ratosh and his group with only passing interest.

The problem for many was the cerebral nature of what Ratosh was offering. According to Avneri the romantic appeal to a distant past, much less one based on ideological abstractions and discriminations, ultimately did not meet the needs of the practical-minded Palestinian youth. They wanted action, and, ironically, the encounter with Ratosh's poetry and personality spurred them to see the Lehi as the place to find it. Those who became active in the committee were those who appreciated the centrality of ideology. Avneri writes:

> In the whole group there was not one who had a serious grasp of politics, who saw in politics his way of life, who had any expertise in the history of revolutionary movements or in the art of political action. I think that the surplus of poets and the lack of politicians determined to a great extent the path of the Canaanite group, with its romantic and dogmatic excesses and its political, ideological, and practical failures.[80]

Thus it happened that in the four years following the apperance of *The Opening Discourse* until the proclamation of Israeli statehood, Ratosh did not press his agenda as vigorously as in the years 1939–44, following his return to Palestine. Now began his lifelong disappointment that the Lehi never emerged as anything more than a coalition of activists of various kinds without a clear ideology. In fact, with the arrival of statehood, the Lehi disbanded instead of becoming the embodiment of Ratosh's hopes for a Hebrew revolution.[81] Furthermore, in 1946 Avneri decided to implement the insights he had received (not so much from Ratosh as from reading Horon's articles in *Shem*) by organizing an overtly political group, one that ostensibly was competing with Ratosh's committee.[82] As conditions deteriorated in the last years of the British Mandate and the actual battle for statehood eroded the stability of daily life in Palestine, Ratosh decided to suspend the committee's activities.[83]

IV

Ten years after Ratosh had demanded immediate Hebrew sovereignty over Palestine, the State of Israel came into being, as a Jewish, Zionist state with, compared to what the maximalists had wanted, truncated borders. In one sense Ratosh clearly had failed and was defeated. In another, though, his vision had prevailed, at least its first stage: the foreign occupier had been evicted and the role of the nativist sensibility that he had articulated in *Looking Towards Sovereignty* and for which he had ceaselessly proselytized, could be seen as having been instrumental in achieving this. The Lehi was the small wheel that had engaged the larger wheel of the Irgun into motion, and those two, in turn, had meshed with and driven the Haganah.[84] It is worth noting, though, that during this entire period Ratosh did not participate personally in the Lehi. His role, as we can see, was that of an intellectual terrorist, an ideologist in search of his legions.

When statehood came it was clear to Ratosh that there had been a revolution in form, not in content. A foreign entity was still in charge. The Hebrew revolution was farther away than ever and its cause again needed to be advanced. There being no need now for a clandestine group, the committee was reorganized as a visible movement, the *'Ivriyim hatse'irim* (Young Hebrews). Its members were still few, and so Ratosh decided to utilize the printed word as the primary method of disseminating his ideas to the public, only now not in convert manifestos but in a review.[85]

Thus was born *Alef,* a publication that from November 1948 through April 1953 served as the vehicle for Ratosh's thought and the "Canaanite" movement as a whole. During this time twenty-three issues appeared, sometimes monthly and sometimes bimonthly. Initially Ratosh listed himself as the editor, but *Alef* was always produced collectively. Editorial policy and content were formulated by a small group, generally following Ratosh's leads, and Amir functioned as a kind of "managing editor."[86] During its existence *Alef* had a small circulation, never more than about five hundred, but its influence in the new state was noticeable. An analysis of the content of the twenty-three issues, important as it is for tracking the details of the development of the "Canaanite" movement, is beyond the scope of this survey of Ratosh's life. In general the publication had everything in it that would reflect its view that the state that had been created was not a continuity of any kind but, as the name *Alef* and what it symbolized implied, a new beginning.[87] There were spacious expositions of the "Hebrew" ideology in all its ramifications by Ratosh and Amir, translations of essays by Horon, poetry and fiction by budding writers, book and drama reviews, pictures of sculpture, inquiries from readers about "Hebrew" identity and ideology, and reports about the progress and how it was being reported and viewed in both the Israeli and overseas Jewish press. Even today, at a distance of over three decades, *Alef* makes for lively reading and provides an interesting retrospective view of the issues that came to the fore during the first years of the new state.

The "Canaanite" movement was now beginning to have some impact. Ex-members of the Lehi and the Palmah, the *dor Tash'ah* (generation of 1948), whose nativist inclinations were being disappointed by the new reality that was taking shape, found their way to the "Canaanite" banner, if only temporarily.[88] Zionism had no claim on them as an ideology; they saw it as something artificial, "Zionism in quotation marks." Like the Lehi in its day, "Canaanism" was as much a matter of style[89] as of substance, and sometimes of mystique and notoriety.[90] Ratosh, however, was determined that the substance of the movement would prevail. In the light of the measurable response "Canaanism" was getting, he and his closest followers announced in the autumn of 1951 the formation of a public group—the *Merkaz ha'ivriyim hatse'irim* (The Center for Young Hebrews).

The Center was to be the closest Ratosh would ever come to translating his vision into political action. "Canaanism" now moved from the privacy of a salon into the public arena. It sought to become an identifiable option within the Israeli body politic. "The Center for Young Hebrews will work as a public body, within the framework of a democratic organization. It will seek to project its influence on the political life of this state. But with all this, it is not a party."[91] This last point was decisive. Ratosh eschewed running a list for the Knesset in accordance with the Israeli electoral system; that would have meant playing the Zionist political game. Instead, the center offered itself not as one more party but as a force above the petty squabbles of contending factions, as a rallying point of patriots who saw themselves primarily as members of a distinct nation in a distinctive part of the world.[92]

This approach was to prove fatal. The only concrete things the Center would produce were a manifesto and a twenty-four point program. These are important in the long run; as we shall see in the next chapter, they are valuable indicators of how the "Canaanite" critique of Zionism might be translated into reality. In the short run, however, they were at best premature, at worst naïve and utopian, since they were not grounded in the political structure and social realities of Israel of 1951.

For this reason, and perhaps for a host of others, "Canaanism" as an overt movement and an articulated ideology began to decline from this point on.[93] The Center did not become a political force of any kind, and by the middle of 1953 *Alef* ceased publication. Those who were in the movement for the ideological speculation it afforded now suddenly found themselves with less time; the pressures and compromises of family and career made themselves felt. There was no small stigma in being identified with a group that was looked upon as a "lunatic fringe," possibly subversive.[94] Those who had found in Ratosh's circle a chance for self-expression and an escape from "cultural provincialism" now did not have such needs.[95] And those who were impatient with the political ineptness of the whole thing or who had differences with Ratosh over doctrine and strategy left in disappointment. The human and material base to fuel the movement, never copious to begin with, now eroded.

Ratosh, who by all accounts was an optimist by nature, does not give the impression of having become embittered at the way things were turning out. His big disappointments had come at Prague in 1938 and with Stern and the Lehi between 1940 and 1948. In the wake of these letdowns his expectations of the Zionist state were few. His prediction that the failure to found a Hebrew nation-state based on secular principles would inexorably lead to "the Destruction of the Third Commonwealth" was a matter of public record,[96] and all he could do now was await the time when the alternative he had conceived would triumph by default. Boaz Evron is perceptively correct when he says that "the time when the 'Canaanite' sensibility and consciousness was at its height was *before* the War of Independence."[97]

The rest of Ratosh's life from 1953 until his death in 1981, while quantitatively great, is really all of one piece. "Canaanism" essentially disappeared as a manifest movement from the Israeli scene, even as its presence as a latent force continued[98] and, as we shall see in chapter 5, continues even today. Ratosh had no new ideas to add to his already fully formulated system. Only twice did the events of the day stimulate him to reopen his case against Zionism and make a new attempt to press his "Hebrew" agenda.

The first was the war of 1967. What galvanized Ratosh into action here was the interpretation that was being given to Israel's unexpected victory and to the new geopolitical situation that victory presented. On the very eve of the war he and Uzi Ornan hastily revived *Alef*.[99] Then, when the fighting stopped, Ratosh published a small book analyzing the war, *1967 umah hal'a?* (1967 and what next?).[100]

The tone here is angry, and a sense of being vindicated pervades every page. Ratosh construes the long weeks of waiting and indecision that preceded the war as the weakness born of the Diaspora Jewish mentality that cowers before the Gentiles. Likewise, the popular interpretation of Israel's lightning victory as a "miracle" was to him an admission of Jewish powerlessness. It was to him convincing proof that Zionism and Zionist politicians looked at the world through Jewish glasses, a perspective that in the long run would be fatal to the nation-state. On the other hand, Ratosh saw the decision not to wait any longer, the victory itself, and, most important, the subsequent territorial conquests as the fruits not of the Zionist politicians but of the Hebrew spirit and power at work in the young people of the military. The need of the hour, he argues, is to save the emerging nation from the politicians and from the dangers of coalition politics where Jewish and Zionist religio-ethical interests are served and not the territorial interests of a secular Hebrew nation. Ratosh advocates the temporary appointment of a *nagid* (chancellor)—perhaps the chief of staff—to ensure that in the negotiations that will follow the maximum will be demanded.[101] The strains of *Looking Towards Sovereignty* of three decades earlier are still audible.

The Yom Kippur war of 1973,[102] specifically its aftermath, was not surprisingly the other moment when Ratosh saw an opening. Now he could point to the mood of depression and the sense of vulnerability that hung over Israeli society as the inevitable result of the Zionist compromise with Judaism. Except now the military leaders were implicated as well. Ratosh at this time edited an anthology of "Canaanite" thinking, a source-book that would lay before a new generation of Israelis the "Canaanite" alternative.[103] The preface Ratosh wrote for this volume was a recapitulation of everything he had been saying for nearly forty years. Now, however, he could fathom the beginnings of "the Destruction of the Third Commonwealth" that he had predicted.

All the evil sicknesses of the Israeli regime and [its] policies are now visible to the naked eye in all their manifestations. Domestically, all the ties that bind are coming apart; the social ethic, society itself, is disintegrating; the economy is bankrupt; the gaps between socioeconomic groups are becoming clear; emigration increases; the establishment—the government, the Knesset—is in a crisis to the point of admitting the bankruptcy of the system itself and the yearning for the strong hand of a government of experts, for an emergency government; and [there are] voices calling for a change in the structure of the parties, for their dissolution, for the dissolution of the Knesset, for the solution of dictatorship. . . . We are transforming victories into standoffs and standoffs into defeats. . . . The State of Israel as it is now has no chance.[104]

The anthology was in press in July 1976, when the rescue at the Entebbe airport occurred. Ratosh appended a section to his preface in which he tried to assimilate this apparent victory of Zionism and corroboration of its effectiveness into his anti-Zionist system. The rescue, he said, was indeed evidence of the inherent valor, daring, strategic brilliance, and technological superiority of the Israelis. The only problem was that these qualities were being applied exclusively to Jewish problems, in this case the religious commandment of "redemption of captives." They were not in evidence in regard to the larger matters and policies of state, especially Israel's attitude and relationship to non-Jews: those who wished to settle there were discouraged and presented with difficulties, and those who, like the Druse in Syria and the Maronites in Lebanon, were natural allies were abandoned to the Arab sphere of influence.[105]

This was to be Ratosh's parting shot. His ideas, if taken seriously at all, were dismissed outright, as they had been all along by the intellectual and political consensus, with the exception of a few ex-disciples and secularists who saw constructive possibilities in the "Canaanite" approach. I shall consider some of these figures and possibilities in chapter 5. Later in his life Ratosh had vague aspirations of becoming a political advisor to Gen. Ariel Sharon,[106] but it is hard to know if this notion was anything more than a fantasy. We can gauge the difference between the estimation of Ratosh's political thought and the estimation of his poetry from the recognition that was accorded him on December 31, 1980. At that time a symposium was held at Haifa University commemorating the fortieth anniversary of the publication of his first and most celebrated volume of poetry, *Huppah shehorah* (Black canopy).[107] We can perceive this event as the payment of a debt long overdue by the Israeli literary establishment, but there may have been something else here as well: by the end of 1980 the ideology Ratosh had propounded all his life was apparently judged to be so remote from the actualities of Israeli society that it was no longer viewed as a threat of any kind, and it was now, as it might not have been before, safe to pay honor to him as a poet.

For his part, Ratosh, while he enjoyed the fete, was not deceived. His last months were spent in the same modest circumstances he had lived in for years, reading proofs for various publishing houses in his favorite Tel Aviv coffeehouse and, with his ever-present bottle of cognac within easy reach, contemplating the discrepancy between what he had envisioned and what he now saw around him. Perhaps the cognac helped dispel the discrepancy. In the weeks before he died he disclosed in two extended interviews[108] his final thoughts about this discrepancy, together with some hitherto unknown details about his life (adduced throughout this chapter). There is a prescience about these interviews, as if the interviewers sensed that Ratosh the recently honored poet and Ratosh the scorned ideologist could not be separated so neatly, and that the ideology itself, curiosity and "period piece" that it had become, was somehow not so unrelated to Israel of 1981. When asked why there were so few "Canaanites," Ratosh answered in the same terms that introduced the life story I have sought to outline in this chapter and that fairly summarize it now that it has reached its end:

> A new ideology never conquers hearts immediately. . . . I'm sorry but I believed it was quite simple and, in fact, I think it *was* very simple. One of the central questions, maybe the major question of the young Hebrew intelligentsia in the forties, was the question of identity. This is, of course, a question that no one really deals with, but it eats at our hearts even today. There is no one who knows exactly what our identity here is, even though the establishment always has a very clear answer, and a very Jewish one.[109]

Yonatan Rotash died in his sleep in March 1981. To the end he was uncompromising in his refusal to be co-opted by Jewish communal and religious usages. There were no Jewish funeral rites and there was no burial; he willed his body to science. "In the last analysis," he once wrote, "a person is free to be free only to the extent that he is willing to pay the price."[110]

IV

YONATAN RATOSH AND THE DECONSTRUCTION OF ZIONISM

We are now ready to examine more closely the critique of Zionism that Ratosh developed as well as the details of the ideology he fashioned in its place. The broad outlines of these concepts are, it is hoped, visible from the foregoing survey of Ratosh's life. Now we can identify and analyze the specific arguments involved and assess their significance. First, though, a few observations are in order about some general features of Ratosh's thought as they emerge from the preceding chapter.

The major premise from which Ratosh's life and thought must be seen to proceed is the notion that the national enterprise that began among the Jews in Palestine at the end of the nineteenth century constitutes a break with their past and the beginning of a revolution in all aspects of their life—consciousness, content, and form. To the extent that Zionism represented and promoted this rejection of the Jewish past, to the extent that it understood itself as a purely secular force and not as a religious one, to that extent was it on the right track. When, however, it made its peace with the past, when it made a place for the past in its program, when it secularized the religious past and then appropriated it in order to use Jewish history to validate itself, Zionism compromised and thus betrayed its revolutionary nature and nullified its radical goals. All these are "givens" for Ratosh.

We cannot say definitely that Zionism was ever understood by its leaders and protagonists in such an unalloyed way. The ambiguous relationship with the Jewish religious past that I have described seems to have been intrinsic to Zionism from its outset. The only identifiable element within its ranks that gives any indication that Zionism's true agenda was the reconstruction of Jewish existence on a totally secular basis is that broad element for whom the question of "culture" was even more pressing than the question of territory. The figure most obviously suggested here is Mikhah Yosef Berditchevsky, and that connection is true enough. But as Almog makes clear, Berditchevsky really is only the extreme expression of the larger quest for a transvaluation of Jewish values that characterizes all of that general tendency—it was never an organized movement—we know as cultural Zionism.[1] Indeed, the struggle against Jewish religion was an essential part of the program of the *Demokratische Fraktion* that walked out of the Fifth Zionist Congress in 1901 as a protest against the pragmatic political conception of Zionism that Herzl was advancing. At its own conference in Heidelberg in 1902, this small group of westernized intellectuals formulated as its program that

> Zionism is the striving for the liberation of the Jewish nation from historical pressure, the solution of the problem of the Jewish individual, and thus also of the economic problem of the Jewish nation and the political Jewish problem. . . . The introduction of religion into the argumentation for, and [into] the program of Zionism is inconsistent with the national character of Zionism. . . .[2]

Vital's description of the brief and ineffectual career of the *Demokratische Fraktion* is, *mutatis mutandis*, a rather accurate description of the "Canaanite" coterie in Palestine a half-century later:

> The Democratic Party [Vital's term] was perhaps . . . too remote, in spite of the origins of its members, from the actual east European scene, and . . . [was] composed of men who were too intellectual in cast of mind and too fastidious in taste to make a thoroughgoing stab at power or power-sharing—even if such a thing had been feasible in the years of Herzl's supremacy. . . . None the less, the Democratic Party did leave a mark. It helped to make open, vocal opposition to Herzl somewhat more respectable than it might otherwise have been.[3]

This, then, is what we may generalize about Ratosh's ideology in its larger sense: when we accord it a status beyond the mere working out of inner, personal, and psychological needs—and since this is not a psycho-historical study, it is not my concern whether this was or was not the case—we can see it as a throwback to that tendency in the development of modern Jewish nationalism which put the emphasis on cultural revolution and on the cultural content of the nation-state in the making. Typologically and functionally, Ratosh bears more than a superficial resemblance to Berditchevsky and perhaps even to Ahad Ha'am.

In any case, whether this linkage adds to or detracts from our understanding of what his long-range goals were, it is clear what the starting point for Ratosh is: Zionism was intended as a break with the past, and when it returned to the past, however dialectically, that return generated a critique and the development of an alternative vision that effectuated the break and rationalized it.

I

The best place to see clearly where, how, and why Ratosh takes issue with Zionism is the *Mas'a hapetihah* (The opening discourse) published in 1944. Although we actually could refer to almost any essay by Ratosh to recover the essential points, *The Opening Discourse* is the single most sustained and systematic polemic against Zionism that Ratosh ever wrote. That fact as well as a number of unique stylistic features combine to make *The Opening Discourse,* in my view, one of the most remarkable and important documents of Jewish intellectual history in this century. This is what I think Uri Avneri means when he describes it as "the summit of Ratosh's life. . . . It was the first and last great creation of the 'Canaanite' school. It may be that in days to come it will be regarded as a historical document."[4] Before looking at the arguments in this long essay, we would do well to take note of some of its stylistic features. They help shape the raw conceptual material of the arguments and reinforce them.

There is first the matter of the considerable amount of anti-Jewish invective in the *Discourse.* Ratosh speaks here of "the stupor of the ancient Jewish poison that eats away, . . . for day by day and hour by hour this poison continues to corrode every pen and every mouth and every heart." Judaism and Zionism are a "sickness" and a "leprosy" that have infected wide areas of the body politic of the nation that is aborning in Palestine.[5] The phenomenal powers of Jewish survival in the Diaspora are compared not to the legendary phoenix that rises from the ashes and takes flight but to the worm, "an invertebrate which has no skeleton that can be broken and no bones that can be scattered. . . ." The more it is cut up into pieces, the more it survives intact, "for each successive piece can continue its groveling existence regardless of where it is cast or of who steps on it."[6] In describing traditional Jewish life Ratosh sounds like Tacitus:

> This is a religious community of people one of whose central and sym-
> bolic holidays—Yom Kippur—has as its high point, for centuries now, a
> kind of prayer called "Kol Nidre": an atonement for false oaths the Jews
> have sworn in order to save themselves from the Gentile oppressors.
> Their other key holiday—Passover—has as its clear ideological core ever
> since the Jews came into existence [the idea] that a people and a land are
> two different things . . . [that] a land is not the home of the people nor is it
> a dwelling place. The land in the Jewish conception is some far-off holy
> place where strangers live, some distant country which, because of the
> righteousness of society and [of] bygone ancestors and [of] the grace and
> mercy of a God, is destined for this people. For the people was not born in
> the land and does not belong to it. It became a people in some other
> country, a foreign land, separated by seas and deserts from its promised
> land. And only through the divine promise and miracles, which God

performs for the Jews while they are silent, and through the power of a
great . . . man of God . . . can the people . . . merit its promised land.[7]

In describing the Jews Ratosh sees around him in Palestine, his *Discourse*
takes on tones reminiscent of *Mein Kampf*:

> Here in the Hebrew land the Jew has removed the furry tails [i.e.,
> "shtreimel"] from his head, cut off his side-locks, learned to mouth the
> Hebrew language and to mutter slogans about a homeland and na-
> tionalism. But let us look with open eyes. He is the same Jew, the eternal
> Jew of the eternal Diaspora. In France he pretends to be a Frenchman, in
> Germany a German. Here he plays his game in Hebrew. . . . He is the
> enemy within who eats up all the best parts. He is the one who tramples on
> the feelings of the best of our children with his obsequious special plead-
> ing and fund-raising. He is the one who trades with his rhetoric on all we
> hold sacred. He is the one who brings upon us the continuation of the
> Jewish catastrophe.[8]

Near the end of the *Discourse*, Ratosh refers to another classic anti-Jewish
tract, the *Protocols of the Elders of Zion*, and its charges against the Jews.
"Of course," he says "all these [charges] are vain insinuations and empty
words." The Jews have "neither the power nor the boldness" to take over
the countries where they live, nor the desire to change the status quo
there.

> But there is one land in the world and one nation where the legend of the
> Elders of Zion is not a legend at all, where there does exist a branch of an
> international organization, where world Jewry does seek to gain control,
> and which world Jewry wants to subjugate to the concept, spirit, and inner
> needs of the Jewish world, the world of the Diaspora. That land is the
> land of Hebrews and that people is the Hebrew people.[9]

How do we account for such verbal excess? Can we make any sense out
of it at all? Several possibilities can be adduced. The most obvious one is
to ascribe everything to the oft-mentioned phenomenon of "Jewish self-
hate"[10] and to conclude that this rhetoric, as well as the ideology it cloaks,
are nothing more than the fruits of a pathology.

Furthermore, if Ratosh, for whatever reason, lacked what Gonen calls
"the ego resources for an identity organization that can tolerate . . .
diversity and even outright contradictions," and his "rage is of an infan-
tile origin,"[11] then the ideology he developed can have no claim upon us
or, for that matter, upon anyone who fancies himself or herself rational
and well adjusted. But since, as I have said, I am not a practitioner of
psychohistory, I am not inclined to base my analysis on such an interpretation and to pass judgment on what is psychiatrically sound or sick.
Particularly since such an approach can serve to deflect the one who

takes it from coming to any terms at all with the implications of Ratosh's ideas.

We are on firmer ground when we understand Ratosh's rhetoric in stylistic terms. A reading of some of Ahime'ir's or Greenberg's articles of the late twenties will illustrate the point that use of such invective was an aspect of intra-Zionist polemics of the period. There is no doubt that Ratosh was intimately acquainted with this writing. Moreover, it is not just in the arguments against Labor Zionism and Labor Zionists by those who defected from their ranks that we find such "Jewish anti-Semitism." The concept of *shelilat hagolah* (negation of the Diaspora) is one of the staples of classical Zionist ideology, and in expounding it many a Zionist writer would heap denunciation and contumely upon the nature of Diaspora life and upon the Jews who were forced or who chose to live it.[12] Whatever the psychological issues at work within this Zionist literary tradition or convention, Ratosh should be seen to be writing within it.

But there is even more to it than this, and now we come to the heart of the matter. If we recall the context in which Ratosh penned *The Opening Discourse* and the audience to which it was addressed, we can understand that he would want to use every device possible to get their attention. If this meant setting up a "we/they" dichotomy between those who felt themselves indigenous to the *Yishuv* and the Jews of the Diaspora and appealing to the long-standing prejudice the former held against the latter—a prejudice I shall discuss a bit later on—then so be it. This is because for Ratosh the central function of the *Discourse* is to transform consciousness. Everything in it—the arguments, the rhetoric, the tone— is in the service of inducing in the reader to whom it was pitched the same transformation of consciousness and identity that Ratosh had experienced with Horon in Paris. That is why the *Discourse* speaks of the importance of "proselytization, liberation of the heart, opening the eyes, and basing action upon thought."[13] If anything, it reads like a religious tract, and its concern for doctrinal purity and the relationship of creed to deed is as intense as anything in Luzzato's *Path of the Upright* or any book of the *Musar* school.

> Winning over people is not a one-time activity. After a person has shown an initial attraction, he is prey to second thoughts. . . . Repeatedly the cerebral Jewish scepticism returns to the immature heart, and questions which had apparently been resolved . . . return and consume and put to flight peace of mind. Deceitful Jewish sensitivity and mendacious Jewish fidelity arise against him to destroy him. . . . Every individual can expect such repeated attacks. It is not enough to win him over—he must be diligently watched.[14]

All this is what Ratosh means by the term *gibbush* (formation or crystallization) and what he intends by that process: the formation and the crystallization of a new consciousness. The name of the group he created is in this sense elliptical; its full name should have been "the Committee for the Formation of the Consciousness of Hebrew Youth."

This is a crucial point in understanding Ratosh and one that was lost both on many of his critics and on practical-minded followers who abandoned him. The Hebrew revolution was not first and foremost a political construct but an internal matter, an act of the imagination. It is the imagination that transforms consciousness. Only when one's consciousness had been transformed would one's identity undergo metamorphosis, and only after that would political forms in the external world be changed. Ratosh, as we have seen, thought this process would come about in a relatively short time, especially since it was an inevitable process to him. But it is clear in the *Discourse* that he does not regard his efforts as anything more than a beginning.

It is in this context that we can comprehend another feature of *The Opening Discourse* that attracts our attention: its contemporaneousness with the destruction of the Jews of Europe and the attitude it displays to that destruction. The *Discourse* was written just at the time when the details of the Nazi death camps had become known in Palestine and just after the Jewish uprising in the Warsaw ghetto. It is probably more correct to say that it was written in the face of those events. Thus the Jewish resistance in the Warsaw ghetto, which could be seen as a contradiction to Ratosh's constricted view of the Jews as weak and obsequious, is minimized as a sop to Zionist aspirations: "And as a sublime example of valor they [the Zionists] point to the heroism in the war of the ghetto, that heroism of rabbits who also will fight with all their limited strength, and to the last breath, when they are trapped inside the recesses of their warrens and have no way to escape."[15] As far as the Nazi slaughter of the Jews goes, it has "touched only the human sensibilities" of the Hebrew youth. Their real fear about it—that is, Ratosh's fear—is that the Zionists will make political capital out of it. With the decimation of the Jews of Europe will come a corresponding decrease in immigration to Palestine; the Zionists will see that Jewish immigrants will not, in fact, outnumber the natives, and then their continued hegemony in Palestine will be in doubt; therefore they would redouble their efforts to Judaize the consciousness of young Hebrews. "But in the heart of the Hebrew youth nothing of all this will remain. In spite of all the indoctrination and proclamation and reportage and literature and speakers and staged demonstrations, nothing will penetrate except into their heads alone."[16] For Ratosh, then, the destruction of the Jews of Europe is a human tragedy, not a Jewish or even a Hebrew one. It is this perspective that enables him to repeat in the *Discourse* a key sentence from the "Open Letter to the Hebrew Youth": "the tie that binds the generations of Judaism cannot be loosened; it can only be severed."[17] In a Jewish context these words would be too painful to bear. We can only conclude that Ratosh knew this, and by writing what he did he redefined the context in which he was thinking, or alternately, forced the readers of the *Discourse* to do that. On the one hand, there is a boldness and an ideological consistency about this approach that are extraordinary. On the other, this was not an expository strategy that had much respect for the sensibilities of the majority of those who might read the *Discourse*. In retrospect such a strategy, not to mention the anti-Jewish language and rhetoric we have noted, did not stand Ratosh in good stead, to say the least. It is doubtful if those who gravitated toward Ratosh and his movement had their consciousness changed by these elements of *The Opening Discourse*. The actual arguments it presents are another matter.

II

About midway through the *Discourse*, after he has expatiated on the difference between a Jew and a Hebrew and all that this difference implies, Ratosh attempts to deal with Zionism in a systematic way. This effort is part of the emphasis on doctrine that is so pronounced here. Ratosh lays down five theses that he says are the essence of Zionism. In spite of the fact that there are many varieties of Zionism—and he indicates a full awareness of the ideological spectrum that runs from Magnes to Weizmann to Jabotinsky—Ratosh posits the following five points as the foundation of the Zionist consensus:

Zionism stands on the belief that:

—the Jews are a people, either greater than other peoples or particularly sick or both great and sick at the same time, but first and foremost—a people. . . .

—this Jewish people desires this land as a homeland, and has been linked to it all its days, whether actually or potentially. . . .

—this Jewish people, as a people, has the capacity to set up a movement of national liberation.

—this movement of Jewish liberation is Zionism. . . .

—the Hebrew settlement in this land is a direct result of Zionism and a limb of world Jewry [literally, "the Jewish dispersion"] . . . [and its purpose is] to solve the question of the Jews and of Judaism (whether physical or spiritual or psychological). . . .

And the fitting symbol for this is the Zionist tallit, which the Zionists hastily seized at the last minute before their first Congress, as a substitute for a flag.[18]

All this to Ratosh is inherently false, since no true nation ever leaves its territory to return to it. The "Return to Zion" is an event in the history of the Jewish religion; it is not a national phenomenon. This leads him to propound five countertheses:

All the fundamentals of Zionist belief are refuted at their source:

—The Jews are not a nation and never were. They are not a nation but a faith-community [literally, 'edah] whose existence is in the Dispersion and whose homeland is the Dispersion.

—This Jewish faith-community has a Holy Land as do many faith-communities. But it has no homeland, nor does it need one, nor does it want one, neither this land nor any other land.

—A faith-community by its very nature does not have the capacity to establish a national liberation movement. The various groups of fighting zealots it can produce from time to time are not movements of national liberation . . . nor do they have a chance of fulfilling national goals . . . [or] national needs or [achieving] national freedom, which are [for a faith-community] unnecessary, if not superfluous.

—Zionism, as a Jewish phenomenon, as a phenomenon within a faith-community, can absolutely never, from its beginning to any form it will assume in the future, be a movement of national liberation or a national movement at all. . . .

—The Hebrews in Palestine are in no way the direct result of Zionism. Among those who immigrated there, only a small number did not come out of necessity, and these were pilgrims, whether religious or secular, [who have] come to the Jewish Holy Land. . . . But the great majority of Jewish immigrants, whether Zionists or not, and most of the pilgrims among them, did not immigrate to this land because of Zionism or its influence but because of the pressures on Jews to emigrate . . . to many lands. As long as the gates to other countries were not closed, only a tiny part of the waves of worldwide Jewish migration came here. . . .[19]

Now a close inspection of these theses and corresponding counter-theses will show that the decisive one in each case is the first. The respective arguments as Ratosh structures them are circular: once the Jews are defined as either a people or a faith-community, everything else follows. The point we need to concentrate on is the first one. Ratosh's entire conceptual system rests on the assumption—only for him is it a fact—that a nation is constituted solely by a specific territory and a common language. These alone determine its history and its culture. As we have seen, Ratosh learned from Horon how the history of the ancient Near East could be seen both to corroborate this assumption and to serve it. Armed with the approach and the findings of higher biblical criticism and archeology, Ratosh is able to construct a new historiography, one that relativizes the absolutes of the biblical understanding of the Jews or, more precisely, sets up new absolutes. We may define Ratosh's polemic against Zionism as essentially historicist in nature, akin to modern historicist arguments against the Orthodox interpretation of Jewish religion and *halakhah* (Jewish law).

How correct or valid is this interpretation of the past? Can we determine exactly what a nation is and what the true criteria for nationhood are? Can we say objectively just what or who the Jews are, whether people, nation, religion, or civilization? I think not. Students of various disciplines have addressed these questions for what is now centuries, each utilizing the particular methods, insights, and biases of their specific fields, be they history, anthropology, theology, philosophy, political science, or sociology. Clarity and consensus have been slow in coming. I am persuaded that the *social* nature of all questions is crucial, if not decisive.

> Nationalism depends upon a particular social definition of the situation, that is, upon a collectively agreed-upon entity known as a particular nation. While political scientists have tried to arrive at some intrinsic elements required for nationality (such as common territory, common history and the like), the definition of a particular group of people as constituting a nation is always an act of social construction of reality. That is, it is always "artificial." This is as much the case with France as with, say, Zambia. The difference between France and Zambia is not that the former is in some way less "artificial" a construction than the latter, but rather that the construction has been around for a longer time.[20]

This analysis gives us a useful perspective from which to grasp both the flaws and the insights of Ratosh's argument. It is not that he is necessarily wrong in his understanding of the Jews and of Judaism; it is that this understanding is a private construction of reality, not a social one. Conversely, it is not that Zionist historiography is correct; it may well be that Zionism at the end of the nineteenth century discovered or invented a Jewish polity or, more accurately, secularized aspects of peoplehood that are implicit in Jewish religion in order to "conquer the communities."[21] But the fact is that it did conquer the communities, for the rudiments of Jewish peoplehood were "around for a longer time," to use Berger's language, than those of the "Hebrew" nationhood Ratosh put forth. Moreover, if Zionism did conquer the communities, it was more by the press of historical events than by the cogency of its conception of the Jews, with all the blurring of the religious and the secular that this view promoted. In the last analysis, both Zionism and the Hebrew alternative Ratosh held out in its stead are "artificial" and need to be seen as relative constructs. The social matrix in which they developed was the decisive factor in determining whether they were viable or not.[22]

III

Here we come to an essential quality of Ratosh's thought and why it was he had so much difficulty with Zionism. This quality is what I call "nativism." In its totality Ratosh's outlook may be seen as the efflorescence of a sensibility that goes back to the earliest days of the *Yishuv*. Its roots are certainly social and can be found in the difference in perspective that obtained between those who had been or had arrived in Palestine earlier and those who came later. Exactly when one had come was not the issue; rather it was the general pattern: those who were there first or earlier tended to see themselves as the autochthonic element of Palestine and exhibited a more or less negative or condescending attitude toward those who came after them. This difference was not always expressed in just this way but rather as a distinction between the few who understood themselves to be in Palestine and to have come there out of pure Zionist motives, to achieve the Zionist ideal of self-realization *(hagshamah)*, and the many who came later out of necessity. A Zionist historian of the Second *Aliyah* period discussed the First *Aliyah* as follows:

> From one side [it was] the fruit of Zionist propaganda. From the other side [it was] one current of the powerful stream of emigration to America which hoped to find in *erets yisra'el* what their more numerous brothers sought in America—the possibility of a trade or business or a profession.
> . . . There was confusion among the people in Palestine who were Zionists who yearned for more settlement and now opened their eyes to behold a development they did not want: instead of *'olim* [settlers]—immigrants! Instead of Zionist builders of the land—Jews seeking a livelihood and not a homeland.[23]

In general we may say that Zionism as a movement was irrelevant to the *halutsim* (pioneers) who came in the early decades of this century. It has already been noted that the Second *Aliyah* had a tenuous connection to the Zionist movement, and some of its major figures were critical of it.[24] Berl Katznelson states that he came to Palestine "not out of a Zionist belief but only out of insult, stubbornness, and an unwillingness to be a party to this generation [of Jews] which does not have the strength to die with honor."[25] Yig'al Elam's analysis of Zionist history makes it clear that this was true not only of the Katznelsons and the *halutsim:*

> The State of Israel sprang from the same source that Zionism came from in its time—from the problem of the survival of the Jewish people. Neither the situation of Palestine nor the situation of the Jewish *Yishuv* in Palestine, but the situation of the Jewish people in the world—this is what put the State of Israel on the stage of history.[26]

It is therefore possible to look back and discern a historical cleavage between those Jews who had become "native" to Palestine, Zionists though they were, and the institutions, apparatus, and ideology of the Zionist movement, which was, in their eyes, an agency of immigration and resettlement, a foreign entity. That this sensibility found its fullest expression in Ratosh is, considering what we know about him, neither accidental nor surprising.

Berl Katznelson's statement shows that there is more to this nativist outlook than a denigration of institutional Zionism. The prime motivation for people like him and other pioneers of the Second *Aliyah* was to become a new type of Jew, to fashion himself into a "natural" man who had liberated himself from the "unnatural" existence of the East European Diaspora. This is what Brenner means when he talks in his novels of getting beyond "life in quotation marks."[27] In a sense this use of the metaphor of "quotation marks" prefigures the disparagement of Zionism as "Zionism in quotation marks" in the outlook of the *dor Tash'ah* (generation of 1948).[28] The essence of the nativist sensibility is feeling free, free from the claims and the manifestations of the Jewish religious past.

This attitude implies secularism. But it was a distinctive kind of secularism—militant, rationalistic, and positivistic. The Second *Aliyah* saw the continuation of the polemic against religion that had begun in the *Haskalah* (Enlightenment) and reached its peak in Eastern Europe in Warsaw and Odessa. I have already noted the efforts of Brenner and Syrkin *inter alia* in this regard. The problem with religion for them is that it is irrational, nonempirical, imperialistic, and is altogether a repressive and regressive force.[29] There is no sense that religion or Jewish tradition has anything to offer, be it anthropological validity, social bonding, psychological insight, or existential illumination. These would be learnings that would come only later in the twentieth century. As Ahad Ha'am tried to show, at best what could be extrapolated from Judaism were some sublime ethical values.

Ratosh epitomizes the history of this positivistic secularism. Perhaps more than anyone else he personifies its origins in Warsaw and Odessa and its rootedness in the consciousness of the *Yishuv*. We noted above his description of Jewish holidays; elsewhere he describes Jewish religion as a deception, an exclusivistic illusion.[30] In its time the "Canaanite" movement became the locus of this antireligious secularism. Both Ratosh's brothers were no less vociferous than he in their denunciation of the evils of Jewish religion.[31] From a North American perspective three or four decades later, it is easy to assess this view and treatment of Judaism as anachronistic. But the reality is that it prevails even today among a large segment of secular Israelis. Ratosh is important for showing that a rejection of religion is as integral to the nativist sensibility as is an antagonism to Zionism.

There is, however, yet another blind spot in this understanding of Jewish religion. It ignores the territorial element within the biblical tradition itself. Throughout the Bible it is clearly enunciated that the religious vision embodied in it cannot be concretized other than in the territory of *erets yisra'el*.[32] This is an important point. Even if we accept Ratosh's contention that the Jews are a religious community and not a polity, it is undeniable that an essential component of the religion—indeed a reading of the Bible shows it to be a requirement—is territory. True, Ratosh concedes the existence of a Holy Land, but the Holy Land is not for him and for other such secularists a homeland. Nationhood and religion have nothing to do with each other. Judaism is therefore consigned and confined solely to the domain of the ethereally spiritual.

Once again, this is not something Ratosh invented. It is an aspect of the kind of secularism his thought crystallizes, a legacy of the Zionist secularism that flourished at the beginning of this century. The negation of the Diaspora was synonymous with the negation of Judaism, and Jewish nationalism had nothing to do with Jewish religion. Strains of this bifurcation (and of Ratosh) are audible in Eliezer Ben Yehudah:

> The Jewish religion will no doubt be able to endure even in alien lands; it will adjust its forms to the spirit of the place and the age, and its destiny will parallel that of all religions. But the nation? The nation cannot live except on its own soil; only on this soil can it revive and bear magnificent fruit, as in the days of old.[33]

Judaism is thus construed (or misconstrued) as a wholly extraterritorial religion. If it had any role at all it was simply to serve as the interim means of keeping the Jews in the Diaspora together. As Klatzkin (and in a different way, Ahime'ir) would later argue, the demise of religion in the face of modern secularism necessitated that the Jews, if they were to survive and cohere as a people, adopt a territorial existence; or, conversely, the initiation of a Jewish national effort rendered Jewish religion obsolete.

All this—a consciousness of oneself as not being an immigrant, a feeling of the irrelevance of Zionism, a positivistic antireligious outlook, an awareness of having an identity different from the Jews of the Diaspora—all this, which as we have seen had been in the air of the *Yishuv* for nearly half a century as the inchoate sensibility of secular nativism, all this Ratosh synthesizes in his thought into an ideology. In the light of what I observed earlier about the decisiveness of a social matrix in defining nationhood, we can understand *The Opening Discourse* and all of Ratosh's writings and efforts as an extended attempt to galvanize the social construction of a reality that already existed privately within him and his followers.

IV

All this is what lies behind the deterministic distinction Ratosh makes between a "Hebrew" and a "Jew" and his call for the formation of a Hebrew nation.

> There is no Hebrew other than the child of the land of 'Ever, the land of the Hebrews—no one else. And whoever is not a native of this land, the land of the Hebrews, cannot become a Hebrew, is not a Hebrew, and never was. And whoever comes from the Jewish dispersion, its times and its places, is, from the beginning to the end of days, a Jew, not a Hebrew, and he can be nothing but a Jew—good or bad, proud or lowly, but still a Jew. And a Jew and a Hebrew can never be the same. Whoever is a Hebrew cannot be a Jew, and whoever is a Jew cannot be a Hebrew. For a member of a nation cannot be a member of a faith-community which sees this nation of his as a faith-community, and a member of a faith-community cannot be a member of a nation which sees the very existence of this faith-community of his in the nation's homeland as being opposed to that nation's existence because of the essential nature of that faith-community from its beginning to the end of time. For the native's homeland is not in the dispersion, nor can he ever regard the dispersion as his homeland. And someone from the dispersion has no feeling of a homeland, nor is there any place in his heart for this natural feeling.[34]

There is an almost mathematical determinism here, and I shall presently examine the nature of this "either/or" mentality.

It leads Ratosh to deduce that "the first of the Hebrews of modern times" was Avshalom Feinberg (1889–1917), one of the major figures in the Nili organization. Ratosh and Aharon Amir find in Feinberg all the qualities that constitute the nativist sensibility: birth in Palestine (to parents of *Biluim* of the First *Aliyah*), a visceral hatred of the Ottoman Turks as outsiders, a daring and fearless disposition that led him to begin working to subvert the Ottoman rule (which cost him his life), an almost physical relationship to the landscape and its non-European essence, and a negative attitude to Jewish religion. The fact that Feinberg was an erstwhile poet and, more important, like Ratosh had spent some formative years in Paris (where he became close friends with Jacques Maritain and Charles Péguy) only confirmed that he was the prototype of what Ratosh had in mind for the youth of his time.[35] And the fact that Feinberg's body was discovered in the way it was—under a palm tree that had grown on the site near Rafiah where he was shot, from seeds he was carrying with him at the time—and was reclaimed by the Israelis in 1967 and reinterred at a state funeral in the soil from which it sprung, all this for Ratosh and Amir corroborated the essential validity of the myth of the native Hebrew.[36]

But Feinberg was a precursor. He was only the first generation.[37]

> The Hebrew sensibility beat in its [the first generation's] heart courageously but vaguely. The Hebrew consciousness could not yet ripen in minds, and so it could not infuse its spirit into the rest of the Yishuv. . . . It is the third generation of immigrants in a new country, not to mention the fourth, that can already crystallize the sense of a new nation. . . . And we here, in this land, are the third generation of immigrants.[38]

And so Ratosh designs a new flag to proclaim the new Hebrew nation that is now emerging. Instead of the "Zionist *tallit* taken from the *bet midrash* [house of study] . . . to cover its nakedness," Ratosh prefers the letter *alef*, written in its ancient Hebrew or Canaanite form, emblazoned in gold on a field of blue and purplish-scarlet *(tehelet v'argaman)*. These colors affirm for Ratosh the royal glory of the ancient Hebrew past as well as the blood that would need to be spilled in the present in order to resurrect that past. The *alef*, which originally denoted a bull, is a "primeval symbol of strength and majesty—our power to begin anew, from *'alef.'*"[39] Unlike other new nations that have no history or symbols they can call their own (e.g., Americans really cannot relate to native "Indian" culture), the new Hebrews have a ready-made past.

> The power of the national Hebrew revival provides us with a great and expansive land on which the seal of our Hebrew fathers is stamped, and the golden age of kings who ruled over land and sea, and the brilliance of wars of valor and freedom, and images of people of spirit and instinct in both their goodness and their wickedness, and examples of coups and revolutions, and a great world of legends and gods which, in spite of the Jewish distortion . . . and disparagement . . . unwittingly committed by our teachers, . . . live on within us and inspire us. If we only [would] brush off the Jewish dust from our eyes and pierce the darkening Jewish fog, then the whole great world of the Hebrews of ancient days will assert its full power in us and in our spirit.[40]

But unlike other new nations, the new Hebrew nation faces a major difficulty: the primary stock from which it is being formed is not a heterogeneous collection of immigrants from various lands and places, as in America, but a homogeneous group of members of one faith-community, that is—Jews. Instead of assimilating into the new society to which they have come, they persist in perpetuating the values and outlook of the dispersion and threaten to turn Palestine into simply another locus of the Jewish Diaspora.[41] This is really the nub of Ratosh's quarrel with Zionism: in compromising with the spirit and the institutions of Judaism, it becomes the major impediment to the formation of the incipient Hebrew nation. Its confused, contradictory agenda, made possible by the dialectical relationship it maintains toward the Jewish religious past, retards the development of the secular nativist sensibility and society. Ratosh's ultimate fear is that the territorial element within Jewish religion—an element we have seen he recognizes—when absorbed into the messianic illusions of the Zionist enterprise, would lead to Zionism's inevitable conclusion: the establishment of the Holy Land as a Jewish theocracy. It is on this basis that Ratosh could pronounce darkly that only two choices faced the *Yishuv*: either a Hebrew state ("New *'Ever*") or the Destruction of the Third Commonwealth. In other words, either a secular state that would be viable or a theocracy that would be unable to function effectively as a modern nation-state and would therefore be doomed.[42]

This notion that anything but a secular state could not survive is a corollary of Ratosh's entire argument, and it is important to understand it. The Jewish religion to him, while it can countenance a Holy Land, does not really require a state to transmit its ideals. Nor is a condition of freedom even requisite to its functioning, as it has proved over thousands of years. "If it should happen . . . that a state should come about as the result of the great powers, and the Hebrew youth will not suffice to drive out the Judaism that would come and overtake it—this state of the miserable Jews will not be viable or last very long."[43] After all, Judaism could not hold its first two commonwealths; why, Ratosh asks, will it do any better or find the staying power demanded in sustaining and preserving a third? When it will become clear what is really involved in fighting for and maintaining a homeland, the Jews in the new land will, like their ancestors, get back into their boats and seek out their real, historical homeland—the Diaspora.[44]

Ratosh was, of course, wrong in his predictions. The Hebrew youth did not drive out the Jewish spirit and the nativist element did not prevail. Three generations proved to be insufficient a time for a Hebrew secular national consensus to establish itself. What Ratosh had projected in *The Opening Discourse* in 1944 was, by 1948, overwhelmed and swept away by the tide of massive Jewish immigration attendant upon the proclamation of Israeli statehood. We shall yet have to address the question whether from the "Canaanite" perspective statehood came too soon, whether the process that was so inexorable to Ratosh was now nipped in the bud or simply postponed. For now it is sufficient to recall Peter Berger's insight that how a nation defines itself "is always an act of social construction of reality." To be sure, an individual and an elite can be important in this construction; whether they are indispensable or necessarily decisive for it is a question that is at this point premature.[45]

V

The critique of Zionism and the alternatives that Ratosh and the "Canaanites" developed did not exist solely in the realm of historiographic and social theory. The advent of statehood ensured this, for it provided a real context to which the critique could be addressed. Indeed, the state that came into being in 1948 was so different from what Ratosh had in mind that not to have formulated a concrete alternative program would have meant to accede to what was now being built. We get a vivid sense of just how Ratosh and his followers viewed the heady first days of statehood from the following passage from the lead editorial in the first regular issue of *Alef* (after four intermittently published issues had come out). The editorial opens by noting that in the new order the military and underground organizations—the Haganah, the Palmah, the

Irgun, and the Lehi—which were not only fighting organizations but socially the seed-bed of young Hebrew sensibility, were all gone.

> In general, friends, things are no good.

> We stand before a broken watering-trough. All the fields are now flooded. . . . Around us are noise and clamor and a tremendous commotion. . . . Around us scaffolds hang, machines clank, houses go up, money flows, forests are planted. Thoughtlessly, inattentively our hands also do the work. But our hearts are not in it, our hearts are empty. But our hands do the work.

> Leading us are generals. Old generals, Zionist generals. From the exile [*golah*], from the dispersion. From yesterday. Jews. . . . And before us is a Jewish Agency, facing us and this whole state. . . . At our doorstep are want and economic strangulation and mass unemployment. At our doorstep is a new enslavement, doubled and redoubled: enslavement to the American dollar and to the American *Jewish* dollar. At our doorstep are political isolation and a second and third round [with the Arabs]. And at our doorstep is Levantinism. Jewish Levantinism.

> Something must be done. . . . Everything is inherently messed up.

> We need to begin with something new. A new, another "beginning" is necessary. We need to build things differently from the ground up. With different material, with a different spirit. The state, the society, the economy, the educational system, the culture, the literature. The foreign policy and the domestic policy. The world of values and the concepts by which we live.

> Everything, everything. Without Zionism. Without Judaism. On the foundations of a nation. And there is no one to do this work except the Hebrew youth, no one but us. Not our parents, not our teachers, not the United Jewish Appeal and not the Soviet Union, not Zionists and not immigrants. If the Hebrew youth doesn't do this work, it won't get done. But if it will be started, it will be possible to live here, in this land. . . . This new, other beginning, this *Hebrew* beginning, this starting from *alef*—is the mission of our generation, the generation of natives of this land and its products. It is our destiny.[46]

There is still plenty of rhetoric here, but the awareness of the necessity to take specific steps so as to alter the very framework and institutions of society begins to be visible here. To this end *Alef* in 1951 took a position calling for a halt to unrestricted immigration. An unplanned Zionist "ingathering of the exiles" would be inimical to the organic growth of the new state.[47] Several members of the *Alef* group demonstrated in Jerusalem at the opening of the Twenty-third World Zionist Congress in August 1951, carrying placards such as "Zionists out of the State of Israel!"[48]

Finally, in the autumn of 1951, with the establishment of the *Merkaz ha'ivriyim hatse'irim* (Center for Young Hebrews), the rudiments of a positive program were formulated and promulgated. The point of departure of the Center's platform was that the new state was not independent. Its connection to world Jewry led to an economic dependence on it, which, in turn, led to "a rule of corruption, an economy based on philanthropy, accompanied by domination, monopolism, protectionism, communal discrimination, and religious coercion."[49] The only salvation lay in economic independence, which would only come about through liberation from the ideology that had led the state into its condition of economic subservience. What Israel had to do to achieve such independence was to "establish its life on a modern, national-secular basis: to institute an equality of obligations, rights and possibilities for every citizen, without regard for differences in religion, faith-community or origin, in all sectors of the law, the economy, education and society."[50] This outline was translated into a twenty-four point program. I reproduce it here in its entirety because it is an important source for assessing what the "Canaanite" critique of Zionism ultimately implies and what possibilities it offers.

The Center for Young Hebrews calls for:

A.

1. the promotion of self-definition of all the inhabitants of the State of Israel, regardless of religion, faith-community, or origin, and the recognition of the differentiation from Judaism of the nation that resides in the State of Israel

2. a policy founded on the recognition of the similarity of fate of the State of Israel and its neighbors, and of the role of Israel and of the other constructive forces in the region (known as "the Fertile Crescent") as vanguard in the struggle for the revival, liberation, and development of the entire region

3. the removal of religious and communal barriers which incite animosity and instability . . . in Israel and its neighbors, dependence on foreign powers and [a state of] continuous material and spiritual crisis

4. the separation of religion from state, liberation from all manifestations of theocracy, a secular way of life, and the institution of a completely secular authority in all areas of life

5. official granting of full political, civil, and social rights and obligations to all citizens of the state, regardless of religion, faith-community, or origin, on the basis of a recognition of the fundamental freedoms and civil rights of all residents of the land

B.

6. a foreign policy founded on the integration of the interests of the countries of the Middle East and on the similarity of the emerging tendencies in each toward independence: tendencies toward national . . . revival and against faith-communities, toward the formation of a secular,

territorial [consciousness], toward liberation from dependence on foreign powers and forces, toward development, modernization, and redemption of the masses from feudal-colonial manipulation and social oppression

7. integration and accommodation of the efforts of Hebrew liberation with parallel forces of secular national liberation in all the countries of the Middle East, such as those in Turkey, Egypt, and Iran

8. cooperation with all the elements which oppose Pan-Arabism in Lebanon, Syria, the Jordanian kingdom, and Iraq; and providing a unified expression to the struggle of these emerging forces in Israel and in those countries

9. a federated unity of Israel, Lebanon, and the mountain Druse, a unity that will put an end to the general economic asphyxiation, will remove the continuous military threat, will spur the initiation and organization of other constructive forces of revival in the entire region, and will serve as the nucleus for a general unity

10. the full integration of "minority troops" into the state's armed forces and the development of the unique military-political potential of elements of this type

C.

11. the liberation of the State of Israel from subservience in its domestic and foreign policies to overseas Jewish appeals and freeing the economy and development policy from the orientation of these philanthropies

12. the denial of any official and recognized status to the World Zionist Organization in the State of Israel and the transfer of all its possessions and monetary assets, especially the Jewish National Fund, to a local authority and developmental administration

13. an Israeli policy of absorption and development in accordance with the state's interests alone, [one] based on the productive use of the manpower and capital of the immigrants, with no religious or communal discrimination

14. the fostering of self-sufficiency in basic foodstuffs through directing appropriate manpower into extensive agriculture and applying the full potential of production [capacity], encouragment of assistance programs and agricultural industry, and the establishment of a network of federally sponsored model enterprises

15. the reduction in the cost of living through the abolition of customs duties on imported food staples, raw materials, and machinery essential for production

16. a taxation policy designed to stimulate production, abolition of the income tax as part of a larger effort to spur [the] labor [effort], and full use of productive and export capabilities through the assistance of federal guidance offices

D.

17. the integration of the non-Jewish economy into the framework of the total development and the placing of every professional organization on a nonsectarian basis

18. the development of local and regional governmental agencies and an expansion of their authority along with the apoliticization of the bureaucracies that manage the economy, settlement, agriculture, the cooperative enterprises, and the trade organizations

19. an apolitical bureaucracy for the government, the army, and the police, and the removal of the influence of political parties from the schools and their students

20. the institution of a citizenship law that would make the conferral of citizenship conditional upon permanent residency in the country, knowledge of its language, and observance of its laws, and that would restrict the right to vote in the general elections to citizens of the state alone

21. the obligation for every immigrant to learn at no charge the Hebrew language and the stipulation that every authorization to deal with the public in Israel is conditional upon [attaining] a minimal knowledge of the language

E.

22. a secular-national reform of the educational system in accordance with the principles of territorial self-definition and the Hebrew revival

23. an obligatory secular, nonsectarian public school education within a single framework and content

24. a stimulation of the culture of the homeland based on the national Hebrew revival, drawing on the values intrinsic to this land, and transmitting it to all its inhabitants.[51]

We can see at once that, although there is a discernible authoritarianism here (e.g., the insistence upon a homogeneous citizenry and the regulation of language, education, and culture), the operative principles are those of Western democracy. In this respect a few observations are in order.

First, it becomes clear that what "Canaanism" ultimately envisions has little, if anything, to do with the pagan past, polytheism, or archaism. When Ratosh and his associates finally spelled out their objectives, ancient Hebrew tribalism with all its values and culture turned out to be secondary, perhaps even window-dressing. It is only the very last point in the program that harks back to the past and this in a most undefined way, as if to supply some intellectual or emotional ballast to the larger conceptual framework it concludes. What is primary is very modern: the individual, his or her civil rights, a secular egalitarianism.

Second, it is in this light that we can begin to evaluate the non-democratic tendencies that are so apparent in Ratosh. There is his background in maximalist Revisionism (originally led by an Ahime'ir, who once proposed the title *"duce"* for Jabotinsky).[52] There is his active involvement in applying to Mussolini for help in the fight against the British. There is his call in the uncertainty of the tense days before and after the 1967 war for the interposition of the army's chief of staff as "chancellor" to provide the needed strong hand. Just before his death Ratosh explained this: by "chancellor" *(nagid)* he meant a "dictator in the Roman sense of the word. An example is Fabius in the Second Punic War."[53] But in that same interview he makes it clear that "As for me, it is hard for me to see myself as part of a system of rule that is not demo-cratic, liberal, in which my people is not granted a maximum of personal freedom including the rights, actually the obligation and the ability, . . . to rise up against a government that betrays its role."[54] If anything, Ratosh felt that Israel was not a real democracy since all power is ultimately in the hands of the political parties and, because of the nature of coalition politics, a small party could dictate policy. His call for a "chancellor" (which he later modified to advocating the appointment of a "presidential" or "executive" council), he explains, was designed specifi-cally to neutralize the power of the legislative parties in the Knesset.[55] What Ratosh's political outlook most nearly approximates is what latter-day African states call, perhaps euphemistically, "a guided democracy."

Finally, it is possible to construe the "Canaanite" program as not inherently antireligious. But here, too, some qualifications must be made. To be sure, the powers of religion are contained by a secular democratic system; religion is made into a personal matter. As such it would be theoretically possible to practice religion in an Israel of the kind outlined in this program. The questions this possibility raises, however, are: how would Judaism specifically fare in such a state?[56] Would it be possible to restrict it to the context of being one of several faith-communities to which individuals could freely belong, as in the West? Would adherents to Judaism in a society fashioned from the kind of positivistic secularism described above be as unostracized as their counterparts in secular America? Could the national and territorial elements that are so deeply rooted and affirmed in traditional Judaism be contained? Could the presupposition of Jewish religious pluralism that is implicit here ever be acceptable to those Orthodox Jews for whom Torah and state, the State of Israel and the Land of Israel, are coter-minous?

VI

A few final observations about Ratosh are in order before we sum up his critique of Zionism. From all that we now know about him it is questionable whether it is totally accurate to describe his thought as "romantic" or even "Canaanite." We can certainly appreciate why he bridled at Shlonsky's term. Once we understand that polytheistic antiquity is actually secondary to what he wishes to propound and is a use of the past different in content but no different in function from that of Zionism, then Ratosh emerges not as a romantic whose thought, like some of his poetry, represents an escape to the past.[57] On the contrary: like his poetry, his thought reveals itself to be thoroughly modern in nature and engaged with the realities of the present.[58] How *realistic* it is, is another question, but there is no doubt that it is grounded in an experienced reality even as it seeks to change that reality. What endows Ratosh's ideas with an air of impracticality and permits many to dismiss them as wishful thinking is the fact that they are the result not of rigorous training in political and social theory or of direct political experience but rather of a belief "in the power of words to effect social and cultural transformation."[59] To see Ratosh's critique of Zionism as the fruit of a nonpragmatic, poetic mind is, however, not necessarily to dismiss it. It can be seen as metapolitics, providing the general principles with which more pragmatic politicians can operate and the broad goals toward which they can strive.

Likewise with the "either/or" mentality that pervades Ratosh's writings. In drawing conclusions about the poetry Miron notes that "his view of the world is marked by a peremptoriness and a totalism. . . . The world of Ratosh's poetry is a world of forcible laws which manifest themselves in everything and acknowledge no importance to that which is distinctive, private, or characteristic of specific times or people."[60] This is exactly the case with his system of thought. It brooks no ambiguities, contradictions, or dialectics. That is why Zionism is either a complete break with the Jewish religious past or, failing that, a continuation of it in secular guise. "Since in the whole history of nations there is not even a remote instance of a nation returning to Zion like this, the Zionists had finally to focus on this central point of the Jews as an exception to history."[61] One is either a Jew or a Hebrew. A nation is either defined by a common territory and language or it is not a nation. The new state will be either "a new *'Ever*" or a theocratic "Third Commonwealth."

This "either/or" outlook means that there are no halfway measures. The ties that bind the Jewish generations cannot be simply loosened; they can only be peremptorily cut. To encounter Zionism is to see its "fullest power and corruption" at its "deepest roots"; when the new Hebrew consciousness is arrived at, it will "totally remove the vestiges of . . . reprehensible education" and assert its "full power."[62] But any attempts to use language or concepts in order to hold onto both ends of the proverbial rope are *ipso facto* deceitful. Thus the word " 'Israeli,' like the very name "Israel," is a blurred and obfuscating term. In fact, that is why it was chosen: in order to evade the choice between 'a Jewish state' and 'a Hebrew state'—the choice that was actually available at the [time of] the proclamation of statehood."[63]

Such a mentality is not so much dualistic or reductionistic as it is doctrinaire and totalistic, qualities we have already discerned in Ratosh. It is admittedly not an attractive feature and one that has repelled many. Gonen sees it as a function of the "negative identity" he finds at the heart of the "Canaanite" approach.

> The psychological toll exerted by a negative identity is a heavy one. For one thing, it is hard to maintain a sense of identity in the face of a society which suppresses rather than condones the norms upheld by the negative identity. This leads persons with negative identities to develop rigid ideologies so as to be able to sustain their sense of negative identity even in the face of stiff opposition. Unfortunately, the clinging to ideologies carries with it the danger of totalistic thinking which is typical of many ideologies. It is in their nature to engage in total inclusion of persons and ideas that are "in" and complete exclusion of all those that are "out".[64]

Moreover, in its own way this totalism offends against the very intellectual honesty it finds lacking in others, for things are never as simple or as "black and white" as Ratosh makes them out to be, certainly not history in general and Jewish history in particular. It is hard to consider as serious a system of ideas that is built on oversimplification.[65] But flawed though it may be, Ratosh's ideology is useful precisely because of its inherent rigidity. In providing a clear ideological mold into which the State of Israel does not fit, "Canaanism" gives us some concrete conceptual tools with which to take hold of the Israeli phenomenon and to comprehend its vagaries more fully. When we understand why Israel did not develop in the "Canaanite" direction, we know a great deal about the forces and ideas that are at work and at stake in the Jewish national enterprise.

Then there is the related matter of Ratosh's iconoclasm. It is an iconoclasm born of several personal or emotional tendencies that led him away from the majority. "There was in him an unusual rigidity. It was impossible to sway him from his position or outlook. Even if you thought that your arguments were right and most convincing . . . you sometimes didn't know if this was . . . [simply] stubbornness."[66] During most of his life as an active poet Ratosh was not a member of Israel's *Agudat Hasoferim Ha'ivriyim* (Association of Hebrew Writers),[67] nor was he ever awarded any of the honors or prizes that so many poets of like stature frequently receive in Israel. His self-perception was not that of a "lone wolf" as many saw him, but that of "an isolated wolf," surrounded, as he says, by a society of immigrants and influences that were foreign to him.[68] Yet those who knew him well describe his utter lack of self-pity at this isolation, his thorough awareness that it was the necessary price of advancing the views he held, and his readiness to pay this price.[69]

It may well be that the estimation of this aspect of Ratosh, and perhaps of his thought as a whole, is a function of space and time. That is to say, those who were near him (with the exception of some very few) saw him, perhaps out of necessity, as a "kook." What they saw were a romantic primitivism, a totalitarian strain in his outlook and mode of expression, and an uncompromising antagonism to Jewish religion. These elements and what they implied could only militate against his ideas being taken seriously. But those who are further away are less apt to be affected by the dissonance of these qualities and thus are more open to the issues Ratosh sought to address. The isolation in which his iconoclastic thought was formed is not an automatic bar to its validity; indeed it is quite possible that any human creativity that is significant and lasting is forged only in what Marin Buber called "the ice of solitude" and is often ignored or denounced in its original context. Considering the range of the agenda his thought encompasses, it may not be too much to understand Ratosh's isolation as "the loneliness of the long distance thinker."[70] Binyamin Tammuz, one of Ratosh's earliest followers, has suggested that Ratosh is a figure who needs a lot of time. After all, it took forty years for the public officially to acknowledge the stature of his poetry; his ideas may require even more time. Tammuz writes:

> Amidst empty chatter designed to throw sand in people's eyes, the voice of Yonatan Ratosh reached few ears. But anyone who heard it was never again at peace. Anyone who heard it heard the footsteps of approaching retribution, intuited the full measure of the price that would be exacted for the abominations, sensed the shame of the discrepancy between words and their meanings, between speech and deed, and looked, shocked, at the mediocrity that effusively celebrates itself.[71]

VII

These words of Tammuz provide a good approach to a summary of Ratosh's critique of Zionism and Israel. They confirm what I hope has become clear from this discussion: that what Ratosh's thought constitutes is not a political program—at least not at this time—but a "voice," a message, a warning. To use another image, it is like a specific type of lens that, when placed over the instrument of vision, focuses reality in a specific way and renders certain things that were either invisible or blurry, sharply defined. To be sure, such a lens, because of the distinctive way it refracts the light of reality, will also cause other things to become distorted or to be overlooked or to disappear. Let us note what these various items are.

The limitations of Ratosh's thought, as I have noted throughout this chapter, are many, and there is no need to detail all of them again. In general, it is not that "Canaanism" rests on a historiography that is

debatable or even spurious; it is that this historiography has not been
socially validated and accepted as normative by a body politic. In Peter
Berger's terms, it may not be any more or less debatable than the
reconstruction of Jewish history that Zionism offers. But it has been
around for less time and, to put it differently, it is much less compatible
with the theistic norms of Jewish religion than is Zionist historiography.

In addition Ratosh underestimated the power of certain phenomena
that have turned out to be crucial in shaping the nature and direction of
Israel's history, politics, and culture. For example, he did not anticipate
the emergence of the State of Israel for the majority of Diaspora Jews as
the *sine qua non* of their existence as Jews. To the empirical observer, this
event is not a religious one at all—which is how Ratosh understood it—
but rather the fruit of the increased secularization of world Jewry. It has
for a while now been established that the State of Israel has replaced
Jewish religion as the linchpin of Jewish life and consciousness in the
Diaspora.[72] This development has blunted the appeal of an ideology
that seeks to dichotomize the relationship between the secular polity (the
Israelis) and a religious entity (world Jewry). Both parties are highly
secularized. Second, Ratosh simply did not foresee the power of Arab
nationalism and the religious element within it. The problem here is
twofold. The resistance with which non-Jewish entities in the Middle
East would meet the "Canaanite" notion of integrating them with Jews
on a Hebrew basis—were it ever actually communicated to them—renders the notion itself preposterous. Then there are the effects that a
militant Arab nationalism would come to have on the Jews of Israel
themselves, not to mention the countereffects Jewish nationalism would
have on the Arabs. The two nationalisms and the religious basis for each
have, in a sense, played into and strengthened each other, and the result
has hardly been supportive of the kind of thinking Ratosh reflects.

But in many other ways this thinking is of great significance and
consequence. What it did take into account more than balances what it
did not. The course of Ratosh's life and thought sheds a great deal of
light on the nature of the Zionist enterprise and on the relationship
between Zionism and Judaism.

The conventional perception is that Zionism and Judaism are two very
different matters. Zionism is secular Jewish nationalism focused on a
specific land; Judaism is a religious tradition and legal system. Ratosh
forces us to see that the two are not unrelated at all and, in fact, may be
two sides of the same coin.

> The Zionists were Jews who went out to the culture of the Gentiles
> because of an inability to find satisfaction in Judaism, but not because of
> the ability or the desire to take leave of it. Or perhaps they did seek to
> leave it but couldn't overcome the obstacles in doing so. So they sought to
> define Judaism for their purposes as a polity, as a nation among the

nations in which they lived, in a world that is based on the principle of nationalism, as a . . . substitute . . . for the nationalism of the Gentiles which they found lacking in themselves; in other words [the Jewish Zionists were] bereft of any grounding in society, uprooted in a world of nations. Zionism from the outset came into being as a substitute for this need. It was created out of a vacuum, in the emptiness of the Jewish heart, in order to fill it with a substitute, in order to provide the possibility to continue to live as a Jew among the Gentiles.[73]

A better description of Zionism would be hard to find. The essential word here is "substitute." Zionism in its classical manifestation *was* a substitute for Judaism. This is common wisdom among historians and everyone familiar with the modern Jewish experience. The power of Ratosh's thought is that it ceaselessly reminds us that Zionism, because it was at bottom something *ersatz,* rests on false premises. For you cannot found Jewish life and identity on a secular basis without taking leave of Judaism and transforming them into something brand new.[74] Maybe Ratosh is insensitive to the pressures of the hour that required the Jews of Europe to forge this secular substitute out of their religious past, but a great deal is accomplished by calling the child by its true name. The integrity of the original, i.e., Judaism, is not in question (even as its validity and relevance are denied by Ratosh at every turn). It is only Zionism that is a fictive construction.

This view suggests some inferences that can be made about a number of significant and perplexing phenomena. Since Zionism is nothing but a secular substitute for Judaism, it has, as we have seen, nothing to do with Jewish emigration to Palestine or Israel. The polity that is evolving there neither got there because of Zionism nor is it sustained in its life there by it. Conversely, the Diaspora is understood to be not an illegitimate but the natural mode of Jewish existence. If it is a despicable mode, as it is for Ratosh, it is only despicable because it involves living as a Jew, that is, as a religionist member of a faith-community. That is why he defined himself differently and changed his name and his identity. But for the majority of those who were born Jews, who are comfortable with the identity conferred upon them by birth, the obvious locus of their lives as Jews is indeed the Diaspora. Further, that the Jews are primarily a religion has been established by history; that they are primarily a polity has not. Ratosh's thought thus provides a most plausible answer to the question why it is that so few Jews followed Zionism to Palestine before statehood and why, nearly four decades after the availability of a Jewish Zionist state, such a relatively small percentage of Jews have elected to go there to live. The Diaspora is the Jew's historic and natural habitat. This is a much more plausible interpretation of the Jewish will to live there than that which sees it as the result of some hypothetical mass neurosis or some other psychological defense mechanism.[75]

Furthermore, to Ratosh the Diaspora is eternal. The presence of a

Jewish religious group affirming specific values, be they theological or ethical, is for him a permanent phenomenon. To be sure, Ratosh looked upon this phenomenon with disdain. But it is not a necessary disdain; this persepctive can be seen to explain and validate the inherent tension between Jewish religion and nationalism. The millennial Jewish suspicion of human power, even if enfranchised in a nation-state, is explained and upheld, just as the necessity for the exigencies of statecraft to be controlled by *realpolitik* and territorial interests is legitimized.

But when Judaism and nationalism come together, as they have in the Zionist movement and now in the State of Israel, then is the vagueness of the state's agenda exposed. We may say that Ratosh's unmasking of Zionism is valuable in uncovering the religious and messianic goals that lie under its secular visage. Ratosh's thought invites us to take seriously the possibility of Israel's evolving into a Jewish theocracy. If Zionism does not stick to its original guns to become a full-fledged *alternative* to Judaism but only a secular *substitute* for it, then the fundamental confusion at its heart will never disappear.

In this way does "Canaanism" cast all the problems Israel has had and is having into a new light: its relationship to the non-Jewish world, its treatment of non-Jews within its borders, its problems of religion and state, the nature of its relationship to the Jewish world, the nature of its culture, the nature and the content of the identity it instills in its citizens. All these are seen as fraught with confusion and tension, as they were in 1948.

VIII

Ratosh never tired of pointing out the discrepancies between the rhetoric of Zionism and the realities it created. "Next year in Jerusalem!" does not obligate any Jew to do anything. "In the last analysis any Jew can carry Zion in his heart wherever he is, just as generations upon generations of Jews have carried it. Changing the emphasis of the slogans, whether to the extreme or to the moderate side, will not subvert them. Slogans can be changed every morning."[76]

In its fullest sense Ratosh's thought signifies not so much an ideological destruction of Zionism as a kind of deconstruction. Deconstruction is a fashionable term these days to describe a process of interpretation whereby rhetoric, the means a text uses to achieve its meaning (be that text a poem or a historical event), is subverted by "putting in question received ideas of the sign and language, the text, the context, the author, the reader, the role of history, the work of interpretation, and the forms of critical writing. In this project a past crumbles and something monstrous emerges: a future."[77] Ratosh's ideological writings serve to do just this. They dismantle the verities and the assumptions upon which supposed certainties rest. Deconstruction is an enterprise born of a deep scepticism. It has been "dismissed as a harmless academic game" and "denounced as a terrorist weapon."[78] The "Canaanite" critique of Zionism that Yonatan Ratosh developed can be described in similar terms. It is the ultimate expression of his lifelong quest to drive out the foreign element using not the bombs or guns of the Irgun or the Lehi but, as befits a poet, language and ideology. Whether this critique is only "a harmless academic game" is a question we must now consider.

V

"CANAANISM" AND ISRAELI POLITY AND POLICY

Were we to understand "Canaanism" strictly as a set of ideas and its resultant critique of Zionism purely as an intellectual construct, this book could end right here. After all, although the ideas Ratosh developed did crystallize into an ideology and the ideology did take on the semblance of a movement, all this happened over a brief and specific period. The "Young Hebrews" movement as a manifest force in the Israeli body politic never went anywhere and it never sought to advance its twenty-four-point program through the means of a political party within the Israeli political system. As we have seen, Ratosh and his followers explicitly eschewed this path. This policy was a source of disappointment to some of those who were initially attracted to the movement. Looking back at its earliest years, Amos Kenan could reflect:

> The Canaanites were a kind of vegetarian entity . . . neither meat nor milk, neither fish nor fowl. . . . They were the pristine church of pure thought. . . . I cannot forgive Ratosh, Aharon Amir, and all the rest . . . of the Canaanite movement for the fact that they chose to live as parasites on the back of the underground organizations, and yet in time they would say and take pride that they actually had influence on Ya'ir [Stern], Hakim [sic], and Bet-Tsuri.[1]

To be sure, there is the case of Uri Avneri, who did attempt to translate his version of "Canaanism" into political terms. But that is what it was: a version, an emphasis on selected elements of the Hebrew ideology, not to mention that it was undertaken not so much without Ratosh and his followers as in opposition to them. This is not to deny the importance of Avneri and his efforts, and I shall return to him later in this chapter. But the fact remains that the vast and revolutionary social, political, and cultural agenda that are implicit in Ratosh's thought were never pursued in any sustained systematic and organized way. The preceding two chapters suggest a number of reasons why this was or had to be, and I shall not repeat them all here, save only to say that we need to locate the sources for "Canaanism"'s failure to challenge Zionism and develop into

76

a serious alternative to it both in the "Canaanite" ideology itself and in the historical and social realities of the society to which it was addressed.

In spite of all this, we cannot close the book on "Canaanism"—at least not this one. To do so would be to gloss over or minimize a whole range of problems and issues that continue to face Israel and Zionism: the nature of the Israeli identity and the dilemmas it imposes upon those who bear it; the nature of the Israeli polity and the way it handles such matters as the relationship between religion and state and the treatment of non-Jews within it; the roots and posture of Israel's foreign policy, especially the way it understands itself in relation to non-Moslem entities in the Middle East; and the nature of the relationship between Israel and world Jewry. In essence these are all questions that flow from the Jewish nature and component of the State of Israel and the unresolved tension between the secular and the religious that lies at the heart of the Zionist enterprise. As we have seen, "Canaanism" perceived and spoke to all these matters and pressed for their resolution.[2] Because it did so and because these issues are still alive, "Canaanism" continues to exist as a *latent* force among those who are concerned with them. To put it bluntly, it is not so much that "Canaanism" has failed as an alternative to Zionism; it is that Zionism has not succeeded in reconciling the contradictions and dilemmas it created in the course of achieving what it has so far achieved. It is not so much that the answers "Canaanism" offered to these problems were so good; it is that the questions it raised still remain. That is why "Canaanism" is far from dead as a topic of discussion among some intellectuals in Israel today.

In this chapter we shall look at these issues, analyzing them and examining the Ratoshian perspective on them. We shall see how Ratosh's ideas, when applied to these issues by such diverse official and unofficial followers as Aharon Amir, Boaz Evron, Amos Kenan, Uri Avneri, and Ezra Zohar, undergo a transmutation. In this way do I hope to show that, far from being irrelevant to Israeli society and statehood, "Canaanism," when transmuted or reinterpreted in these different ways, offers some very cogent possibilities for Israel and can serve as a potential corrective to some of the dilemmas facing it. If this statement sounds excessive I would say that at the very least an application of the "Canaanite" thesis, refined at the hands of its contemporary protagonists who are in touch with the realities of current Israeli life, can do for Israel in the fourth and fifth decades of its existence what it did at the outset of statehood in the late forties: not so much transform Israeli polity and alter its policies as promote their clarification by making a substantial and honest ideological fuss.[3]

I

At the core of Ratosh's ideology is an insistence on a new identity for the nation that is emerging in Palestine and Israel. The first of the twenty-four points of the Center for Young Hebrews was a call for "the promotion of self-definition of all the inhabitants of the State of Israel . . . and the recognition of the differentiation from Judaism of the nation that resides [there]." All this was predicated on the idea and the values of what I have termed and described as nativism. Even more to the point, it rested on the assumption that there was an element in the populace that already understood itself in this way—the younger generation that had been born in the land—and on the hope that these "Sabras" would rise up and act upon the implications of their new identity.

In the late forties this hope was not unrealistic. It was the younger generation that had fought in the 1948 war for Israeli independence, and if it was anyone's state it was theirs. And yet among significant sectors of this youth the war left not euphoria but a bitter taste and a profound emotional upheaval. For the first time many of them saw death and encountered the tragic dimension of life. An astute American-Jewish observer, writing just after the war, describes this generation:

> The presence and predominance of Israel's youth—in a swaggering, wholly physical sense—in the streets of Tel Aviv, in the settlements, and in army and government offices . . . is overpowering. It sweeps in on the newcomer to the land with the suddenness of a breaker. . . . But though the sabra may seem, at first, self-assertive and cocky, his manner is a deceptive veneer, and he is as insecure in his own way as his parents in theirs. His own publications indicate that he is confused; craving affection he receives adulation, and instead of love he reads worry and doubt in his parents' eyes.[4]

The source for this malaise is suggested when we discern another detail through Teller's sharp eyes:

> The sabra uses the term "Zionist" in mockery, and Israel's political parties are still Zionist in orientation and even in structure: their roots have been world Jewry, not the territory of Israel, they are still the Israeli branches of world-wide movements, and their platforms are loaded down by the ballast of "Zionist" thinking which derived from the needs, frequently regional, of Jewish communities outside Palestine.[5]

Note here how Teller twice places the word "Zionist" within quotation marks—as if to suggest its artificiality, remoteness, and irrelevance to the consciousness of the young people about whom he is writing. This was exactly the attitude of many of the more sensitive and articulate youth who had fought in the 1948 war. There was the feeling that this war, in which so many of their friends had died, was not the same war that was now being popularized, and in their view stereotyped and vulgarized, as so much Palmah heroics. We get a sense of this feeling in a powerful and important piece Ya'akov Aschman wrote for the second issue of *Alef.*

"This was not a national war. It was a war that was forced upon the individual, a war of individual self-defense; and the individual, in his isolation, was shattered in the struggle with his [own] egoistic instinct for self-preservation." This is a very different picture of the 1948 war from the one commonly painted. According to it, that war was no transcendent Zionist peak experience, nor was it the great adventure of daring togetherness and joyous collectivism of Palmah jargon that was celebrated in the work of Natan Shaham and Yig'al Mossinsohn. Rather it was the fight of individuals for their land and a terrifying induction into the realization that one faces death utterly alone. It had little to do with Zionism and Zionist leaders, who in any case did not fight but sat in their offices and imposed their vision on the whole thing.[6]

It is difficult to measure just how representative or widespread this interpretation of events is or was.[7] Clearly, though, the feeling that Zionism was just so much rhetoric was pervasive enough for an American like Teller to pick it up. It is important to stress, however, that this attitude was a matter not so much of philosophy and doctrine as of identity.

> Putting Zionism in quotation marks in and of itself does not yet transform it into something that rests on a different emotional basis. To put something into quotation marks is a sign of despair and of the inability to express yourself. Self-definition is to find the definition of yourself, not to put in quotation marks a definition that someone else forces on you. If you are not a Zionist, then say what you are. Don't be a Zionist in quotation marks.[8]

An essay by Amir written in 1950 provides an interesting perspective on the confusions of Israeli youth of the time. He notes its proclivity toward a pragmatic operationalism and its paucity of intellectual resources on which to found an ideological basis for its identity. Moreover, with the massive immigration that is streaming into the new state—the Jewish population exploded from 589,300 in 1948 to 1.48 million in 1953[9]—it is no longer either the youngest element of society or the center of attraction, as it was before 1948. And the fact that the only context in which this youth is organized is a military one (viz., the Israeli army) does not help it.

> It almost never attempted—perhaps it didn't have the strength—to establish a movement, to set up a leadership, to formulate the essentials of its existence, *to define itself.* It *sensed* its power, *felt* its primacy, *was aware of* its distinctiveness, but wasn't wise enough or never sought *consciously* to take note of these things and base them on a conception of life, a world view, on an approach to the fundamental problems of this land and of the national Hebrew reality.[10]

It is easy to see why the Young Hebrews movement would appeal to those who did care about this matter of identity and self-definition. Boaz Evron has put this very well:

> The fact [is] that this sense of a Hebrew homeland sought out an ideology for itself. Zionism is an ideology of an ethnic group that lacked a territory and sought one in order to solve its problems. But from the moment a territorial structure was created, the moment when its inhabitants felt that their *territorial* basis was the main thing and on that basis they built their society and their *true* world view (in contradistinction to a ritualistic world view they acquired from educational systems and social propaganda to which they related only by rote with no inner conviction)—from that moment on they were in need of an ideology that would express this movement . . . and this is the explanation for the joy and the relief that we felt when we first encountered these ideas. . . . This ideology was important [evidence] of a tremendous intellectual hunger of which we were not even conscious. It defined for us why we rejected Zionism, why we felt that we, children and products of this land, were intrinsically different from Jews in the Diaspora, whose thought processes and sensibility seemed qualitatively foreign.[11]

In the light of all this Shavit's judgment that the "lost generation of *erets yisra'el* youth" of 1948 is a "myth" must be seen as tendentiously incorrect.[12] A more accurate reading is that a new national identity had begun to develop but never got beyond its first stage. Whether this identity was "Hebrew" or exactly the one Ratosh had in mind is open to question, but the sense of a new entity emerging does not seem "mythic" at all. Kenan points out the important fact that "Canaanism" in the years immediately following 1948 began to attract followers from the left even though, as we have seen, it originated on the right. His explanation for this is that those on the left had greater expectations of what the new state would be like and, therefore, their disillusion with it was much greater than among those on the right.[13]

Kenan and Evron, who are both of the "generation of 1948," each offer related reasons why this new identity never developed. Kenan feels that it was quite literally decimated in the 1948 war. He notes that fully one-third of all the Jewish students in Palestine were killed in this war. "In a certain sense *Erets Yisra'el* died in '48. It died then. . . . Just as the Holocaust was to Judaism, so was '48 to us."[14] Those who survived felt betrayed. They had fought in a war the meaning of which was in the process of being, in their view, distorted and romanticized, and the incipient nation for which they had shed so much blood was not being embodied in the state that had resulted. Yet they could do nothing about this, for very soon their sense of betrayal was neutralized by the new reality—and by their own human aspirations.

You also faced the huge machinery of the Zionist movement, the enormous amount of money. And you also faced something else, which was perhaps sociologically very important—and this is something which the generation of the War of Independence, which was really my generation, felt: here was a country, a new country. Suddenly—mass immigration, and suddenly opportunities opened which you could hardly find in any other country. Suddenly, you know, a person who continued, like his father, to be a clerk was offered a job managing big enterprises. So that generation, if it was ready to forego its self-awareness as a group, as a new thing, as a separate nation, and accept the ruling ideologies and the ruling system, was enormously rewarded. Very quickly. Suddenly people rose like rockets. If you were in the right place. . . . Again and again members of my generation talk about a sense of betrayal. People felt that something enormous was betrayed and don't know what it is. Something, our real being, was bartered off. Our basic feeling was of personal success and historical defeat.[15]

We are left with the notion that the 1948 war and the generation that fought in it are the watershed from which the issues and the problems of the definition of the Israeli polity flow. The attainment of statehood and national sovereignty was not accompanied by any corresponding ideological clarification; all the contradictions suspended in the emulsion of the dialectics of Zionism were carried forward. This is what Kenan means when he says,

That war [of 1948] actually has never ended. All the things that bothered us then, of which we did not want to give an accounting to ourselves, have arisen and are arising even more forcefully. . . . The problems which faced us before '48 are, in the last analysis, those which confront us today. . . . But it is clear to me that in general our entire literature, our culture and our whole political and social reality are nourished from '48. And whenever we do not return to that time to see what went wrong there, we shall be unable to continue and to progress.[16]

II

Since 1948 the nature of the Israeli polity and the questions of identity it raises have been grist for the mill of many sociologists. All who have studied and written about these matters have dwelled on the tension between the national and the religious, that is to say between the Israeli and the Jewish, elements in the self-understanding of the new state and its citizens. The conclusions of the French sociologist Georges Friedmann, reached after his studies of 1963–64, became well known.

There is no Jewish nation. There is an Israeli nation. The state that came into existence as a result of Herzl's prophecies is not a "Jewish state". The

> Israeli state is creating an imperious national community that is conscious
> of itself, but does not include in that consciousness belonging to a "Jewish
> people". There seems to be a widening gap . . . between the part of the
> population that sees itself as essentially Israeli and the part, consisting of
> the orthodox, that regards itself as essentially Jewish. . . . There is a great
> deal of truth in the caustic saying that in Israel the 'olim [settlers] are more
> or less rapidly turned into Israeli patriots, "Hebrew speaking Gentiles"
> about whom there is nothing Jewish except the memory of their origins.[17]

This thesis quickly fell into disrepute, for it was advanced literally on the
eve of the 1967 war, and the conventional view is that that experience
effected some permanent changes in the way Israelis saw themselves.
This is the upshot of Simon Herman's study of Israeli high-school
students done in the years 1964–68 and published in 1970. Herman
found that "Israelis are not—as some observers have claimed and as
some Israelis would have it—an entirely new people. The majority of the
Israelis in this study see themselves linked to the Jewish people and to its
past. The thread of historic continuity has not been snapped. . . ."[18]

Now while this finding may be correct, Herman's work is long on
empiricism and short on theory, even sociological theory. The recent
work of Liebman and Don-Yehiya posits and analyzes the presence of a
civil religion in Israeli society whereby the *materia* of traditional Jewish
religion are appropriated into "a symbol system that provides sacred
legitimation of the social order" so as to integrate and mobilize the
individuals that make it up.[19] Thus the Jewishness that Herman finds in
such abundance may be nothing but "the nationalized Judaism" of Israeli civil religion, "whose symbol system is, however, so close to that of
traditional Judaism that it is often misleading."[20] This is something quite
different from a nonempirical self-understanding of what it *means* to be
a Jew in Israel and the existential question of the *meaning* and *value* of
Israel as a Jewish state.[21] Such subjective data are hard to get at in an
interview and even more elusive to quantify in statistical analysis. To be
fair to Herman, he sets down his findings without any triumphalism and
is careful to point out the softness of the Jewish component within the
Israeli identity of the high-school youth he studied (i.e., the large nonreligious sector) and the tenuousness of its attachment to the Jewish past
and to the Jewish Diaspora.[22]

Dan Segre's more recent treatment of the subject shows that the 1967
and 1973 wars have only served to abet the confusion resulting from the
ambiguities inherent in the Israeli identity. Segre writes:

> It was to be expected that the question, the Jewish question of Israel,
> would explode in all its intensity with the establishment of the State.
> Against all logic, however, it did not: for three main reasons. The first was
> the Arab hostility, which created in the new and fragmented Israeli society
> a strong reflex of unity for survival. The second was the astonishment of

the Israelis, old settlers and newcomers alike, at the reappearance of Jewish political sovereignty. . . . The third reason was Ben-Gurion, who not only acted as midwife to the state but imposed on all parties, much against their will, the historic decision of not deciding on any essential problems of the State: not on a constitution, not on the national borders, not on the ideological character of the State. . . . But it was an attitude which saved Israel from grave internal dissension in the first very difficult years of her existence. The extent of the military victory over the Arabs in 1967 changed all this. It relieved the State from the Arab menace of physical destruction; the conquest of populous Arab areas obliged Israel to define itself in relation to its enemies: what it meant to be "Jewish" or Israeli in the occupied areas, how the "redemption of the land" could serve or be justified by the redemption of the people. . . . Thus, to the old, insoluble problems new ones were added, but in a situation which no longer permitted postponing the fundamental debate on the nature and task of the Zionist State. . . . The coalition government of Premier Levi Eshkol, and even more those of Mrs. Golda Meir, adopted a policy of military, social, economic, and above all psychological and ideological immobilism, the sole result of which was to sweep under a carpet of conformism and righteous platitudes the old and new problems of identity, legitimacy, institutions, and ideology facing the Israeli State as a State of the Jews. . . . Like the centipede in the Indian tale, who found himself unable to walk the moment the parrot asked him to explain how he co-ordinated the movements of all his feet, so a kind of emotional-psychological paralysis overtook the Zionist movement and the State of Israel the moment they found themselves forced to analyze and define their own nature in response to external pressure. They could not reach any inspiring consensus, and they lacked the time for reflection and the socio-economic tools to analyze their problems. Those they had—as in every colonized society—were alien, imported, and unfitted to explain to a people, which had largely cut itself off from its own national culture, what that culture was and what their new State was meant to achieve.[23]

Can we not conclude, then, that the understanding of Israel as a new polity with a new identity has in fact been borne out? Has not a secular nativism, even if it is not precisely the "Hebrew" one originally envisioned by Ratosh, implicitly developed? Or, to put the question in a slightly different way, if it has not come about, why not? If nativism is a function of the incremental growth of an indigenous populace, surely by this time, after nearly four decades of statehood, it ought to have crystallized?

Just as there are a number of ways to ask the question, so are there a number of ways to answer it. It is possible to say that the "Canaanite" analysis, if not the specifics of its ideology, has indeed over the years proved itself a serious challenge to Zionism, much more than the official numbers of those who openly declared themselves its protagonists would indicate. That is precisely why in 1957 the Israeli government felt itself obliged to introduce a program of "Jewish consciousness" into the school system.[24] Alternatively, it may be that the development of secular nativism has been impeded by the press of history. The animosity and the firepower concentrated and, in 1948, 1967, and 1973, used in war against Israel by its Arab neighbors has, psychologically and politically, mitigated the "normalization" process that the early Zionists had hoped for and turned much of Israeli existence into not so much the living out of a new reality as a continuation of the millennial Jewish struggle for acceptance and survival in a hostile world. The "state of the Jews" has become the "Jew of the states."[25] If the Israeli experience to date discloses anything, it is that a Zionist state has not been able to escape Jewish history. The quintessential quality of Jewish identity—distinctiveness— was, from the start, imposed upon it from the outside more than it was chosen by its founders. All of which is another way of saying that an Israeli nativism has certainly developed since 1948, but it is a nativism in which the Jewish component has persisted with increasing strength.

And so it is that at this writing secular Zionism remains as vulnerable to a challenge to its integrity and its adequacy as a basis on which to found a nation-state as it was in 1948, if not more so. The issues that Ratosh and the "Canaanites" raised when they formulated their platform are as cogent now as then. In the words of one Zionist intellectual, "the main question of relevance in the ideological discussions facing us is the question of the relationship between the territorial-political identity and our religio-national identity."[26] To the religionist there are various possibilities to bring the two elements into line (of which *Gush Emunim* [Bloc of the Faithful] is only one), and we must be careful not to hypostatize the religious position and oversimplify its complexity and variety. But to the secularist who rejects the "Canaanite" approach, the dilemma is acute.[27]

In truth secular Zionism does not and cannot solve it. Nor, when it is intellectually responsible, does it seek to do so or even wish to evade the impasse. Rather, as we have seen above in chapter 2, it accepts it and celebrates it. We see this position poignantly formulated in some essays of the poet Hayim Guri, one of the well-known figures of the "generation of 1948." For Guri the dilemmas of Israeli identity are central, to the point where he confesses to a lifelong obsession with them. In an excellent symposium on the nature and meaning of the whole Israeli experience in the light of the 1973 war, sponsored by the review *Keshet* (of which Amir was editor), Guri notes:

> The Israeli is the "product" of this soil, of the sun and the language, the life-style, the labor and the wars in this land. . . . But all this is not sufficient to define his identity. He is also the fruit of an entire history, the continuation of many generations that lived through powerful and painful life-experiences in other lands. He is also memories. To be a civilized

person means to contain a past, to go beyond the merely biographical, to live whole generations. There is within us a bitter rebellion against those generations; we are actually both parricidal and in search of our father. This duality among those born in this land is not only a cause for tearing [us] away. It can also be a source of richness. And so it has been decreed that we must live out our doubleness, our colorfulness, to the utmost limit, not to diminish the Israeli reality. Cutting the "Gordian knot" is liable to pull us into a destructive and impoverishing cultural escapade.[28]

Guri adamantly refuses to accept the "either/or" ultimatum that both Orthodox Judaism and "Canaanism" present to him, an insidious ultimatum he feels has been tacitly accepted by all of Israeli society, just as he rejects no less resolutely all the apocalyptic implications that the choices impose: either life or death, either holding the occupied territories or peace everlasting, either "Massadah" or appeasement, either a democratic Jewish state within reduced borders or catastrophe, either a Greater Land of Israel as a Jewish state or total destruction, either *Gush Emunim* or *Shalom 'Akhshav* (Peace Now), either Yonatan Ratosh or Rabbi Goren, either a "New *'Ever*" or "the Destruction of the Third Commonwealth." All of these threats and the mentality that underlies them Guri categorically rejects as "an orgy of clarity. The problem is that the clarity isn't always 'objective' and the alienation of the extremes continues to precipitate madness among us." Instead of "either/or," Guri affirms "both/and," and he has no hesitation in living with contradiction and "belonging to the confused majority" even as he knows that Israel "will have to decide who it is and what it is and what it is saying to its minorities and what, in the long view of the Israeli revolution, it wants to say to its neighbors, its enemies, and those who want to destroy it."[29]

In the course of the *Keshet* symposium Guri declares that as a secular Jew he supports the separation of religion from state in Israel (a subject I shall presently examine). This draws a sharp response from his most articulate antagonist in the symposium, another poet, Shin Shifra, who along with Aharon Amir expresses a "Canaanite" perspective here.

> Out of a fear of confronting reality face to face, of defining and shaping it, we abstain from an honest reckoning with the problem of our self-identity. Young people sense the contradictions, the emptying out of content from [key] concepts. . . . On one hand Guri speaks of the historical continuity of the Jewish people, but over against it he subverts this continuity and kills it when he proposes the separation of religion from state. I am absolutely in favor of such a separation, but then we have to be consistent down the line to the end.[30]

The push for self-definition is as vigorous here as it was when Ratosh proclaimed it as a first principle of his ideology. The implication is that unless the polity that has begun to take shape in Israel boldly *defines itself* in contradistinction to Judaism, it will *be defined by* and *within* the religious and theological categories of historical Judaism, and thus the original Zionist ideal of the people no longer being the *objects* of history but its *subjects* will not come to pass. We can see, then, how Ratosh's thought continues to serve as a challenge to and a critique of the diffuse national identity that Zionism has fostered. The ultimate contention of this line of thought is that the Zionist state is not yet a fully sovereign nation, as the following words of Boaz Evron indicate:

> Most people in Israel accept the official line that they are Jews and they get confused in their mind: "We are Jews but we are separate. We are Israelis but we are also better Jews [even if we are] without any Jewish content, whatever that means. And all the world hates us. And therefore we have to be strong and we have no obligation to anybody. (That's a Sharon idea, you know.) We're always right. We're entitled to kill Arabs and drive them out because we are Jews and they are all out to destroy us." This is a very primitive mishmash, in the fostering of which there is no difference between Likud and Ma'arakh [the Labor alignment] and most Zionist groups, including Mapam. Now if you are a Jew, why is it better to be a Jew here [in Israel] and not in America? It's more comfortable in America, so why be here? Because here you are more Jewish? In what are you more Jewish here? Because you are a nation? Because of your religion? People have no clarity about this. . . . I say that . . . an Israeli identity doesn't yet exist. It exists in potentiality, if we create a state, a real state. A state with a constitution.[31]

III

The lack of a formal constitution as well as the problem of the relationship of religion and state (which is both a cause and an effect of the lack of a constitution) shows us that the unclarity of the Israeli identity leads to a corresponding fuzziness in some of Israel's domestic policies. While the absence of a constitution per se is not a necessary impediment to a nation's ability to function (viz., England and the United States from 1776 to 1793), it is a sufficient one; the failure to formulate and ratify a written constitution can bespeak a fundamental failure or a fundamental unwillingness to achieve national consensus on basic principles and issues.[32] "Canaanism" and its adherents have had some trenchant things to say about and do with these matters. I shall confine this discussion to two crucial relationships: that of religion and state and that of the non-Jew to the Israeli polity.

There is no question that as a sovereign entity the State of Israel is secular in nature. Authority and government are derived from human sources. Yet because "the ethos of the new nation is derived from the theology as well as the history of Judaism,"[33] the relationship between the secular state and (Jewish) religion has been significantly tighter than in other Western secular democracies. Although Judaism is not the state religion, neither is it merely *primus inter pares* with respect to Islam, Christianity, or other religions extant in Israel.[34] Part of the reason for this situation has to do with the ongoing necessity for coalition politics in order to permit governments to be formed (a fact that in itself is testimony to a lack of consensus within the Israeli body politic about what kind of state it wants). The ongoing consequence of coalition politics has been to empower small Orthodox religious parties to prosecute their theopolitical agenda far beyond the proportion of the population they represent. This has meant that almost from the beginning of statehood there has been an unresolved tension between the claims and requirements of Orthodox Jewish religion and *halakhah* (Jewish law) on the one hand and the sensibilities and needs of a largely non-Orthodox citizenry on the other. This is the "perpetual dilemma" of which Abramov writes, and in the light of the disputes and the mutual distrust it has engendered between various sectors of the Israeli populace, not to mention its effect on world Jewry, it is hard to understand how Abramov can describe this dilemma as having "exercised a fructifying effect on its [world Jewry's] thought and action."[35]

On the face of it, one would think that the domestic history of Israel can be described as essentially one extended *Kulturkampf.* Abramov notes that "it has been one of the more notable achievements of Orthodoxy that it has succeeded in attaching to all shades of non-Orthodox opinion the label of secularist, thus implying that there is no Jewish religion other than the Orthodox. From this it logically followed that secularism was the only ideological alternative to Orthodoxy. . . ."[36] Social scientists who have studied this subject have concluded otherwise. Nonobservance is not necessarily a function of nonbelief, antireligiousness, or a conscious secularism (just as observance is not always grounded in religious belief or theological self-consciousness). In his examination of Israeli society Samet has found not a polarity between a secular majority and a religious minority that seeks to impose its will on it, but a continuum of positions along a broad spectrum, one that exhibits much more good will and tolerance of Orthodox norms than would be expected. Furthermore, the Zionist movement's historical accommodation of the Orthodox in the prestate period, both in the Diaspora and in the *Yishuv,* embedded the values and the institutions of traditional Judaism so deeply into the soil of the Zionist enterprise that the possibility of the separation of synagogue from state in Israel is nonexistent. Samet concludes that if one has any quarrel about the role of Jewish religion in the Jewish state, it can only be in regard to its *extent* and *form,* not in regard to its essential presence.[37]

But again this kind of analysis seems oblivious to the phenomenon of civil religion that Liebman and Don-Yehiya have described, and it may be confusing it with traditional religion. This mistake cannot be made, however, when we look at the "Who is a Jew?" controversy of 1958–59 and its implications. Here the conflict truly was between the norms of a secular state and traditional Judaism. When Yisra'el Bar-Yehudah, a secular Labor Zionist and then minister of transport, directed that anyone who said he or she was a Jew should be accepted and registered as such for the purpose of being issued a state-required identity card, he was only meeting the needs of a secular state, even if he was, in effect, separating Jewish nationality from Jewish religion. Conversely, when the National Religious Party (NRP) opposed this directive to the point where its ministers resigned from Ben Gurion's cabinet, they could only claim that

> it is impossible to create two types of Jews—those who are kosher according to the *halakhah* as opposed to those on whom the State of Israel confers their Jewish identity. The new regulations will split the people in Israel and will sever the state from Jewish history and from a large part of the Jewish people outside Israel.[38]

When the issue was finally decided in favor of the NRP and the halakhic view that a Jew is only one "born of a Jewish mother who does not belong to another religion, or one who has converted in accordance with *halakhah*"—even if the decision was based largely on the exigencies of maintaining a coalition and was not a permanent law ordained by the Knesset but a temporary administrative order[39]—it was made clear that the needs of the tradition and the religious system prevailed over the interests of the secular state. What is more, the fact that Ben Gurion asked forty-five eminent Jewish scholars all over the world their opinion on this question testifies not so much to his statist desire to proclaim the centrality of Israel for Jewish life as it does to "a recognition of the subservience of the state to the tradition in basic questions of Jewish identity."[40]

In this respect the grounds for a *Kulturkampf* between religionists and secularists do indeed exist, just as they have existed since the inception of Zionism. But it is unlikely that the battle will erupt with any more ferocity than it already has. One of the many reasons for this is the differential between the two camps: "Unlike the 'religious,' who are an organized community with a defined identity, the 'secularists' do not comprise a distinctive entity within Israeli society."[41] Because it itself possesses one, Orthodoxy imputes to secularism a clear and rigorous identity—but this is not the case.

It is here that "Canaanism" enters the lists. Not as a romantic escape into pagan mythology or as a militaristic advocate of a Pan-Hebraic imperialism, as it is so often construed,[42] but as a force for the galvanization of a considered, explicit secularism on which to base the domestic policy of a secular nation-state. The fourth point in the program that the

Center for Young Hebrews enunciated was "the separation of religion from state, liberation from all manifestations of theocracy, . . . and the institution of a completely secular authority in all areas of life." This particular agenda was developed not only within the narrow framework of the Young Hebrews movement. In 1950 Uzi Ornan founded the League for the Abolition of Religious Coercion. Organized to deal with issues that the Jerusalem municipal elections of that year were raising, the league sought to attract a diversity of people from across the political spectrum, including even those religionists, Orthodox and non-Orthodox alike, who were unhappy at the role religion was assuming in matters of state. This is one of the few instances where the exponents of the "Canaanite" approach devised to advance their goals through coalition-building around a single issue. The league in time became quite visible on the Israeli scene, especially in Tel Aviv and Haifa. Its numbers were never large but it did succeed in calling public attention to those many cases where it felt that the infringement of Orthodoxy was insufferable, such as the SS *Shalom* kitchen controversy of 1963–64 and the Rina Eitani citizenship affair of 1965–66.[43]

One of the league's biggest problems was that it was widely perceived as the "League for the Abolition of Religion," a perception that greatly blunted its appeal. To counter this image, it at times tried to function not as a political lobby group but as an educational agency. To this end it attempted to provide a forum for the exposition of non-Orthodox approaches to Judaism, which, because of their American ties and ethos, were entirely comfortable in advocating the separation of religion from state. In all its utterances and leaflets the league never tired of pointing out that freedom of religion and conscience were explicitly guaranteed in Israel's Declaration of Independence.

The league disbanded in 1968, apparently overwhelmed by the Judaization of Israel that the 1967 war precipitated. From 1977 to 1980 an attempt was made to reorganize it under the rubric of the Israeli Secular Movement, but when the secular humanism of the majority of its members inclined toward pacifism, Ornan withdrew.[44] The group is no longer in existence. Secularism in Israel remains to this day a vague and unarticulated position. Those who define themselves as *hiloniyim* (secularists), as opposed to *datiyim* (religionists) and *mesoratiyim* (traditionalists) are on the defensive and in the minority.[45] It is a situation that is antipodal to Palestine of the Second *Aliyah*. The irony is that in *The Jewish State* Herzl had seen the dangers religion posed to his vision:

> Our community of race is peculiar and unique, for we are bound together only by the faith of our fathers. Shall we end by having a theocracy? No, indeed. Faith unites us, knowledge gives us freedom. We shall therefore prevent any theocratic tendencies from coming to the fore. . . . We shall keep our priests within the confines of their temples in the same way as we

shall keep our professional army within the confines of their barracks. . . .
They must not interfere in the administration of the state which confers
distinction upon them, else they will conjure up difficulties without and
within.[46]

But the awareness of this irony and what it portends is not a mass
concern. The failure of the League for the Abolition of Religious Coercion or the Israeli Secular Movement to become a "grass roots" vector on
Israeli policy in matters of religion and state suggests that it is largely
within the intellectual and the academic sectors that a consciousness
exists of what is really at stake in the conflict between religion and state in
Israel.

A primary source here is Gershon Weiler's study of the philosophical
roots of the Jewish political tradition.[47] The value of this work is that it is
a longitudinal analysis; it makes clear that the confrontation between
religion and state in contemporary Israel is not of recent origin but
grows out of the background of Jewish political experience and thought
in late biblical, rabbinic, and medieval times. Weiler's conclusions are of
great import to this discussion. I do a disservice to the range of his
scholarship and the richness of what it implies when I abstract here but
two salient points that emerge from his work.

The first is the total incompatibility between the halakhic system of
classical Judaism and a modern secular nation-state. The *halakhah* knows
only one kind of authority: that of God and those who interpret God's
Torah; therefore the secular state, in that it derives its sovereignty from a
human source, can be either antagonistic or, at best, ancillary to the
concerns of the *halakhah*. In short, the *halakhah* does not need a state to
enfranchise itself and to advance its interests. If there were one it would
have to conform to theocratic principles, since the Jews are understood
as *subjects* of a theocentric system and not *citizens* of an anthropocentric
one. Any political tradition Jews have is predicated upon their collective
fealty to religious norms from which they are *not free* to abstain. The
modern state, however, is predicated upon the secular freedom of man,
who is understood to be bound only by the claims of reason. Spinoza, the
first secular Jew, is the first one who made all this clear (in the *Tractatus
Theologico-Politicus*), as he did the terrible danger that lurks at the heart
of a Jewish theocracy: in looking out for its own particular interests, it
will be oblivious to the interests of the state *qua* state; in fighting its
enemies from within, it will be too preoccupied to pay attention to
problems and dangers outside its borders.[48]

A second insight to which Weiler's work leads relates directly to the
relationship between Zionism and Judaism. In its original conception
Zionism in essence was an attempt to legitimize Jewish existence in
radically different terms from the past, terms that, because they were
political and secular, were antithetical to the *halakhah*. But the secular
Zionist leaders never declared their program to be this antithesis. After

all, they were not philosophers and may not even have understood the challenge their new ideology posed to the hegemony of the *halakhah* as the ground of Jewish existence.[49] Instead of publicly proclaiming their opposition to the *halakhah* and its advocates, thereby risking a major row and a fundamental cleavage in the Jewish ranks, they adopted the conservative strategy of attempting to co-opt the religionists into their cause and thus functionally papering over the differences between them. For their part, the halakhists immediately and correctly saw the threat for what it was and never gave Zionism any real sanction (with the exception of Rav Kook, which explains why he is so revered by secular Zionists).[50] If religionists have joined the Zionist enterprise, it was and is more out of a political strategy to influence it, to advance their one-item agenda within it, and ultimately to appropriate it to conform to their norms. The result is that Zionism has never really been legitimized in secular terms, even though Israel is a secular state. In spite of the fact that a majority of Israeli Jews do not accept the ontological status of the *halakhah* as Divine Will, nor do they observe its most important tenets, it is the *halakhah* that has served to define and regulate the usages of Israeli society.

The consequence of all this is not just the crisis of Israeli identity that we have examined but a more profound crisis of Israeli legitimacy.[51] When we put the two points I have abstracted from Weiler's study together, we see that the door to theocracy in Israel is wide open. It is the logical outcome of understanding Israel not as a secular state but as the Holy Land. The *halakhah* brooks no authority other than its own and those who claim to speak in its name; the state is nothing more than a means to very specific ends. Weiler suggests that in using the content and symbols of the Jewish religious tradition and in drawing on the *halakhah* to legitimize itself, Zionism is precipitating its own downfall. The choice really is between a truly secular state (in which religion, Judaism included, is strictly a private or communal matter and not a societal one) or a theocracy in which Torah and state are coterminous.

Gershon Weiler is a professor of philosophy at Tel Aviv University with no apparent vested interests in the "Canaanite" movement. Yet his study *Jewish Theocracy* provides a remarkable confirmation of what Ratosh's thought achieved intuitively, with skimpier historical analysis, thirty-five years earlier. All of Ratosh's bold contentions—that secular Jewish nationalism and Jewish religion can never be reconciled, that Judaism is not really committed to a nation-state, that the needs of the polity that has emerged in Israel are very different from the needs of Jewish religion, and that so long as Israel does not transform itself into something that is different from the Jewish Diaspora in content as well as in form it will not be viable—these ideas can be seen to be validated by Weiler's historical study. This is why Weiler reaches what I think is the most penetrating appraisal of Ratosh's ideas: "Canaanism" he says, possesses "one great truth and many falsehoods," while Zionism turns on "one great falsehood and many truths."[52] Weiler's work leads to the realization that what I have been describing as Ratosh's critique of Zionism was in actuality an analysis of the crisis of legitimation that has overtaken Jewish nationalism.

As before, the last word here goes to Boaz Evron, both because he summarizes incisively the "Canaanite" perspective on the matters I have been discussing, without the rhetorical or ideological excess that characterizes some of Ratosh's writing, and because his remarks are relatively recent. Writing about the problems Zionism faces a century after its inception, he notes that the secular-religious conflict was quite visible right from the outset:

> The opposition to their ideas that Herzl and other early Zionists encountered . . . among nearly all orthodox Jews should have warned them that something was wrong. These religious Jews did not find their existence "a problem", as did Herzl and his free-thinking colleagues, nor did they consider themselves "abnormal." . . . To the orthodox Jew, the worhsip of God exists for its own sake; it is a sacrilege to view it as a means to a secular end, even if that end is the preservation of a people. Jews have a meaning only as servants of God, not as an ethnic group. The Zionists were wrong. Religion was not a substitute for nationalism. Religion was positive, self-determined, unequivocal.[53]

That is why we cannot discount the possibilities either that Israel will evolve into a theocracy or, if secularism takes itself seriously and persists, that the long-postponed *Kulturkampf* will break out.[54]

IV

A related issue is the relationship, legal and attitudinal, of Israeli Jews to the non-Jews among and around them. Here too "Canaanism" led to a critique of Zionism that has implications for Israel's domestic and foreign policies.

When Zionism looked to Jewish religion as the legitimator of the corporate framework it sought to redeem, it took with it one of the main philosophical principles of Jewish theology, one expressed at every turn in the *halakhah*—the notion of Jewish particularism. Jewish law rests on the idea that the Jews, in that they have been chosen for the role, are in covenant with God. Hence their status in Jewish legal matters is distinctive from the status of non-Jews. The nub of Ratosh's objection to Zionism in this area is that instead of nullifying what is to him a regressive dichotomy, Zionism has perpetuated it. This is why he repeatedly scores Israeli leadership for its ethnocracy, which he identifies as exclusivism and isolationism. The Law of Return is the most blatant example of this attitude, but it is manifest no less in the general posture of Israeli policy, domestic and foreign. For Ratosh secularism *ipso facto* implies universalism. If Israel chooses to give preferential treatment to Jews and to foster Jewish distinctiveness, then that is the proof that Zionism is perpetuating the pre-Enlightenment ghetto pattern of the Diaspora, when religious differences and categories were decisive. As Uzi Ornan puts it: a society that discriminates against Moslems and Christians will, of necessity, be more conscious than it should of "Moroccans" and "Yemenites."[55]

In place of this the secular, non-Zionist society "Canaanism" advocated would be egalitarian. Citizenship would have nothing to do with religious or ethnic background. As in the United States, religion would be a private matter; all members of society would be assimilated into a new, secular polity. The American paradigm is central: in the wake of the 1967 war, when Israel's demographic problems were keenly felt, the "Canaanite" proposal was to solve it by calling for unrestricted immigration and a radical opening up of Israeli society to all who would be attracted to it, Jew and non-Jew alike. After all, argued Aharon Amir, who put forth this idea, if the United States had at one point decided to accept only Anglo-Saxon Protestants, it would never have attracted the diverse and talented population that eventually enabled it to become a continental nation and a superpower.[56] And in this new Israel there would be one educational system with one language, in which Jew and non-Jew, religious and nonreligious, would all participate together.

This vision has several implications and I shall consider some of them below, when we examine what happens to relationships between Israel and world Jewry in the light of the "Canaanite" thesis. For now suffice it to note this facet of it as perhaps even more "utopian" than its call for the separation of religion from state. Whereas that call was concretized for a while in the League for the Abolition of Religious Coercion, there is no evidence of any public support to bring about the dissolution of the distinctions between Jewish and non-Jewish identities and cultural patterns within Israel. Where this element of the "Canaanite" ideology did find some response was in the implications it held for Israel's foreign policy. Here the "Canaanite" position attracted individuals from the political left who saw in Ratosh's critique of Zionist-Jewish ethnocentrism (which on the left was apprehended as racism) a confirmation of their universalism.

It was here that the "Canaanite" thesis underwent perhaps its most interesting transformation. The key figure in this connection is Uri Avneri, whose political trajectory over the past four decades has been from right to left, although his "dovishness" is not nourished by any Marxist roots. We noted earlier that Avneri had been influenced by Horon in a manner similar to Ratosh. But the two never made common cause together. There were at least three reasons why Avneri chose to go his own way. First, he understood Horon's ideas somewhat differently. "The main feature of the Hebrew idea was, in our view, the fact that it was at once both national and regional. Ratosh grasped the national aspect and exaggerated it in a dangerous way. We placed the emphasis on the regional aspect."[57] Second, Avneri was interested in a political action group, not in a coterie that would sit and intellectualize about history, culture, and identity. "Canaanism" under Ratosh, Avneri concluded, was "an overture after which there came no opera."[58] And third, the two quite simply did not like each other. After their apparently one unhappy meeting, Avneri and a few others made their own way.

The initial effort was to divest the notion of a new Hebrew nation from the Pan-Hebraic imperialism that Ratosh was articulating. The idea of foisting a Hebrew identity and culture upon the Arabs and other non-Jews seemed ridiculous. In place of Ratosh's "Land of the Euphrates" *(Erets Haperat)* the group that Avneri founded in 1946, *Bama'avak* (In the Struggle) (named after their periodical), fastened on the concept of a "Semitic Region" *(Merhav Hashemi)*. The Hebrew national movement, having foresworn Zionist separatism—this much is clearly Ratoshian—would affirm its Semitic commonality with the Arabs and form a regional Semitic Federation. The hope was that the Arabs, on seeing that Israel had renounced Zionism, would understand this to mean that it had renounced expansionism, and would in turn themselves renounce Pan-Arabism in favor of the new Semitic bloc, thus "melting all our differences into one great movement toward national liberation, social reform and planned regional progress."[59] To Avneri this Semitic Revolution would be the final stage of the process that began with the Zionist Revolution (which he felt had accomplished its goals and had dissipated) and continued with the Hebrew Revolution (of which Ratosh's thought and work, like Horon's, were but early expressions). "We felt that we were the wave of the future, the authentic new voice of Hebrew youth."[60]

The *Bama'avak* group rejected the United Nations partition plan of 1947 not only because of Jewish nationalism but because of Arab nationalism as well. As long as the needs of both nationalisms were unmet, the conflict would go on until Semitic unity would be achieved.[61] In this respect it is possible to say that Avneri's break with Zionism was even sharper than Ratosh's, for Ratosh, in his refusal to acknowledge Arab polity, was much closer to the standard Zionist position. Avneri, in contrast, accepted the legitimacy of Arab "otherness." In time this attitude led him to define his political vision in more precise terms: if a grand Semitic Confederation was an unrealistic dream, then what could be called for was the partition of Palestine into a secular federation of an Israeli state and a Palestinian state. This was the platform of *Hape'ulah Hashemit* (Semitic Action), the group that Avneri, together with such left-leaning ex-members of the Lehi as Natan Yellin-Mor, Boaz Evron, and

Amos Kenan, organized in 1958. The platform was laid out in a 126-point "Hebrew Manifesto" *(Haminshar ha'ivri)* that this group published. "Semitic Action," of course, had no immediate impact on Israeli policy, but in retrospect it, like the League for the Abolition of Religious Coercion, represents a discernible adaptation of "Canaanite" thought in the direction of a post-Zionist ideology. Avneri's more recent activities, notably his meeting (together with Gen. Matti Peled and Ya'akov Arnon) with Yasir Arafat in Tunis in February 1982, show us the permutation of the territorial definition of a Hebrew nation and of secular nativism from what Shavit calls a "national-cultural unifying principle" into a "political-civil" one.[62] In spite of the mutual antagonism that always prevailed between Avneri and Ratosh and the declared differences between them, the two need to be linked and seen as expressions of the same ideology.[63] This is especially true as the crucible of their disagreements—Palestine of the mid-forties—fades into the past and the disagreements can now be seen largely as differences in emphasis and style rather than in substance.

Now if we affix to Avneri's approach to surrounding non-Jewish entities the label of "revisionist Canaanism," that of Aharon Amir can be termed "pragmatic Canaanism." In general Amir has been the most consistent and vigorous pursuer of the "Canaanite" agenda, in a certain way even more than Ratosh.[64] For whereas Ratosh's doctrinaire approach led him to regard any cooperation with Zionists and Jews as compromise, Amir has always understood the value of strategic alliances, and this has enabled him to inject the "Canaanite" perspective into a variety of issues and arenas. For our purposes here the most important is the relationship to non-Jews in light of the 1967 war and, more recently, the 1982 incursion of Israel into Lebanon.

When the "Six Day" war ended Israel found itself in control of a million Arabs. What from a Zionist viewpoint appeared as a threat to the "Jewish" basis of Israel looked in "Canaanite" terms like a real chance to alter the nature of the national entity that called itself Israel.

> With the war I saw a spontaneous occasion to keep all this, to solve the refugee problem. A chance to integrate the Arabs as far as possible into Israeli society. An opportunity to help achieve the de-Zionization of the state on a secular non-denominational basis. Abba Eban said after the war that the choice was to be great or to be Jewish. Eban chooses a Jewish nation; I choose a great one.[65]

In other words, a tangible step toward the formation of a secular United States of the Middle East, which is implicit in Ratosh's vision of the "Land of the Euphrates," its imperialistic overtones notwithstanding, could now be taken—if Israel would retain sovereignty over the newly acquired territories.

Accordingly, Amir quickly reorganized the "Forum for Hebrew

Thought" into the "Action Staff for the Retention of the Territories" *(Mateh Hape'ulah Lehahzakat Hashetahim)*. This group consisted mostly of such self-conscious "Canaanites" as there were at that time and a few who were not. Shortly thereafter, however, a much larger, broader, and more "main-line" coalition was organized to influence Israeli policy, the "Greater Land of Israel Movement" *(Tenu'at Erets Yisra'el Hasheleimah)*, into which not only Revisionists entered but also Orthodox and some penitent (wayward?) Labor Zionists. Amir sought to bring his group into this coalition as well. What happened subsequently is most interesting: while the Orthodox element had no problem accepting and working with the "Canaanites" within the new movement—according to Amir they were even prepared to see him as its executive director—the secular Laborites demanded that the "Canaanites" be expelled because they were not Zionists. Clearly the "Canaanites" represented less of a threat to the religious groups, who had no problem about their identity and could exploit Amir as readily as he could exploit them, than they did to the secular Zionist groups, who evidently were deeply challenged by a nationalist view that unequivocally broke the links to Jews all over the world, links that to such Zionists were undefined.[66] The Laborites, who were the most vociferous in wanting the "Canaanites" out and who were the crucial component of the whole "Greater Land of Israel Movement," had their way.[67]

The Lebanon episode began before the 1982 war. In March 1978 Israeli troops entered southern Lebanon and launched Operation Litani. The objective was to drive out the forces of the Palestine Liberation Organization that had been harassing settlements in northern Israel and inflicting many civilian casualties. When the brief campaign ended, Israel found itself for the first time since before statehood in real contact with the Christian Lebanese population, who, at that point, welcomed the Israelis and the relief they provided from the attacks of the Moslem Palestinians. Like many Israelis, Amir had fond memories of Lebanon from his youth. In 1942 he had worked in the Christian village of Marj 'Ayoun, an experience he was to remember as one of the best of his life. But to a follower of "Canaanite" theory propounded by Horon, Lebanon held even more meaning. A contiguous coastline united Israel and Lebanon into one geographical unit, western Palestine. History, too, told of a close working relationship between the Phoenicians and the Israelites, who, as we have seen, were both "Hebrews" in Horon's view.[68] And the modern descendants of these people, the Israelis and the Maronite Christians, both represented forces for pluralism and nonconformism in the Pan-Arabic Middle East. For all these reasons Amir saw new possibilities for Israel's relationship with its northern neighbor and, attendant upon these, for the advancement of the "Canaanite" program. Thus he argued (this last point only implicitly) in his introduction to an anthology about Lebanon, which he edited in 1979 in order to acquaint

Israelis with the country and the people with which it was now in day-to-day contact.[69]

But Amir, as we can imagine, could not confine himself to writing about Lebanon.[70] Shortly after Operation Litani he organized a group of six Israelis, which, with the Israeli army's permission and assistance, visited southern Lebanon. There contact was made with a corresponding group of Lebanese Christians, both Maronite and Greek Orthodox. Together the gathering hatched the idea of setting up a body of thirty Lebanese Christians and Shiite Moslems and a similar number of Israelis, not all of them Jews, which would develop cooperative programs and activities fostering communication and humanitarian relief. In this way would the human relationship between Israel and Lebanon be cemented constructively. The proposal was taken to lower-echelon officials in the Israeli Ministry of Defense and, according to Amir, there was some interest. A budget was drawn up for the project, the logistics were arranged, and the matter sent for approval to the desk of Ezer Weizman, then minister of defense. There it stopped. Amir and his group never received any response or explanation why the idea was vetoed, if it ever officially was, but Weizman apparently effectively killed it.[71]

It was, however, resurrected in the summer of 1982, when Israel conducted a full-scale invasion of Lebanon. Now the outlook was different and it appeared that the proposal might have a chance. In early July, before the Israeli army's siege of Beirut, Amir and his colleagues, again with military assistance, went to the Lebanese capital and held talks with a number of Christian intellectuals. Two of them, the poetess Mayy Morr and her husband, Alfred Morr, a historian, returned to Israel hosted by Amir. Amidst a good measure of media attention they met Menahem Begin and other Israeli government officials. This meeting set the tone for continued talks throughout the next several months. The result was the establishment of an official group called "Interaction—the Lebanese-Israeli Council for Friendship and Development" with offices in Tel Aviv and Beirut. At its height the group included several scores of Lebanese and Israeli members. In spite of the rising debate over the efficacy of the Israeli initiative in Lebanon, the council began to conduct in both cities a number of intensive discussions and parlor meetings over the questions the new political situation posed for both societies. In Beirut, for example, there was a joint meeting of economists from universities of both countries. On one weekend a group of Israeli medical personnel sat with a few Lebanese intellectuals. All this interaction took place quietly, in private, with no publicity. Then in February 1983 the Israeli authorities began to block the project. Again, no explanation was given. Very soon the council died. It was by all indications a completely unnatural death. Amir is convinced that if it had not been stopped by the Israeli government, it would still be continuing.

Leaving aside whatever immediate strategic or political considerations
may have been behind the decision that caused the project to be aborted,
this episode bespeaks a fundamental confusion about the nature of
Israel's relationship to its neighbors who are not in a state of war with it.
The same is true of the entire Israeli experience in the West Bank. Does
Israel come to these people as friend? As conqueror? As ally? As occupier? As savior? As manipulator? The answer at this writing is as
unclear as the *telos*—to which it is related—of Israel as a Jewish state.[72]

It is here that the clarity of the "Canaanite" approach stands in sharp-
est contrast to that of Zionism. We shall have to consider just how
important ideological clarity is in the long run. Nevertheless, a few
speculative questions present themselves here. If the Jewish historical
experience is one of living "outside the pale" of the nations of the world,
if the Jewish religion is predicated on the notion that the Jews are "a
people that dwells alone," and if Zionism and Israel have defined themselves largely by and within the hermeneutics of Jewish history and
religion, is the die not cast for future Israeli policy, domestic and foreign,
and the kind of society it will produce? Perhaps we must invert San-
tayana's oft-quoted dictum: those who persist in remembering the past
are condemned to repeat it. How much has Israel itself, besides the
Arabs, fostered the state of siege it has lived in since 1948? How much
does it actually want such a situation? How much does it actually like it
and need it?[73] If Israel decides that the United States of America is an
inappropriate paradigm, is there not a danger that it will develop as a
Middle Eastern Albania? Further, what does all this imply about Jewish
religion and *halakhah*? Do they do best in a state of siege, where "we/they"
is the operative category of reality? What happens to the humanistic and
universalistic currents within Judaism? Can they be expressed only in a
Diaspora context? Are they necessarily assimilationist? Must openness to
non-Jews necessarily be a function of how far one is from the traditional
religious position? These are some of the questions that the "Canaanite"
thesis forces in this context.

V

What then becomes of the relationship between Israel and world
Jewry when the ideological link connecting them is cut with the knife of
the "Canaanite" thesis? An initial answer is that since Ratosh's thought
takes the idea of *shelilat hagolah* (negation of the exile) to its furthest limit,
Diaspora Jewry simply drops out of the Israeli consciousness, left to
wither on its rootless, stateless vine. That is certainly a possible answer,
but it is not necessarily the only one. In the *Zionist* working out of the
"negation of the exile," world Jewry outside Israel is indeed consigned to
the inexorable forces of assimilation and, bereft of national sovereignty,

is doomed to the fate of the politically impotent. That is not the implication of "Canaanism." Most ironically, in its negation of Jewish *nationhood,* "Canaanism" actually reaffirms Jewish *religion.* That is, it can be seen to uphold, if not advocate, the millennial power and validity of religion as the natural modality of the Jewish experience and the Diaspora as its historic locus. In the shrillness of Ratosh's denunciation of both Judaism and Diaspora (which are for him synonymous) one can hear an acknowledgment of their legitimacy. For Ratosh *galut* (exile) as a pejorative term for deracinated existence, which Zionism purloined from the Jewish mystical tradition (where it denotes an impaired spiritual condition), does not exist; there is only *pezurah* (Diaspora), which is the "homeland" of Judaism.[74] As opposed to Zionism, "Canaanism" sees Diaspora Jewish life, anchored in the self-sufficiency of the religious tradition and the halakhic system, as viable and even eternal, its survival beyond question.

This position leads to a posture of acceptance of the Diaspora and its essential "otherness" from Israel. This is a posture quite different from that of Zionism.

> In the last analysis it is not we but Zionism which presumes to declare war on communities of Jews wherever they may live. It aspires to subvert their values, to challenge them to personal transformations and to revolutions, to conquer the communities, to force upon them a dual loyalty, and to sanction such loyalty. We have no part in all that. . . . As far as we are concerned the Jews of America, France or the Soviet Union and all the communities of Jews wherever they live are entitled to continue fostering the values of Judaism and to conserve and protect them. . . . Our relationship to Jews the world over is that of respect for foreigners.[75]

To the believing Zionist such words are horrifying and immoral. "To be a Zionist," writes Eliezer Schweid, "means to recognize the moral responsibility towards the whole Jewish people, not only towards those Jews who . . . have already made *aliyah* and have a common interest together."[76] But the argument from morality cuts two ways: what appears to one party as "responsibility" for the other can seem to the latter as manipulation and coercion, an arrogation of responsibility that says, "I will be responsible for you whether you like it or not." The "morality" of this attitude is, at best, open to question.

The "Canaanite" focus is on *interests,* and the nub of its critique of Zionism here is that in the name of such high principles as morality and loyalty what are overlooked are the conflicting interests of both parties. The identification of the interests of those who live in Israel with those Jews who do not (an identification we see clearly in Schweid's definition of a Zionist) and the corresponding identification of the interests of world Jewry with Israeli interests are judged to create problems for both parties. This point was made forcefully in the "Canaanite" stricture of American Jewry after the 1967 war. Underneath the unprecedented outpouring of support, tangible and intangible, for Israel that American Jewry displayed at that time, the "Canaanites," in contrast to the Zionists, who were widely reported to have discovered the Diaspora for the first time, found some rather self-serving motives. American Jewry, they argue, wants to use Israel as a psychological bulwark against anti-Semites to show them that Jews too have heroes. It is

> interested, likewise, in the existence on our [Israeli] soil of a Jewish "Holy Land" . . . [so] that . . . there should dwell Jews who keep the precepts of the Law. . . . [Moreover, American Jews want Israel] to appear "liberal and democratic" and resemble as much as possible a pocket edition of the U.S.A. That would make a good impression on American Gentiles also, while ensuring a complete subservience of Israel to American influence. Last but not least: American Jewry wants to make sure that should any community of "non-European", not to say "colored", Jews need to emigrate and re-settle, they would find a refuge in Israel rather than discredit the American Jew in the eyes of his "white" Gentile countrymen by trying to immigrate to the U.S.A.[77]

Now regardless of whether these charges are in retrospect ludicrous or accurate, the principle behind them contains, I think, an insight that is not at all foolish: that American Jewry, like Diaspora Jews in general, uses Israel to nurture its own particular interests. We could just as easily invert the argument and observe that Israel, under the veneer of morality and loyalty, uses Diaspora Jewry to further its own agenda. The value of the "Canaanite" perspective is that it exposes, to borrow Buber's terminology, the "I-It" nature of the relationship that obtains between world Jewry and a Zionist Israel, even as both parties foster the sense that the relationship is of an "I" to a "Thou." The results of such, let us call it, confusion are actually deleterious to both parties. For Israelis it promotes an attitude of material dependence upon the largesse of Diaspora Jews, a mentality Ratosh described as "the kingdom of *schnorr*," at the same time as it leads to a feeling of moral superiority. For Diaspora Jews it runs the risk of their liquidating all their Jewish assets—material, spiritual, and psychological—into an Israel they condescendingly view as a "poor cousin" without physically going there, thus impoverishing themselves as Jews in all three senses and retarding their development of their own inner resources, indigenous institutions, and sense of involvement as Jews in the societies in which they live.

The "Canaanite" approach rests on the hard-nosed recognition that the interests of the Israeli people as a developing nation in the Middle East cannot possibly be equated with the interests of Jews who live in various kinds of societies the world over. The interests cannot be equated because, subjectively and objectively, the *needs* are different. If Israel's commitment to Zionism obscures this fact, to the mutual disadvantage of both Israelis in Israel and Jews in the Diaspora, then it is only by taking leave of the presuppositions and the institutions that underlie Zionism that the relationship can be defined.

What would this redefined relationship look like? Amir finds that

> precisely because I do not see them [Jews in the Diaspora] as obligated to receive some "message from Zion," [because] I have no preconceived notion of commitment on their part, therefore do I think that I (not I personally but I as a representative of this approach) can find more paths to true and free dialogue than the . . . Zionist who always comes—even though he never says so openly—with the demand "You owe it to me!"[78]

Amir decries the Israeli manipulation of American Jewish public life he says he saw when he visited New York in 1977–78 and worked with the Israeli Consulate there in an effort to help arrange relief efforts for Lebanon. It is a manipulation he compares to that of the Comintern among workers in Italy and in Central America. "I think that precisely because we do not want this kind of an understanding [of Diaspora Jewry], we have nothing to dictate, we are not going to dictate anything."

What, then, would Israel "mean" to American Jews if its Jewish component were excised from it—if there were no obligation for it to proclaim (and correspondingly, no compulsion from American Jewry to receive from it) some "message"? Amir is clear that there would indeed be something to be communicated, especially when the dialogue between Israel and the world would not be weighed down with Zionist value judgments. Israel as a new secular democratic nation would offer a challenge. Not a Jewish challenge, to be sure, but a human, personal one; a challenge for a new life, one that could be physically and spiritually fulfilling. Like America and Australia in their time, it would offer a new frontier, "except for Alaska, the last frontier in the classical American sense," made even more appealing by its unique historical background and the confluence of cultures within it.

> I think that this can be sold to Americans as Americans, not just to Jews. The fact that the approach to the Jews of America can be done as part of an approach to Americans in general is a very great plus. To approach the American Jew as a Jew only brings here those with *payot* [side-curls]. . . . The Jews of America *en masse* will have no motivation to come here. . . . But this is not so if you turn to them as free, open, and liberal human beings and you say to them: "Listen—you are searching for something interesting? Then come here. Not because you are obligated to come. I want people to come here from Nebraska and from Holland. And you, too. You want something interesting? Then come here."

It is important to note the mutuality of needs and interests on which an approach of this kind is based. Amir is clear that his are purely those of a native who wants to see his homeland grow. A secular-democratic society is therefore a much more attractive prospect for this eventuality to occur than the ethnocratic and the possibly theocratic one that Zionism fosters. Similarly, from the perspective of the American character this approach speaks to its need for adventure, mobility, individualism, and pluralism. Israel becomes a place to which there is no "historical reason" or "religious imperative" to come. With this lightening of the ideological load that the State of Israel carries comes a corresponding reduction in the level of expectations and demands Israelis and Diaspora Jews have of each other. The "Canaanite" thesis leads to the possibility that it is only beyond a Zionist framework that the two parties can encounter each other as separate entities, that the "otherness" and integrity of each is legitimate and, most radically, that the existence and the survival of one is not conditional upon that of the other.

VI

The agenda of "Canaanism" we can now see was and is truly revolutionary. Though its proponents were keenly aware of this, at no point did they ever organize or advocate seditious activities.[79] Instead "Canaanism" infused its energies into the diverse, short-lived groups and causes noted above—the League for the Abolition of Religious Coercion, Semitic Action, the Action Staff for the Retention of the Territories, and Interaction. Still, there was always a feeling among Ratosh and his followers that there existed "a link between the doubt surrounding the fundamental questions and the failure of the regime, [and that] perhaps the ideational confusion is what dictates unsuccessful policies."[80]

For this reason those who were imbued with the "Canaanite" view would frequently direct their critique not just at the policies of the Zionist government but at the very form and structure of the Israeli political system that enfranchised such policies and perpetuated them. A vivid example of this criticism is the book *In the Vise of the Regime (Bitsevat hamishtar)*, which was subtitled "Why Has No One Risen Up?" by Ezra Zohar. This work was not intended as an argument for "Canaanism," though Zohar was a follower of Ratosh, but it does point in that direction. Instead of dealing in ideology, Zohar focuses on the day-to-day realities of Israeli life. Using a surfeit of facts and figures he concludes that the entire network of institutions and values that make up Israel's domestic existence—the services, the standards, and the attitudes—is inadequate and intolerable. This situation, he says, is due not to coincidence or to incompetence

> but to the system of government by which all the power and the means are concentrated in the hands of the government. Inflation, scarcity, the necessity to run around from clerk to clerk, the lack of consideration for the individual citizen, the petitions, the applications, the permits, the

"committees" that decide on everything, the *protektsia*, the preferential treatment, the "certification" of enterprises, the "fringes," the understandings, the discounts, the dismissals, the grants—all these and the like are nothing but an integral part of that system, of that regime, and only serve to strengthen it and to make *the citizen dependent upon government when the government should be dependent on him.* This regime is what shapes the contours of our present life as it screams at us daily from the newspaper headlines: [labor] sanctions, strikes, embezzlements, scandals, a poor work-ethic, noncompliance with contracts and obligations, a social gap, knuckling under to demands, fast bucks, exploitation of the weak, continuous escalation of taxes and prices, obliviousness to the consumer, and palming off of substandard goods. All these and the like are the results of the regime, the inevitable consequence of a regime that sees its perpetuation as the highest imperative.[81]

It is not surprising that Zohar's book enjoyed a wide readership. Its incisive complaints articulated very well the frustrations of many. Yet, remarkably, the book is all diagnosis; there is no prognosis. Zohar stops short of putting forth any program, political or economic, that might change the situation. It is only when we know his "Canaanite" leanings that we can hear the implications that rise up out of his book. It is a not quite subversive work.[82]

The essential point of *In the Vise of the Regime* is that the resident of Israel is a *subject* and not a *citizen.* This is a conclusion we have already encountered in the discussion above of the social arrangement of a theocracy. From the "Canaanite" perspective it is all one, the necessary and permanent consequence of the identification and union of Zionism with Judaism. The crises of identity, legitimacy, and morale will abide as long as the state rests on the present ideological foundation.

This is what Ratosh had in mind when he called the Knesset, and therefore all succeeding governments, "illegal." For him the solution lay in dissolving the whole apparatus and starting anew. This was a change that in his last years he felt "would not be possible other than through a civil war."[83] His proposal to establish a "presidential regime," while less radical only in a relative sense, was intended at least to diffuse power and reduce the influence of the political parties.

Strange as it may seem, these ideas live on and from time to time surface in Israeli political debate. They represent one more point around which "Canaanism" continues to press its agenda. In 1981, just before the elections for the tenth Knesset, Aharon Amir gathered a nucleus of people to explore the concept of a "Second Israeli Republic."[84] The idea was that in view of the problems created by the existing coalition politics and the resultant inability to generate coherent policy or reach consensus on political and cultural questions, what is needed is a new governmental system. The American model again comes to the fore: in addition to the Knesset there would be instituted an executive branch (the conceptual descendant of Ratosh's "presidental regime"), a written constitution, and with it the process of judicial review (the rudiments of which are already in existence). In place of the system of election by proportional representation would come representation by region. This latter idea is not new and has been bruited about in Israeli intellectual circles for years. What is new is the holistic approach of combining electoral reform with a restructuring of the governmental system. In January 1982 a conference of thirty or forty individuals took place in Tel Aviv to explore this possibility, and then in March there was another one with double that number. The discussions were held *in camera* and the participants agreed to give no interviews to the press. The hope was to set up an organizational structure and an office and not go public until the elections originally scheduled for 1985.

According to Amir, what stood in the way of this project's making any real headway was not opposition among those who participated in the two meetings but the sobering experience of the Democratic Movement for Change *(Shinui)* party (DMC). The DMC had coalesced for the 1977 election on a platform of electoral reform, won fifteen seats in the Knesset, and then proceeded to decline as a coherent party. In the 1981 election it was wiped out. The fate of the DMC had the effect of inhibiting any real impetus to think about a "Second Israeli Republic." Soon after, when the Lebanon war began in June 1982, Amir himself chose to invest his energies in pursuing the possibilities that now came into view, which I have discussed above.

VII

And so it is that "Canaanism" exists, as it has for forty years, not as an organization but as an impulse, a protean force, within Israeli society, an enzyme of ferment, challenge, and change. If its success and significance are to be measured by the numbers it has attracted to its banner or the tangible effect it has had on Israeli policy, it has clearly failed. If the criteria, however, are the importance of the issues it has addressed and the intensity and consistency with which it has addressed them, then its critique is indeed worth pondering.

It is also worth recalling, as we conclude this survey of its engagement with Israeli society, "Canaanism"'s point of departure: the necessity of that society to define itself clearly in secular democratic terms if it was to have any future as a nation. The following words of Amos Kenan, spoken in 1977, sum it all up:

> I really don't know if we have a nation here. And if we have no nation here—then what do we have? I am not seduced into believing that because we have a government and a representation at the U.N. and an army and a

Chief of Staff, we have a nation. I think that the failure of Israeli society and of the Israeli state is the lack of a possibility to create a nation. There is no homogenization of the exiles here. That is one big lie. We are living in a false society whose lies are already not credible to the society itself. I think that our root problem is what it was in the forties: can a nation be created here? When Ratosh and those like him coined the "Canaanite" expression, it was with the idea of crystallizing here the ingredients appropriate to a nation. They were thinking about what attributes this nation would have . . . what its cultural foundation would be. For various reasons, and especially because the nation . . . that was here in '48 did not comprise the backbone of the new state but was only an infant and an accomplice—for this reason . . . there is no nation here but a mixed multitude.[85]

VI

"CANAANISM" AND THE ISRAELI ARTISTIC IMAGINATION

In the introduction I observed that "Canaanism" is generally remembered as a cultural ideology, especially in this country. I hope it is now apparent that such a perception is accurate only in part. Culture, after all, does not exist or flourish in antiseptic isolation but is an aspect and a function of the society that creates it. As the two preceding chapters have shown, the essential agenda of "Canaanism" was social and its ramifications political. Only when the issues that the social agenda raised were addressed would the cultural possibilities that "Canaanism" envisioned become relevant.

Now while this is a logical way to look at it, it may not be a correct description of how Ratosh and his followers approached the matter of culture. There are grounds for thinking that what they really had in mind was a cultural revolution, one that, when launched, would perforce lead to political changes. We remember that for Ratosh the first step was a transformation of consciousness. When this was accomplished by the artistic elite, and the most creative forces in society achieved a new self-understanding and identity, then would the cultural revolution begin.[1]

This construction of what "Canaanism" intended forces into view a range of issues relating to Israeli art, specifically its nature, content, and prospects. By art I mean the imaginative experience in its generic sense, although in actuality "Canaanism" seems to have addressed only the plastic arts (painting and sculpture) and the language arts (literature). The "Canaanite" critique of Israel, therefore, as much as it constitutes a sociopolitical challenge, impinges even more on such subjective processes as creativity and the imagination. This is probably why it appealed primarily to artistic types. It is this manifestation of the challenge that I want to discuss here.

106

I

At the outset I want to say that I have no interest in dealing with the problems of defining the nature of "Canaanite" art and of determining whether there has or has not been such an expression in Israel. These are questions no less theoretical—and no less fruitless, in my view—than the questions of the "Jewishness" of Israeli art and whether there is, in fact, such a definition or esthetic norm as "Jewish art." At least one Israeli critic, after confessing to an initial willingness to discover whether a "Canaanite" art exists, has backed off.

> What, actually, is "Canaanism" in art? A yearning for a defined culture? Hopes for an undefined culture? Apparently [it is] the link between the yearning and the hope. The problem of "Canaanite art" is that those who identify with the future (a distinctive regional culture) do not necessarily identify with the way the [pagan] past is defined, and conversely, those who do identify with the past (for example, those artists who have been interested in primitivism for esthetic reasons) do not seek after a collective cultural future. We are left with a vague middle ground.[2]

For this reason there is really no point in trying to determine the influence of Ratosh's thought on the various modes of artistic expression in Israel. This becomes clear from the 1980 exhibit at the University of Haifa of painting and sculpture on the theme of "the Myth of Canaan: the Influence of the Ancient Middle East on Modern Israeli Art." The works shown there established the fact that the tendency to draw on the local landscape and its past existed independently of the "Canaanite" ideology, and it would be a mistake to link them causally.[3] Melnikov's famous lion monument at Tel Hai, widely hailed as a harbinger of artistic archaism, was created in 1926 and Danziger's statue *Nimrod*, celebrated as the consummate expression of the "Canaanite" sensibility, dates from 1939, when Ratosh was still in Paris.

Literature shows the same thing to be true. In fiction there are few novels that can be said to be thematic treatments of the "Canaanite" thesis. Tammuz's *The Orchard* (1971, Hebrew) and his more recent *Jeremiah's Inn* (1984, Hebrew) come close in a certain way and, in another way, so does Yizhar's *The Days of Tsiklag* (1958, Hebrew), as Barukh Kurzweil pointed out.[4] The most explicitly "Canaanite" novels of which I am aware, not surprisingly, are those of Amir, particularly *Nun*.[5] In poetry, Ratosh's "The Walker in the Darkness" *(Haholkhi bahoshekh)* (begun in the early forties, completed about 1964, and published in 1965) is nothing but an exposition of "Canaanism" in verse. Beyond it there is only the poetry of Amir and Ayin Hillel that can be said to show a distinct "Canaanite" content.[6] As far as the Israeli stage goes, that is the last place we ought to look for manifestations of "Canaanism," for of all

genres it is the drama that is most closely linked to the norms, expectations, and outlook of its society. The Hebrew drama in particular has
most actively served the Zionist vision.[7] If there are "Canaanite" tendencies in such plays of the twenties as Moshe Halevy's "Jacob and Rachel" or
Shoham's "Tyre and Jerusalem" or in what Avigdor Hame'iri had in
mind in his conceptualization of the Hebrew drama,[8] these are but the
theatrical equivalents of what I noted above about sculpture.

II

The questions that "Canaanism" raises about Israeli art are more
profound. They relate to such issues as its nature, its content, and the
sources of its inspiration. "The historical debate about Israeli art is as old
as the debate over . . . Zionism, and it follows the same contours."[9] That
is, in considering the nature of the Israeli artistic experience, we are
thrown back to the root issues we have been concerned with here all
along: continuity versus revolt, secularism versus the sacral, the nature
of the relationship to the past. In the esthetic context, however, this
dialectic takes the form of a tension not so much between past and
present, which is obvious, as between time and space, between memory
and locale. The questions become: which of these elements is primary in
the artist's consciousness? How is artistic consciousness related to experience? And how are these factors related to identity?

The insight that "Canaanism" provides is that the spatial dimension
embodied in the sense of place and rootedness in the landscape is
decisive for the nourishment of an authentic artistic consciousness. "Canaanism"'s assumption and hope are that the nativist experience will
precipitate a cultural revolution.[10] In severing the ties with Zionism, the
Israeli artist will free himself or herself of the confusions and ambiguities that impede the development of a clear identity. And in severing the
ties with Judaism he or she will acquire new wellsprings of inspiration
and new fields for their expression.

Initially, it was the plastic arts, especially sculpture, that provided the
impetus for this hope. That is why Danziger was considered so important and why he was so influential. *Nimrod* achieved a perfect integration
of content and form. Not only did it hark back to the pre-Jewish, pagan
past, but the very materials out of which it was made—Nubian sandstone
from Petra—affirmed nativist values. Moreover, the notion of sculpture
itself as a legitimate cultural expression flew in the face of the Jewish
religious *ethos* and the Diaspora experience.[11]

But because Ratosh was a poet, the major context in which a "Canaanite" esthetics developed was in literature. Here, too, the raw material of language had the potential to reflect as well as to express the
desired transformation of consciousness. This, of course, is what

Ratosh's poetry is all about. I am referring not only to the studied archaism of his early work but also to the colloquial, almost slangy, quality of his later poems. This shift does not signify a diminution of his muse, as some think, or a concession to trendiness, but a recognition that

> every language breathes its own syntax. Hebrew as it is colloquially spoken breathes a syntax quite different from what came before, and this is [a] Canaanite [idea]. . . . Ratosh was perhaps the first person in Palestine who understood that to write in a colloquial language is the beginning of the cultural revolution that one day will be a political revolution.[12]

III

It is testimony to the richness of Ratosh's thought that whatever else it implies for history and politics, it leads to a fairly well-developed poetics. This is one area where Ratosh worked out the implications of his "Canaanite" thesis in a little more detail than in some others. Simply put, the distinction he makes between "Jewish" and "Hebrew" has relevance when it is applied to imaginative literature written in Hebrew. The two terms become full-fledged literary norms. "Jewish" literature is that body of *belles lettres* produced by the Diaspora experience. It is rooted in the problematic of a religious community and interprets reality from that standpoint. That is its *raison d'être*. On the surface this domain endows "Jewish" literature with a patina of universalism, for it exists in many countries, is written in many languages, and knows a great deal about the world. To Ratosh, though, these broad horizons mask the essential narrowness of vision that energizes all such "Jewish" literature. "All these things [it] apprehends in terms of the problems and needs of Jewish existence, and of these alone."[13] In cultural terms such exclusivism is judged to be provincialism,[14] since there is no real connection with the real temporal and spatial worlds. In the Jewish perspective, which we must remember is for Ratosh extraterritorial, the only dimension is time.[15]

In opposition to this category Ratosh offers "Hebrew" literature, which is nothing but the concretization in literary art of the nativist imagination. Here the language of creativity can only be Hebrew because the reality that this literature will depict will be that of the specific place and specific life of an incipient Hebrew nation. Because such a literature will not necessarily be connected to the Jewish problematic, it will be truly universal.

> It will break through the guarded wall, and . . . expand both the historical and the territorial horizon; it will open the heart and the eye to the continuity of time and space. Perhaps ultimately it will know how to relate to a person as a person and not as a Jew, a member of a certain com-

munity, and to the world as world and not as an arena for millennial
Jewish wandering. From the wide, deep, and firm basis of a nativeland it
will be possible to open our eyes and hearts to wide horizons.[16]

Ratosh admits that such a literature exists only in theory as a cultural
potential. At the present time, "we stand . . . impoverished and empty.
The new Hebrew literature . . . according to the definition arrived at
here . . . has only produced and could only produce the first buds. . . .
There are few among us whose mother tongue is Hebrew."[17] What is
worse, "the literary values upon which we are raised are foreign to us;
they give us no sustenance. They do not help . . . to develop the powers
of Hebrew creativity. On the contrary, they help strangle it."[18] The
problem stems from the nature and the definition of the reality that is
taking shape in the new immigrant society. It is diffuse and bifurcated.
The "Hebrew" experience of the native is qualitatively different from
that of the "Jewish" immigrant whose imagination was formed in the
Diaspora. This situation leads Ratosh to see the same choice imposed in
the literary sphere as in the social and political spheres: Israel will
produce either a Jewish literature that happens to be written in Hebrew
or a new Hebrew literature written in the new secular language that
integrates form and content.

Language and literature thus become for Ratosh and his followers
important loci of the *Kulturkampf* they wished to precipitate. This is why,
for example, Ratosh proposed at one point abandoning the conventional
"Assyrian" style of Hebrew script in favor of recasting it in Latin characters. This conversion would formally express the transformation of
Hebrew from a sacral Jewish tongue into a secular Western one. It would
also serve in a practical way to drive a wedge between the younger
generations, who would grow up using the new script, and the sacred
texts of biblical, rabbinic, and medieval Judaism.[19] It is on this basis, too,
that we must understand the energy Ratosh invested in developing
Hebrew neologisms. It is a fact that several widely used words and terms
in current Hebrew usage were coined by Ratosh.[20] Now while this
cultural agenda was directed at promoting the secularization of Hebrew
as a language, it also, at the same time, was intended to preserve its
linguistic independence and autonomy. For Ratosh this meant being
zealous to purify the language by purging it of foreign influences in
vocabulary and spelling.[21] This pursuit was really a working out in
cultural terms of what "Canaanism" called for in its broader vision.

What is most significant about this poetics is the respect for the integrity of the artistic imagination that underlies it. As a poet Ratosh understood that literature, like all art, relies on lived experience for its power
and its authenticity. Since the reality of the new nation was not that of the
Jewish Diaspora, there really was no literary tradition in which "Hebrew"
artists could write and from which they could draw inspiration. The

Hebrew literature of the prestate period was, as we noted above, inadequate. And because it was foisted upon the younger generation, it was harmful. How could a child of Yemenite-Jewish parentage, for example, going to school in Tel Aviv, be expected to identify with the characters of Sholom Aleichem or Bialik? What is worse, how could the creative impulses within such a child ever be nourished by the coercion to identify with these characters that prevailed within the educational system? Better for such a child to read someone like Mark Twain, where the ideological pressure would be off and his or her imagination could float freely, as it must if it is to exist at all.[22] Hebrew literature of the kind taught in the public schools has "documentary," not esthetic, value, and Ratosh would consign its study to the university. What he would have taught at the elementary and high school levels in the absence of a truly "Hebrew" Israeli literature would be the literature of the Italian Renaissance, the literature of emerging nations, and selections from American and Russian literature written during the formative stages of the national life of those countries.[23]

Because it was founded on such a poetics, the "Canaanite" impulse concretized itself into some important efforts to foster the creation of the Hebrew literature to which it aspired. The results here were considerably more apparent and successful than those of its efforts in the sociopolitical sphere. For one thing there was the enterprise of translation. In seeking to expand the imaginative horizons and esthetic criteria of the citizenry of the new Hebrew nation it would be necessary to make available to them in their own idiom the best of what other nations were thinking and creating. This impelled Ratosh and Amir to translate hundreds of works of both fiction and nonfiction, mostly from French and English, into a lucid and beautiful modern Hebrew. It also spurred them to create vehicles for the encouragement of Hebrew literary talent and the publication of its fruits.

The realization of this dream took some time. Originally, in the forties, Ratosh had hoped to put out a magazine of national culture (*Mahbarot latarbut hamoledet*), but the 1948 war intervened. *Alef,* as we have seen, filled this role only in part. It was not until Amir organized and took over the editorship of *Keshet* in 1958 that the implementation of this aspect of the "Canaanite" agenda was accomplished. Ratosh had written that in order for the new literature to come about, "what is required is independence, a liberation from the framework of Jewish literature and its values, content, and the Jewish problematic. . . . Like a chick in its shell it must break through, split it open and take leave of it in order to breathe the air of this world. Otherwise it will be asphyxiated inside."[24] *Keshet* viewed itself as a hatchery for Israeli literary talent. For eighteen years, until 1976, under Amir's tutelage it certainly did serve that function. Many of Israel's major writers such as A. B. Yehoshua, Amos Oz, Yitshak Orpaz, and Yehoshua Kenaz took some of their first literary steps in the pages of *Keshet;* many others were given a chance there to establish that they were of lesser talent. Consistent with his outlook, Amir saw to it that Israeli Arab writers such as Attallah Mansour and Anton Shamass could publish their fiction in *Keshet.* In time the review took on a broader aspect as a shaper as well as a purveyor of native culture. Besides original fiction and poetry, it included essays, translations, documentary material on the history and folklore of the *Yishuv,* and occasional symposia on larger cultural questions. Throughout *Keshet*'s existence Amir saw to it that it remained independent in all ways. This principle made it unique among Israeli reviews, but it also left *Keshet* without any institutional base. Accordingly, in 1976, when Amir felt that the time had come for him to devote his energies to his own writing instead of being the midwife to the creativity of others, he relinquished the editorship and thereby terminated *Keshet.*[25] Whether Hebrew literature is the better for this decision even Amir himself is unsure, but it must be said in retrospect that Amir's efforts with *Keshet* constitute one of "Canaanism"'s signal achievements.

IV

Ratosh's poetics, because of the monism in which it grounded, has one very important virtue: it furnishes a unified theory of modern Hebrew literature.

> If we want to speak of Hebrew literature . . . we cannot speak of a contrast between generations but of a contrast between two different literatures. Hebrew literature, according to this approach, is in its totality simply the creation of Hebrews in the land of the Hebrews, just like any other literature in any other country or in any other language. There is or can be no other general definition.[26]

That is to say, the commonality of language notwithstanding, the difference between the Hebrew literature of Israel and the Hebrew literature of the prestate Diaspora is one not of degree or sequence but of substance. It is a true revolt and not a continuity.

Such a view is the mirror image of one of modern Hebrew literature's major critics, Barukh Kurzweil. For Kurzweil, too, the literary creativity of the new state was devoid of Jewish values, except that what for Ratosh was a positive, liberating development was for Kurzweil the end of the line.[27] Like Ratosh, Kurzweil agreed that religious faith had been the central issue of modern Hebrew literature. Because this issue did not figure in the fiction of native Israeli writers from the Palmah generation down to the younger modernists Oz and Yehoshua, Kurzweil judged the poststate phase of Hebrew literature to be mediocre, inauthentic, and superficial. Without a rootedness in the sacral past these secularized young writers simply skimmed the surfaces of reality. All they could achieve was what Kurzweil called a "literarization of life," which lacked the "dimension of depth."[28]

This is exactly Ratosh's opinion, but from the opposite viewpoint. Like Kurzweil, Ratosh sees Uri Tsvi Greenberg as "the last Jewish poet" writing in Hebrew.[29] But whereas Kurzweil aspires to a literary renewal born of the poetic vision that will unite past and future, Ratosh wants the two to be totally dissociated from each other. Both are agreed, however, in their assessment of the present. What Kurzweil calls the "literarization of life," Ratosh terms "the escape to surface reality." The "dimension of depth" that Kurzweil wants is for Ratosh an "escape to the past." Such "escapes" are for Ratosh defense mechanisms that deflect the Hebrew literary artist away from the natural introjection of the new reality of which he or she is a part. True, this introjection process has only just begun and its literary expression has not yet crystallized. But it is clear that the literary renewal to which Ratosh aspires is born of the poetic vision that comes from a total rootedness in the land, with no immigrant experience or another non-Hebrew mother tongue to interfere with the primacy and the naturalness of the nativist Hebrew perception.[30] Ultimately both Kurzweil and Ratosh come out in the same place: the former's denunciation of the products of the post-1948 period of modern Hebrew literature is matched by the latter's rejection of the works of the pre-1948 Diaspora period. Both await a new creativity that is not now in evidence.

Ratosh's view of "Jewish" literature has affinities also with that of another important theorist of modern Hebrew literature, Dov Sadan. Unlike Kurzweil, Sadan does not separate secular Hebrew *belles lettres* from other nonimaginative, religious literary expressions such as commentaries, responsa, homiletics, scholarly writing, and Hasidic literature. All are holistically seen as diverse expressions of the Jewish mind and spirit, not just with respect to form and content but even with respect to language; Sadan includes within the purview of Jewish literature that which Jews have written in Yiddish, German, Polish, English, Ladino, and other languages of the Diaspora.[31] This is essentially the same conception that Ratosh had of "Jewish" literature. Where Ratosh and Sadan part company is in their understanding of the meaning and significance of the Israeli experience and its literary expression. Sadan, unlike Ratosh and Kurzweil, is thoroughly imbued with a Zionist outlook. For him a Jewish state offers a real chance to reintegrate the religious past and the secular present to achieve a new cultural synthesis. (In this respect Sadan is almost as far from Kurzweil as he is from Ratosh, since he was much more optimistic about Zionism's possibilities as a "continuity.")

This three-sided conjunction of Ratosh, Kurzweil, and Sadan has been observed and discussed by Dan Miron. His conclusion is noteworthy:

These three theories point in utterly different directions. . . . And yet, these mutually exclusive theories emerged from one crisis which all three critics interpreted as the crisis of a new culture negotiating the terms of its existence *vis à vis* its traditions. That Ratosh included among these traditions the so-called "new" Hebrew literature, while Kurzweil identified the emergence of this culture in the second half of the eighteenth century, and Sadan identified a continuous existence of the past alongside and within the new literature, should not blind us to the similarity, indeed, the parallelism of their theoretical constructs. This parallelism reveals the common seriousness and integrity of these three brilliant intellectuals as they fathomed the depth of a major cultural crisis and courageously carried their convictions to their logical conclusions. While popular propaganda culture predicted the glorious continuation of triumphant Zionism, they saw grave dangers and the need for sweeping cultural change.[32]

V

Of course the cultural revolution these theorists each called for did not happen. Israeli culture developed in ways quite different from what Ratosh, Kurzweil, or Sadan expected. A theory is, after all, a network of ideas, and, like a net, it accounts for and catches some things while other things fall through. Of the three parallel visions of Hebrew literary creativity that he describes, Miron observes: "The parallelism also indicates their common rigidity and the limits of their powers of observation. . . . All three shared [a] characteristic . . . insensitivity to reality."[33]

We do not need to explain why and how this is true of Ratosh. The historical and sociological reasons that Miron adduces why the "Canaanite" sensibility did not develop have already been discussed. There are, however, two factors that do need mention.

The first concerns the artistic elite upon which Ratosh predicated his hopes for a cultural revolution. Kurzweil had first called attention to the possibility that, in the absence of any other such elite in the society of the new state, the "Canaanite" coterie had the potential to assume this role.[34] While this was a plausible contention at the time, in retrospect it can be seen to have been unwarranted. Amos Kenan explains the simple reason why it was unwarranted: an elite, if it is truly to function as such, cannot be in opposition to the norms and values of the society of which it is a part.[35] Because the "Canaanites" were by their own definition anti-Zionists, they were in effect cut off from their society, unattached to its basic assumptions and so devoid of cultural influence.

Alternatively, we may note that artistic consciousness is really inseparable from the general experience that shapes society as a whole. Because Israel has not been either willing or able to escape its Jewish destiny, its art has not transcended the reality prefigured by Jewish myth. Israeli literature has perforce been a development of "Jewish" literature as Ratosh defined it. A transformation of consciousness did occur in Israel, but not the one Ratosh sought. The Jewish past has not been expunged from the Israeli literary imagination but instead has endured as a potent energizer of it.

Perhaps the problem with Ratosh in esthetic terms is that he generalized about all literary creativity from the standpoint of the poetic process and was insensitive to the differences between genres. As the most subjective mode of literary expression, poetry has the best chance of living within its own hermetic world without recourse to the collectively experienced reality of society. But even poetry is not solipsism. Hayim Guri, a secular Hebrew poet, attributes his rejection of Ratosh's excision of the Jewish past not to any religious yearnings or like reasons; he sees it, quite practically, as an impoverishment of the imaginative resources available to him as a child and a product of Jewish history.[36] The case is even clearer with respect to fiction and drama. For fiction the dimension of time is even more integral than the spatial. The categories of history and memory cannot be controlled or manipulated as easily as Ratosh thought. And drama, the most public of the literary arts, is, as noted earlier, the most dependent of all upon its correspondence with the collective consciousness of society.

And so we return to the point from which this entire discussion began. For the most part it is not art that shapes society but vice versa. A "Hebrew" art and culture did not come about because the "Hebrew" society Ratosh called for did not develop. Rootedness in the land and in the language is itself no guarantee that a cultural revolution will transpire. This is why "Canaanism" actually has less to say in the cultural than it does in the sociopolitical sphere. Its critique of Zionism cuts more deeply there. What "Canaanism" does imply culturally is more theoretical than practical. It leaves us with the question of the nature and content of Israeli culture in general and Israeli literature in particular. In regard to the latter, Miron professes not to be troubled. Whether in Israel or the Diaspora,

> . . . in investigating the contemporary Jewish literary scene, we should refrain from applying our habitual reductive procedures. We should rather accept it for what it is, a fragmented array of diverse, independent literary developments, which, nevertheless, come into contact in a common artistic commitment to the imaginative probing of the possible significance or significances of the Jewish experience under contemporary circumstances.[37]

But this conclusion leads to another, final question that the "Canaanite" critique of Zionism invites, however indirectly. It is a question not so much about the nature of the culture Israel is creating but about the creative process itself within the Israeli milieu. "Israel," observes

Amos Kenan, "is, from a cultural standpoint, one of the most totalitarian states in the world." The Israeli artist, he explains, is, like every other Israeli, subject to the authority of the army. And so one who is at one moment a free, creating human being, is at the next moment a soldier, called up to serve by and under the jurisdiction of the state. "This teaches a person a lesson . . . that it is possible to take him wherever they wish, to make of him whatever they wish—and he has nothing to say about it." The Israeli artist, whatever his or her medium, must always live in readiness to be called away from artistic freedom and distance, must always be prepared to perform this inner "switch." It is not a situation conducive to creativity.

> This is a system of repression the like of which I am unacquainted with in any other country. It is very subtle, very democratic. There is no secret police or concentration camps. There is simply no need for them. In this state you can't become an other. Now how can a culture grow if a person doesn't become an other? What does it mean to be an other? It means first of all to be who you yourself are. Something that is not uniform. If there is no "you," then there can be no "we."[38]

Here the "Canaanite" insistence on definition and clarity reaches its full expression in the artistic sphere. Its implication is far-reaching. It necessitates in the Israeli artist a critical attitude toward the ideological canons of Zionism and a suspicion of its rhetoric, though not, to be sure, a renunciation of it.

"Canaanism" translated into esthetic terms may not imply a usable poetics but a posture, a style, and maybe even a content. It positions the artist, especially the literary artist, to see, as Ratosh saw, the dangers that lie in the blurring of the sacred and the secular and to call for an accounting of the moral dilemmas posed by such a syncretism.[39]

VII

CONCLUSIONS

What is the upshot of this inquiry into an ideology that, for all its coherence, did not institutionalize itself within the broad spectrum of Israeli political life as an alternative program? What does the "Canaanite" critique of Zionism imply as we look upon a living Israel in its present condition?

I

In order to answer these questions and bring this study to a conclusion, it is first necessary to place "Canaanism" and Zionism side by side and point up both a fundamental difference and a fundamental similarity between them.

The fundamental difference between "Canaanism" and Zionism lies not so much in the way each conceives the content of Israeli national life as in the very way in which the state is understood. I refer here to the difference between understanding the state as "a moral community" and, on the other hand, viewing it as an agent of the interests and needs of diverse individuals, or what is known as a consociational society. "Israel's [Zionist] founders conceived of it as a moral state," one in which the entire body politic is energized by a common vision and a broad consensus about its nature and its goals. The vision was that of Zionism and the consensus was that Israel was intended as a Jewish state, whatever that might mean. "No leader was more explicit or insistent than Ben Gurion in arguing that Israel was created with a purpose beyond the satisfaction of its citizens' needs; but every Israeli political leader shared this conception."[1] That there never was any unanimity about just what the purpose was is beside the point.

Now as Liebman and Don-Yehiya note, "the alternative to the moral state is the welfare or service state—a state that views its primary role as satisfying the demands of its citizens or mediating between the competing demands of citizens or groups of citizens."[2] This is the conception of

Israel that emerges from "Canaanism" as I read it. To be sure, Ratosh originally formulated the "Canaanite" vision of Israel in terms of a "moral community," or, to be precise about it, as an alternative type of moral community to the one put forth by Zionism. But this construct is more a function of Ratosh's own Zionist roots and the universe of discourse in which he operated; it is not integral to his ideas. "Canaanism," as some of Ratosh's followers have implicitly recognized, really translates into a consociational "service state" conception of Israel, one that presupposes a heterogeneous populace and that is much less weighed down with ideological freight.

In the light of this difference it is easy to see why "Canaanism" never had a chance. Ultimately it represented a metamorphosis of Jewish identity into something that had no defined historical precedent or definable content. In other words, when "Canaanism" sought to act on the secular impulses that were so clearly manifested in early Zionism and to actualize them by severing the tie to the Jewish past, it had no available model or context upon which to predicate the new secular self-understanding it asked of its adherents. The appeal to a prebiblical "Hebrew" past was more a fillip than a plausible option. So in essence "Canaanism" was a theory without a praxis. Secularism as the upshot of modernity and the Emancipation could be appropriated by Jews as individuals but there was as yet no way for Jews to do this meaningfully as a collective entity without some recourse to the Jewish past and the Jewish religion, as the Zionist experience shows. "Canaanism" held out a transformation into an unknown world with no real past to structure its vision.

"Canaanism" was seen as a fiction, then, because it was utopian. Those who have critiqued it are fond of depicting it in these terms. Such a description is not in itself incorrect. It helps us understand some of the essential qualities of "Canaanism." For example, the ideological clarity that we have noted as perhaps its outstanding feature derives precisely from its utopian nature. So, too, does the rationalism that pervades Ratosh's thought. In it everything works out neatly, as it does in all utopias: language and territory alone define the "Hebrew" nation; everyone living within the "Land of the Euphrates" will ineluctably agree to this definition. Even if they are Maronite Christians or Druse or Kurds, not to mention Arabs, they will accept the Hebrew language and Hebrew identity.[3] This conviction leads us to identify determinism as another aspect of "Canaanite" utopianism.

But it is not only "Canaanism" that is utopian. In its own way so, too, is Zionism. Herzl's *The Jewish State* is nothing if not clear and rational in the way it lays out the solution to the Jewish question. Moreover, when we recognize that Zionism rests on the assumption that a Jewish state will guarantee Jewish survival and that, with the attainment of this state, the Diaspora will, sooner or later, wither away (to use the language of another utopian ideology), we see that Zionism, too, is at bottom deterministic. And there is more to it than this. Calling an ideology "utopian" does not *ipso facto* invalidate it. It leaves some important questions still open: when is a body of thought deemed arrant utopianism really preternatural boldness? When is a set of ideas that are formed in the free-floating world of theory really the key to new and constructive possibilities? Is rationalism of necessity suspect in the formation of an ideology?

Indeed, it is possible to conclude that any ideology, as a coherent framework of ideas, is inadequate, a "Procrustean bed" into which multivalent reality is squeezed. The fact is that life is more forceful than logic and people have the nasty habit of not always acting rationally or thinking clearly. This is an argument which has justifiably been used to explode the feasibility of "Canaanism"'s vision of a pan-Hebraic "Land of the Euphrates."[4] But it seems to me to be no less applicable to Zionism. Consider, for example, the two phenomena of Arab nationalism and the Nazi destruction of European Jewry. These can both correctly be adduced as having had such a profound effect on the collective Israeli psyche that they have reinforced Jewish historical consciousness and thereby retarded the development of the secular nativist consciousness that Ratosh called for. At the same time both these phenomena have also served to delay, if not divert, Zionism from attaining, through the State of Israel, its goals of security, productivity, economic independence, and a new Jewish social order. The unrelenting persistence of Arab hostility to a Jewish nation-state, combined with the hold the Nazi experience still has on the Jewish sensibility, leads us to ask whether the synergy of the two will not only divert Israel from the agenda of its founders but subvert the agenda itself.

In the long run, therefore, we must wonder whether ideology is or will be quite as decisive as this book imputes it to be in shaping and determining Israeli self-understanding, society, and policy. Maybe in the fluidity of history, ideas and principles count for less than material, empirical, and pragmatic interests and needs. Maybe that is the way it has always been with Zionism.

It is only in this respect that Shavit is justified in concluding that "Canaanism" is "irrelevant" to the present realities of Israeli society.[5] The presupposition on which this study rests, however, is that ideas and ideology are indeed real, with a life force of their own. This is why I believe there is value in analyzing the contradictions of Zionism and in showing why Ratosh addressed them and how he proposed to overcome them. I cannot claim that Ratosh is as important as Ahad Ha'am or Berditchevsky, but some of his ideas, especially as they have been applied by some of his followers, are rife with implications for many of the problems facing Israel. "Canaanism" in this book has served a heuristic

device. We have, in effect, been studying a footnote to the Zionist idea
and the Israeli experience.[6] What is left to do is to determine what the
footnote implies for the text.

II

"Canaanism" is important because of the insight it brings into a problem that was always present but is becoming and will continue to become
increasingly crucial as Jewish national sovereignty establishes itself in the
Middle East and Israel matures as a state. The problem is the relationship between Zionism and Judaism. The conventional understanding is that the two are inextricably linked. Many would say that they are
inseparable. Ratosh himself, as we have seen, holds this, and he founds
his critique of Zionism on just that notion. But therein lies the clue to
what he really believes: in rejecting Zionism for the accommodation it
has made to the symbols, values, and outlook of Jewish religion, Ratosh
implicitly is suggesting that *in principle* Zionism and Judaism should
really have nothing to do with each other. "Canaanism" becomes important because of the ideological wedge it drives between secular Jewish
nationalism and Jewish religion.

This is an instructive perspective at this time. Whether Zionism and
Judaism will continue to cohabit, whether their union is judged to be licit
and sacred or illicit and promiscuous, and whether it will be a fulfilling
and generative union or a manipulative and sterile one—these things
remain to be seen. But a great deal is gained when we are reminded that
in actuality there are two ideological organisms here, two discrete elements that at the outset, a century ago, were opposed to each other. The
developments of the present day, when secularism is on the defensive in
Israel, make it easy to forget that at its inception Zionism was a continuation of the *Haskalah* (Enlightenment) in a national framework.

> The ideal of the Zionists, like the ideal of the *maskilim* [Enlighteners] was a
> new kind of Jew. The distinguishing features of the ideal prototype may
> not have been uniform among all Zionists, but it is possible to point to
> some particular characteristics: the new Jew would be a proud and brave
> fighter, he would abandon his excessive spirituality for a love of nature
> and development of the body, or, as Max Nordau put it, he would display
> a "muscular Judaism." What is interesting is that this ideal was shared by
> political and cultural Zionists alike, and by Zionists from both Eastern
> Europe and the West.[7]

"Canaanism" reminds us of these facts. It invites us to pay attention to
the secular nature of Jewish consciousness and national life in the twentieth century and to take it seriously.[8] It may well be that the particular

ways in which it advocated translating such secularism into reality were bizarre and inadequate and are today forgotten. But the very fact that there arose an ideology that insisted that the Jewish national enterprise be played out solely in secular terms represents to my mind an insight that is as permanent as it is provocative, a challenge that has yet to be met. "Canaanism" in its time amounted to a raising of some fundamental questions about the state that was in the making during the period of the British Mandate and that appeared on the stage of history in 1948. What was to take precedence in the formation of its national policy: the territorial dimension of its existence or the Jewish dimension? Were its primary loyalties and interests with the non-Jews of the region or with international Jewry who did not and might not ever live within its borders, whatever those borders might be? From what values would the political life and institutions of the new state derive: from those of the Jewish religious past and its laws and traditions or from those of Western secular democracy? Could Israel be a "Holy Land" and a homeland at the same time? Could it be both without becoming a theocracy? While it is true that a person or thing can have various modes of existence and be different things to different people, is it possible to maintain multiple identities that conflict with and contradict each other? The dominant strategy of Zionism in dealing with these questions was, as we have seen, simply to postpone their resolution. Perhaps in its time, this decision was correct. But in any case the questions abide and now they have begun to press with increasing urgency. Every day they impinge on what Israel says and does both domestically and in its foreign policy.

The two metaphors that Gershom Scholem suggests, cited in the epigraph to this volume, now come to the fore. They show that Scholem saw the cogency of the "Canaanite" argument even as he did not agree with it.[9] The metaphors are an exact depiction of the issues that "Canaanism" raises and that are at stake in its critique of Zionism. When we consider each one carefully we see that the difference between them pertains not just to the question "are we Jews or Israelis?" as Scholem says, but to matters even more profound. The issue is, in a word, history. How much of a claim does the past really have on the present (and on the future)? What kind of a claim? Does the past determine the present?

These are the true questions, the ultimate questions of modernity. They are the questions Nietzsche saw when he pinpointed perhaps more clearly than anyone else the central issue of modernity as the conflict between man's capacity to remember and man's capacity to forget. Unlike animals, who live unhistorically, human existence is always qualified by the past, by history and by memory. For Nietzsche this weight of the past is sufficiently oppressive so as to inhibit man's vital forces and stifle the juices of creativity. Modernity in essence for Nietzsche means to summon the strength to forget the past so as to act.

We must then consider the capacity to perceive unhistorically to a certain
degree as the more important and fundamental so far as it provides the
foundation upon which alone something right, healthy and great, something truly human may grow. . . . Where are there deeds which a man
might have done without first having entered the mist of the un-
historical? . . . As the man of action, according to Goethe's phrase, is
always without conscience, so is he also without knowledge; he forgets a
great deal to do one thing, he is unjust to what lies behind him and knows
only one right, the right of that which is to become.[10]

This is exactly the metaphysical posture of "Canaanism." Its roots in
Berditchevsky and cultural Zionism notwithstanding, "Canaanism" represents the full working out in a Jewish nationalistic context of the idea
of modernity as defined by Nietzsche. In this respect it is instructive to
compare it not only with normative secular Zionism, which preferred in
the end to remain within the orbit of history, but also with the metahistorical perspective of religious Zionism, in which, as in biblical
Hebrew, there is no real present but only the past and the future.

What will be in the end has already been in the past.
And what has never been will never be.
Therefore do I trust in the future, for I have set the face
Of the past before me; this is my vision and my song.
Selah. Hallelujah. Amen.[11]

In contrast to this view, "Canaanism" relinquishes memory, knows only
the present and "the right of that which is to become." Greenberg is
unquestionably correct when he says that "forgetfulness is the mother of
denial."[12] "Canaanism" 's demand that the link to the Jewish past be cut is
intrinsically related to its negation of Jewish distinctiveness.

But there is another implication of Scholem's metaphors. We may say
that "Canaanism" and its critique of Zionism are significant no less as a
part of the debate over the conflicting claims of time and space. "Canaanism" opted for the latter; the essence of Judaism is its unswerving
commitment to the former. Zionism tries to pacify the furies of both.

As a monotheistic religion Judaism is founded on a deep suspicion of
space and the spatial. It is suspicious of them because they are the
domain of Judaism's archenemy: idolatry. Idolatry can be understood as
the affirmation and celebration of the self-sufficiency of the three spatial
dimensions of existence. In asserting the primacy of the fourth dimension, time, Judaism imposes a stark choice on its adherents: either God
or an idol. Either time or space. Either history and memory or nature
and matter. The only concessions Judaism made to the spatial were in
regard to the status of the Holy Land (*Erets Yisra'el*), Jerusalem, and
Mount Moriah, but even these sites were subordinated to and qualified
by the significance accorded them by time.

Modern secular Jewish nationalism, on the other hand, rebelled against this ultimatum. Whatever else it implied, it constituted an invitation to Jews to reencounter the spatial. This rebellion was expressed in secular currents of early Zionism, but its full development came in "Canaanism." Now the choice originally imposed by Judaism was reversed: either space or time, either a radical new beginning, different in content as well as in form, or more of the same, a continuity of old content albeit in new form, an unbroken connection to the past. As Scholem put it: either the metaphor of a rocket detaching from its booster to achieve independent existence in its own orbit or the metaphor of an organism, the parts of which are linked by memory and destiny. Or as Ratosh put it: either a brave "New '*Ever*" or a "Third Temple" doomed to destruction. In the light of the fact that the ultimatum was originally issued by Judaism, it turns out that the dualistic mentality of Ratosh's thought is not so much the product of a penchant for totalism that grows out of problems in identity formation but is rather an honest expression of the recognition that all who are involved in a secular Jewish national enterprise face *ipso facto* a choice—either space or time.

But Zionism as it developed refused to define the conflict in terms of mutually exclusive alternatives. Instead of "either/or" it attempted to live with "both/and," both the needs of space and the claims of time. In principle this approach was right, for life is lived both in time and in space. This objective was no less bold than anything "Canaanism" or Jewish religion envisioned. In practice, however, it was not so easily accomplished. As we have noted, Judaism is not amenable to subjection to secular Jewish authority, and in the course of the Zionist experience and Israeli statehood it has driven a hard bargain. So much so that a secular Zionist observer, in assessing the Israeli scene in the autumn of 1982, came to the conclusion that secular Zionism is in the process of being repelled and overwhelmed by Judaism.

> In a conversation twenty years ago, my teacher Dov Sadan said that Zionism was nothing more than a passing episode, a temporary mundane phenomenon of history and politics, but that Orthodox Judaism would re-emerge, would swallow Zionism and digest it. At the time, those who heard him thought that Sadan was engaging in intellectual pyrotechnics, as was his way. . . . Although I still do not agree with his prognosis, I cannot dismiss it as intellectual acrobatics.[13]

What troubles Oz and many like him is that the die may already have been cast. Orthodox Judaism may already have become the sole repository of national content and values. In Oz's words, "thirty or forty years have passed and we have left tomorrow behind us and yesterday is here upon us."[14]

In other words, the Diaspora has prevailed, even in Israel. Not only has Sadan been proven correct but so has Ratosh's original prognosis. Consider, in the light of all the problems it faces today, the following description, written in 1949, of what an Israel that would not choose to set itself up as a "New *'Ever*" would look like:

> Or there could be established here a Jewish state in the Holy Land, a community of the Jewish Diaspora. A second version of the Second Commonwealth—closed in by its particularism, shakily surviving, sitting on weapons and on money in a hostile world, relating with millennial suspicion and hatred to the world around it, . . . dependent upon the various [Jewish] communities of the Diaspora, seeking through them the support of the superpowers at no cost [to it].[15]

Yonatan Ratosh was not a prophet and the positive content of his vision has not materialized. Nor is it about to materialize.[16] A more useful perception of him is that of the "village atheist" of the *Yishuv*. Or, less colloquially, he can be seen as a Zionist heretic, one who developed his views by denying the root assumptions of Jewish polity. In this regard he belongs to a clear and respectable line of Jewish nonbelievers who thought themselves out of the Jewish religion and, in Ratosh's case, out of the Jewish community. If Spinoza was the first secular Jew, Ratosh is the epitome of one. In spite of all the vast differences between them in time, in substance, and in intellectual stature, a straight line can be drawn between them.

It may well be that the problems Israel faces today are not solely the result of the contradictions of Zionism. To the extent that they are, we do well to ask after its intellectual origins. We do well to remind ourselves that there was indeed a potential revolution in Jewish history intended by the claims and goals of secular Zionism. As concretized in the State of Israel, it was surely one of the mightiest, most far-reaching transformations history, certainly Jewish history, has witnessed. The "Canaanite" idea serves to alert us to the possibilities that this revolution either died in its infancy or has not yet come to pass. Which one it is, time—and space—will tell.

Excursus

"CANAANISM" AND THE RECONSTRUCTION OF ZIONISM

THE CASE FOR A SECULAR ISRAEL

Having examined some of the ways in which "Canaanism" has influenced Israeli society both sociopolitically and culturally, we come to the realities of the present and the prospects for the future. We must now ask: if "Canaanism" as it has been presented in the previous chapters represents a heuristic device, a challenge to Zionist verities and ideological smugness and triumphalism, what might it mean to accept the challenge? To spell out where the challenge might take Israel in the light of where, as a state and as a society, it is now?

The argument that follows is admittedly and can only be speculative. To be sure, I believe it a responsible speculation, one grounded in an open-eyed recognition that Israel is irrevocably a Jewish state and that its regnant ideology will always be called Zionism. To argue for the immediate adoption of "Canaanite" principles by Israel's society and government would be ludicrous. But I want to probe, however boldly or foolhardily, in that direction.

I

The case I wish to make is that in the long run Israel will be better off when it acts on "Canaanism"'s essential insight and purges the Jewish national enterprise of its religious trappings, content, and aspirations. That is to say, I want to claim that a great deal will be gained when Zionism and Judaism are dissociated from each other and the Israeli polity is placed on a purely secular basis.[1] My contention is that Israel will do better to evolve into an understanding of itself as no longer an ethnocratic "moral community" but a pluralistic "service state."

125

Let me repeat: Israel as it defines itself now and for the foreseeable future is Jewish and Zionist. Any responsible speculation must begin with this reality. The case here is not for the unilateral adoption of "Canaanism" and its policies as the solution to Israel's problems (even though, as has been noted, Zionism is no less utopian in nature and outlook). A transformation of consciousness of this magnitude is unthinkable and probably undesirable. It presupposes some enormous national trauma or a revolution that, while not impossible, is certainly not inevitable.

The question is not one of revolution, whereby the clock is turned back to the *status quo ante* of early Zionism, but of evolution, of the gradual recognition that the interpenetration of secular Zionism and Orthodox Judaism is dysfunctional and inimical to Israel's national interest. The nexus between the two cannot, as Ratosh believed, be severed decisively at this point; just the opposite: it can and might be loosened over time. The important point is that this development could never occur in the explicit name of "Canaanism." Aharon Amir observes that "Canaanite" ideas have always done best precisely when they are naturally arrived at and not self-consciously promoted.[2] It is not unreasonable to wonder whether this process will be spurred when the full implication of Jewish ethnocracy is realized and the immanent spectre of an Orthodox theocracy creates a powerful secular backlash that will propel Israel toward becoming a secular "service state." Uzi Ornan, who in spite of his militance is much less confrontational than his late brother, admits to great reservations about the entire way in which "Canaanism" was developed and presented by Ratosh. In his view "Canaanism" did not necessarily need to break so sharply and irrevocably with Zionism. It could have more positively acknowledged the Zionist matrix from which it sprang and developed its program as a legitimate outgrowth of that matrix.[3]

This is a good perspective from which to examine the case for a secular Israel. The objective is not for Israel to disavow Zionism or to call for it to evolve to a stage "beyond Zionism."[4] That is as unthinkable as asking America to disavow democracy or capitalism or Russia to abandon Marxism or communism. To speak of the "de-Zionization" of Israel is too close to the language of Arab rejectionism and creates a cognitive dissonance that is counterproductive. It is equally unnecessary to speak of Zionism as "dead" and to define the era toward which Israel must move as "post-Zionist," as such neo-"Canaanites" as Uri Avneri and Boaz Evron do.

> This State must stand on two legs. One is its special relationship with the Jewish People. The other is its relationship with other States in the region who also have much in common with the Israeli nation. One cannot contradict the other. The extent to which it does is a function of the 'world

picture' created by Zionist ideology, an ideology which must be allowed to die its natural death.[5]

The real desideratum is to alter not terminology but the content of Zionism, to change the nature of what is done and aspired for in the name of Israeli sovereignty. Here it becomes important to take a developmental view and to see Israel and Zionism not as ideologically static entities but as the dynamic, open-ended processes they are. The 1967 war, for example, revealed aspects and implications of Jewish nationalism that few knew were there. Impulses and ideological wellsprings that had been running silently and deeply suddenly burst and flowed out into the open. In different ways the same thing happened in the 1973 war and more recently in the 1982 Lebanon war. The various and conflicting forces that make up Zionism and Jewish nationalism are still contending and no one can say that anything has really been resolved. Lawrence Meyer, at the end of his account of Israeli society at the outset of the eighties, observes instructively that

> For purposes of comparison and perspective it is useful to remember that Israel is roughly at that point in her history where the United States was when Andrew Jackson occupied the White House. Lincoln and the Civil War . . . McKinley and the Spanish-American War . . . the Great Depression . . . World War II . . .—all that was far into the future.[6]

This insight helps us realize how new and young the Israeli experience is and how recent a phenomenon Zionism is within the totality of Jewish history. If we see Jewish history synoptically, in the same way, for example, as a satellite photo captures a continent spatially, we will notice that the fault line along the Great Divide that separates the modern Zionist experience from the earlier Diaspora one is not all that clear. It has been obscured by the fact that Zionism up to now has used the norms and values of the pre-earthquake period to cover itself. But an earthquake did occur; the foundations of Jewish existence were radically and irrevocably altered when the State of Israel came into existence.

Everything, then, is still in formation. Here we need to recall an idea attributed to Lord Acton: that it is not the nation that creates the state but the state that creates the nation.[7] Because "Canaanism" is predicated upon this insight it can serve not as an alternative to Zionism but as an indicator of the direction in which the ideology and, more importantly, the policies of the Israeli polity—which I believe will always be called "Zionist"—must develop.[8] It is not implausible to think that the nub of the "Canaanite" idea—Israel as a pluralistic secular democracy—could eventually come about. After all, according to Scholem, the nub of the earlier Sabbatian heresy—the subversion of halakhic authority—evolved over time into the *Haskalah* (Enlightenment). In any case, the issue is not whether Israel will call itself "Zionist" or "Canaanite" but the content of its national life.

II

But what really does this new content entail? What does it mean to dissociate Zionism from Judaism?

The operative term I wish to adduce here is "reconstruction." What I am really arguing for is the ideological reconstruction of Zionism in the light of certain elements of the "Canaanite" thesis. In other words, while it is possible to claim that Zionism or whatever ideology that governs the Israeli polity's self-understanding has the capacity to develop into something different from what it is today, no one can say when and how this process will occur. The more immediate task, therefore, is to delineate the details of the intellectual transformation that needs to take place, the terms of ideological evolution.

Reconstruction is a particularly apt term in this context. If we say that Ratosh's thought signifies a deconstruction of the Zionist idea, then the process of integrating its implications is a reconstruction. Moreover, the term and the process have already been fruitfully applied to Jewish religion. The thinking of Mordecai Kaplan and the movement he established illustrates how a body of religious thought and practice can be refashioned in the light of new needs and criteria. That which is judged to be unworkable or dysfunctional is jettisoned, and that which is retained is reinterpreted. The same holds true for that body of political and social thought called Zionism.

There is no question that Zionism is today in dire need of reconstruction. The contradictions that lie at its heart exact a price that has begun to impede Israel's progress—socially, politically, economically, and morally. One by one the versions of "unreconstructed" Zionism have played themselves out. Labor Zionism, the one closest to the ideology for which I am arguing and the one that had potentially the best chance to achieve it (because it was essentially about creating a new society), proved itself inadequate to the challenge of maintaining and implementing its secular vision, although it did build an economic and social infrastructure. Likud Revisionism, with its preoccupation with borders and no apparent vision of what life was to be like within those borders, needed much less time to demonstrate that the deliberate combination of Jewish religious myth and the secular political means to actualize it creates many more problems than it solves, some of them dangerous. In both these cases it was the messianic impulse, rooted in Judaism, that got the better of the secular impulses of modernity. That leaves religious Zionism as the only other available conception of Jewish sovereignty. While it is unlikely that it will ever be enfranchised as the majority force, its influence on the

Israeli polity and policies has become decisive. The emerging alternatives truly are either more theopolitics or the reaffirmation of Israel as a secular state.

If it could be determined that the hegemony of Jewish religion would be a humanizing factor, one that promoted mutuality and dialogical fullness in human relationships, then Israel as a state founded on spiritual ideals might make sense. If it could be assured that Israel as a theocracy would mean that its society was permeated by a moral scrupulousness that concretized what lies behind biblical and Talmudic Judaism, then the definition of Israel as a Jewish state could conceivably be viable and compelling. Holiness would be its hallmark. Furthermore, if there were grounds to suppose that a great Jewish religious reformation could take place, whereby *halakhah* was transformed into a means to achieving the above ends and would not be an end in itself, as it is now for Israel's religious authorities, then it would be easy to argue that the union of Judaism and Zionism is redemptive. But my fear, based on what has been unfolding within Jewish nationalism for nearly a century now, is that religion exists within it strictly as a force for reaction. Within the Israeli context it cannot but oppose any attempts at reform. It is not what Jewish religion learned from its encounter with secular modernity that energizes religious Zionism but premodern myth. Specifically, it is the biblical myth of the Children of Israel as a Chosen People entering the Promised Land. The one spatial fixation of biblical Judaism became the source for an impulse that in time came to be called redemptive or messianic. As long as the Jews lived without a territory of their own, this myth could sustain them; in modern times, when they have attained sovereignty over the ancestral land, its retention is an atavism, an ahistorical fundamentalism that, in the modern world, is an anachronism.

Now just as a central aspect of the reconstruction of Judaism is the rejection of supernaturalism and hence the renunciation of the idea of the Jews as the Chosen People, so, in a related way, does the reconstruction of Zionism enjoin the repudiation of its religious element and hence the renunciation of its messianic aspirations. It means finally admitting that the territorial dimension of biblical Judaism is untenable in a modern context, and that all that that dimension implies is expunged from the agenda of Israel and Zionism. It means that no messianic significance or expectations are accorded to the Israeli national enterprise. It means doing away with the statement, repeated vapidly by many Jews who really do not believe it, that Israel is "the beginning of the dawning of our deliverance." It means abrogating in time the Law of Return, an enactment that has proven more problematical than beneficial to the Israeli state. It means that the ideological furniture of the State of Israel is drawn not from premodern Jewish religious myth but from the values and the insights of the Enlightenment, as befits a state that calls itself

secular. Israel becomes for Jews, in effect, what East Africa might have
been.

This agenda implies the rehabilitation of secularism. Here there is
much work to be done, for secularism has fallen into disrepute. Amos Oz
writes of

> that fateful meeting between Ben Gurion and the Hazon Ish, that meeting
> during which destiny perhaps was met and secular, socialist Zionism
> accepted a unilateral ceasefire in the Hundred Years War against the
> fiefdoms of *Yiddishkeit*. "Two carts, one empty, the other full, meet on a
> narrow bridge," said the Hazon Ish to Ben Gurion. "Isn't it only fair that
> the empty cart bow to the full cart and allow it to pass?" And Ben Gurion,
> out of some strange emotional impulse that may have come from his very
> depths, took upon himself and upon us the verdict of the empty cart.[9]

The harm this verdict has caused over the years is incalculable. It has
led to the regrettable mentality that, as Uzi Ornan puts it,

> a secularist is the person who has no values; the religionist [*dati*] is the one
> with values. And so if I am [a] free[thinker], then that is a sign that I am
> bereft of values, that I am empty. This notion has been successfully
> inculcated in the educational system. . . . "Values" means religious values.
> There is nothing else—no humanism, no rationalism, no science,
> nothing.[10]

A major component of the reconstruction of Zionism, then, will have to
be overturning "the verdict of the empty cart." It is ultimately an offense
against the intellectual and, above all, the moral integrity and responsibility of a significant majority of people in Israel and elsewhere.

This is not to suggest that predicating Israeli nationhood on a secular
foundation would not be without its problems. It is indeed a "lowest
common denominator" on which the polity would rest,[11] and it certainly
does run the risk of being too low. The ills of a secular society—anomie,
rootlessness, loneliness, consumerism—these would all be potential
threats to the mental and spiritual health of the society. But they would
still be preferable, far more preferable, to what would result from the
formal enfranchisement of Orthodoxy. A rabbinic "ayatollism" would
call into question the very values of freedom and democracy, and the
number of casualties that would result would eventually, I fear, far
outnumber those that would arise from the inadequacies of secularism.[12] Israel as a secular democracy, imperfect as it would be, would
still be a happier, less dangerous place than Israel as a Jewish religious
totalitarianism.[13] Furthermore, it is not that religion, its positive salvific
role, and religious values are all to be banished from a secular Israel. On
the contrary, the ironic possibility is that Judaism would get a much
better hearing when removed from the political domain. Stripped of
political authority, the only authority it would command would be a

moral one. Jewish religion detached from the principles of territorial sovereignty and power politics would still have an enormous contribution to make to Jews. In addition to an Orthodoxy whose energies would be freed to pursue very different goals from those it is presently pursuing, the full force of the various non-Orthodox approaches to Jewish religion, which have attempted to honor the claims of modernity, would be felt, as they are not now.

III

Now come the obvious questions: If Israel as a state and as a polity is recast by whatever evolutionary process into secular terms, what is its meaning and destiny as a Jewish state? What happens to its *raison d'être* as a Jewish state? What happens to its role as a guarantor of Jewish survival? Without a "Jewish" Israel, will not Diaspora Jewry lose its main legitimator and yield to the inexorable forces of assimilation? And would a secular democratic Israel really precipitate an end to Arab hostility?

These questions are cogent only within the framework of unreconstructed Zionism. There it is still possible to harbor expectations of the State of Israel that, however secularized, are messianic. When Zionism is reconstructed, however, along the lines I have indicated, and it is understood that Israel can only remain a Jewish state by becoming a theocracy, then do these questions fall away. A strange and ironic truth about Israel suggests itself: in the long run it may not be as decisive for Jewish survival as is now commonly thought. Jewish existence did not depend upon a state in the past and there is no reason to think it is necessarily and irrevocably doomed without one now. That is to say, Israel is a sufficient ground for Jews and Jewish culture, but it is not a necessary ground. The necessary one is the existence and development of Jewish religious life—in all its manifestations and interpretations— wherever it may be, whether in a secular Israel or a secular Diaspora. As it has in the past, Jewish existence remains on a *religious* basis; Israeli life rests on a *secular* basis. Judaism has to do with time, Zionism with space, and never the twain shall meet, unless for some reason a Jewish theocracy is judged to be desirable. One could hope that the insights and values of Jewish religion would inform and have impact upon the Israeli body politic to the end of humanizing its society and policies. But the Israeli state would not be the instrument for realizing territorial dreams mandated by the Bible or by halakhic requirements defined by the rabbinate.

There is no question that such an Israel would force the reconstruction of Jewish life outside Israel. It would lead to some difficult but therapeutic changes there. World Jewry, unwilling and unable to project upon a secular Israel its own failings and illusions, would of necessity be thrown back upon its own resources. Israel could no longer function as the vicarious collective Jew, a role for which it was never really equipped. Those in the Diaspora who would wish to maintain and develop their lives as Jews, both individually and collectively, would have to look not to Jewish organizational activity and its endless round of meetings, dinners, honors, and awards, but to the religious tradition—its calendar, its *rites de passage,* and, above all, its texts. These have always been the substance of Jewish life and, without the distractions of an Israel bent on realizing some messianic or pseudomessianic dream, these things would again, quite literally, substantiate it.

By texts I mean the full spectrum of the inherited tradition as it has developed, been preserved, and been passed down through the generations textually, in writing. The primary energies of Jews would be directed once again to what Jews have always done and always will do in an unredeemed world: studying these writings, interpreting them, reinterpreting them, and seeking to apply their insights to their lives as individuals and as members of a community that interacts with the society in which they live. Such a reconstructed Jewish existence would assume—or, more accurately, reassume—a texture of textuality. I do not mean by this for every Jew to become a rabbi, although the relationship between the rabbinate and the laity might narrow to become merely a gap instead of the chasm that it currently is, and the level of Jewish literacy, and therefore self-understanding, would rise. Nor do I mean to suggest that such a text-centered Jewish life need be exclusively cerebral. The kind of study and interpretation I have in mind involves passion and human concern as much as it does rigor and intellection. It is important to remember that text study is pursued not in isolation but in connection with the other two elements of Jewish life I have mentioned: the calendar and the *rites de passage.* The interplay among the three would suffuse Jewish existence in the Diaspora with a new energy and creativity that is drained from it when it sees itself as a mere appendage to the Israeli state.[14]

It is true that the religious tradition is all that would stand between Jews and assimilation, and some will claim that this is not enough. Such a claim, I think, misreads Jewish history and underestimates the power of Judaism as the historical source of Jewish distinctiveness. The Jews have survived not because of political power but because of the religious tradition they created, transmitted, and developed,[15] and it is this alone that would again validate their existence, not a nation-state that confuses itself with this tradition and, what is more, confuses the world about the Jews and Judaism. A secular Israel that would have no relation to Jewish religion would make it clear once and for all that the national policies and interests of the Israeli state are not connected to and do not implicate or obligate world Jewry. There would be no arrogation of power and responsibility, no manipulative claims and unrealistic expectations in the relationship between Jews in the Diaspora and Jews in Israel.

As for Arab hostility, here I do not believe much will change. We could, as long as speculation holds sway, go all the way and conjecture that an Israel ideologically reconstructed along the lines described here would finally induce the Arabs to make peace with it. But, unlike the developments projected up to this point with respect to Israel, Judaism, and world Jewry, this one is not dictated by the logic of the matter. It is true that moderate Arabs do at times say that Zionism, not Israel, is the fly in the political ointment and when Israel takes leave of Zionism and becomes a secular-democratic state they will make peace with it. But as I have noted, I do not believe Israel will ever renounce its Zionist identity no matter what its content. The roots of the Arab inability to accept Israel, I am persuaded, have as much to do with ideas that are indigenous to Islam and Arab history and culture as they do with Judaism and Jewish exclusivism. Unless the former undergo the same kind of evolutionary metamorphosis that Zionism might, no change in what Israel does or signifies to Jews will remove the source of Arab rejection (although a repeal of the Law of Return would help). The case for a secular Israel needs to be argued from the logic intrinsic to the Zionist idea, not for the ulterior motive of inducing the Arabs to make peace.

IV

Obviously this sketch of what is projected is not commensurate with the profundity of what it implies. To deal with all the questions raised by an ideological evolution of the kind outlined here is beyond the scope of this excursus. My purpose has been more fundamental: to note the general principles for the reconstruction of Zionism as the official ideology of Israel that are implied by the "Canaanite" critique of it. Clearly the specifics of the reconstruction, however vaguely or imperfectly glimpsed, do transport us into the realm of the imagination. But the principles themselves are drawn from the history of the Zionist idea and are rooted in the dynamics of present realities. Consider, for example, the implications of Israel's annexing the West Bank *de jure* as it has *de facto*. The demographic basis of the state would be dramatically altered. Zionism would threaten to become impaled on its messianic sword and the pressure upon it to evolve from a "moral community" with a Jewish "civil religion" into a "consociational" secular "service state" would grow.[16]

To project forward from such a reality, therefore, may be bold but also logical and possible. That the notion of a secular Israel is grounded in the vision of a poet should not in itself disqualify it. By the same token, we ought to have dismissed what the imagination of Uri Tsvi Greenberg brought forth—and yet Revisionism emerged as a potent political force in the seventies. The ideas that both these poets espoused, however they were nourished by (and, in turn, nourished) the poetic muse, are ultimately indigenous to Zionism itself. Like a true organism, the Zionist idea contains many genes. Who can say whether religious messianism is dominant and secular "Canaanism" is recessive? The organism is still developing.

Here Amos Oz's destination, at the end of his ramblings in the spring of 1983, is interesting, although it is not surprising. After surveying the Israeli scene with a lucid candor and finding secular Zionism in decline—"the fiefdoms of *Yiddishkeit* will annex region after region"[17]—he winds up in, of all places, the port of Ashdod.

> A small Mediterranean city is Ashdod, a pleasant city, unpretentious. . . . Not pretending to be Paris or Zurich or aspiring to be Jerusalem. A city planned by social democrats: without imperial boulevards, without monuments, without grandiose merchants' homes. *A city living entirely in the present tense,* a clean city, almost serene.[18]

Here at last is the "normality" that secular Zionism sought. Oz invites us to celebrate it. Here we have an indication of what "Canaanism," when it is stripped of its ideological excesses and its roots in maximalist Revisionism, has in mind. Here we see the first signs of what a Zionism reconstructed in the light of the "Canaanite" critique would look like.

> Perhaps we must limit ourselves and forego the rainbow of messianic dreams, whether they be called "the resurrection of the kingdom of David and Solomon" or "the building of a model society, a Light unto the Nations," "fulfillment of the vision of the Prophets" or "to become the heart of the world." Perhaps we should take smaller bites. . . . Concede heavenly Jerusalem for the sake of the Jerusalem of the slums, waive messianic salvation for the sake of small, gradual reforms, forego messianic fervor for the sake of prosaic sobriety. . . . Not "the land of the hart" and not "the divine city reunited" as the clichés would have it, but simply the State of Israel.[19]

Perhaps, then, to project forward from such a reality, however bold, is logical and possible.

But it is not inevitable. Nothing in human history is inevitable, neither revolution nor evolution in a specific direction. Ratosh thought it was.

> Indeed, I am optimistic. Even a bumbling leadership like the one we have, regardless of its achievements and failures, regardless of the damage it will do, will not be able to hold back forever the natural development of the new secular Hebrew nation. What reason will not accomplish will be done by time. The vision will surely come about in its appointed time.[20]

Such determinism is unwarranted. The reconstruction of Zionism, like the notion of a Second Israeli Republic or its equivalent, is a possibility, not an inevitability. Consider the reconstruction of Judaism: the steps that Mordecai Kaplan laid out a half century ago have not led masses of religious Jews to abandon supernaturalism and to reinterpret their tradition systematically and holistically in the light of modern thought. Similarly, there is no guarantee that Israel and Zionism will undergo the changes that "Canaanism" as I have interpreted it implies. Ashdod, after all, does not exist in a vacuum. Rather, it lies within the orbits of both Jerusalem and Tel Aviv and what each of these places signifies; it is qualified by both. We do not yet know which place holds the ideological balance of power.

NOTES

Works by Ratosh frequently referred to in the notes and Bibliography have been abbreviated as follows:

RH—*R'eshit hayamim: petihot 'ivriyot* (The first days: Hebrew overtures) (Tel Aviv: Hadar Publishing Co., 1982, Hebrew). This book is an anthology of some of Ratosh's key essays, most of which first appeared in *Alef*. The introduction (pp. 7–31) is the important but fragmentary autobiographical memoir Ratosh composed in 1980.

MP—"Mas'a hapetihah" (The opening discourse). This piece was written in 1944 and is reprinted in RH, pp. 149–203. All citations are from RH.

E—"'Ever hahadashah o bayit shelishi?" (A new 'Ever or the third commonwealth?). This piece was originally published in *Alef* in October 1949 and is reprinted in RH, pp. 204–19. All citations are from RH.

N—*Minitashon lemapolet: me'asef Alef* (From victory to collapse: An *Alef* anthology), ed. Y. Ratosh (Tel Aviv: Hadar Publishing Co., 1976).

The original titles of all material in Hebrew noted below are transliterated in the bibliography.

Preface

1. Eliezer Livneh, Yosef Nedavah, and Yoram Efrati, *Nili: The History of a Political Audacity,* 2d rev. ed. (Jerusalem & Tel Aviv: Schocken Publishing Co., 1980, Hebrew), p. 13.

2. James S. Diamond, *Barukh Kurzweil and Modern Hebrew Literature,* Brown Judaic Studies Series (Chico, California: Scholars Press, 1983).

3. See below, chapter 1, section III and note 19.

4. See below, chapter 6, end of section IV and note 32.

5. "There is a line among the fragments of the Greek poet Archilochus which says: 'The fox knows many things, but the hedgehog knows one big thing'" (Isaiah Berlin, *The Hedgehog and the Fox: An Essay on Tolstoy's View of History* [London: Weidenfeld & Nicolson, 1967], p. 1).

6. Ibid.

I: The Importance of "Canaanism"

1. The eminent historian of Zionism, David Vital, considers this the crucial question. See below, chapter 2, end of section II.

2. Arthur Hertzberg, *The Zionist Idea: A Historical Analysis and Reader* (New York & Philadelphia: Meridian Books & Jewish Publication Society, 1960), p. 18.

3. In his introduction to *Between Faith and Heresy* (Tel Aviv: Massadah Publishing Co., 1962, Hebrew), Ephraim Shemu'eli writes: "The history of heresy accompanies the history of belief. The charge of heresy was raised in every major theological debate. Yet the heroic-tragic history of heresy and heretics in Israel has not yet been analyzed."

4. Two representative examples of excoriation are: Shlomo Grodzensky's essay "The Great and the Small Canaan" written in 1951, reprinted in *Considerations: Political and Social Essays* (Tel Aviv: Hakibbutz Hame'uhad, 1975, Hebrew), pp. 34–37, and Maurice Samuel, *Level Sunlight* (New York: Alfred A. Knopf, 1953), pp. 205–208. The "Canaanite" periodical *Alef* frequently reprinted some

of the hostile attacks on it; see issues number 3 (June–July 1950), 6 (Nov.–Dec. 1950), 16 (Nov.–Dec. 1952), and 17 (Dec. 1952).

5. The implication is that Zionism is functionally a religion. The confusions resulting from this intermingling of secular nationalism and Jewish religion are explored in the next chapter. The postulates of Zionism have been shown to form an integral part of the civil religion of the North American Jewish community.

6. There is no one source for all the ideas mentioned in this brief summary of the "Canaanite" thesis. The essentials can be seen in MP, especially pp. 181ff., and E, especially pp. 213f. The dissimilarities between the entities mentioned here are obvious. But "Canaanite" ideology lumps them together, probably because it perceives all elements that are not Sunni Moslem as one potential grouping. See, for example, the essay "At The Gates of the Land of the Euphrates," originally published in *Alef,* November 1948, and reprinted in RH, pp. 63–76.

7. Yonatan Ratosh, MP in RH, pp. 149f.

8. The nickname was bestowed pejoratively by the poet Avraham Shlonsky. Uri Avneri notes that in the late forties, when "Canaanism" was fairly widespread among Israeli youth, a rumor circulated through the country about the reenactment by some Palmah members of ancient fertility rites. Avneri names the writer Matti Megged as the originator of the rumor. (*The War of the Seventh Day* [Jerusalem: Daf Hadash Publication Co., 1969, Hebrew], p. 150. This is a Hebrew version of Avneri's *Israel Without Zionists: A Plea for Peace in the Middle East* [New York & London: Macmillan, 1968], but the chapter on the "Canaanite" movement does not appear in the English original.)

I place "Canaanism" in quotation marks not to be pejorative but to differentiate this modern ideology from the Canaanites of the biblical period. Moreover, since the term is most inadequate to convey the true content of the ideology, the quotation marks can serve to remind the reader that "Canaanism" is really a signifier like a number or an equation. It expresses the whole complex of assumptions and values of the secular nativism I shall present and discuss.

9. Of "The Opening Discourse," Avneri writes: "certain passages could have been copied verbatim from the pages of *Der Sturmer*" (*The War of the Seventh Day,* p. 157). For further discussion of this "self-hating" aspect of Ratosh, see below, chapter 4, section I.

10. David J. Schnall notes that "almost by their nature, dissenters tend to band together in smaller groups, demand ideological purity and decry compromise in the name of political gain" (*Radical Dissent in Contemporary Israel: Cracks in the Wall,* Praeger Special Studies, [New York: Praeger, 1979], p. 5).

11. Two good discussions of this issue, both from the standpoint of normative Zionism, are the following reviews of N: Moshe Atar, "The Sweet Dream of the Canaanites," *Ha'arets,* Nov. 12, 1976, in Hebrew, and Eliezer Schweid, "A Question of Identity," *Yedi'ot Aharonot,* Oct. 22, 1976, in Hebrew.

12. "First Person Plural—Literature of the 1948 Generation," *The Jerusalem Quarterly* 22 (Winter 1982): 106.

13. Atar, *Ha'arets.*

14. Rael Jean Isaac, *Party and Politics in Israel: Three Visions of a Jewish State* (New York & London: Longmans, 1981), pp. 167–87.

15. Ibid., p. 201. This statement is not quite accurate. There have been several anti-Zionist expressions within the Israeli political arena. For a survey of some of these, see Schnall, *Radical Dissent.* He looks only at those groups visible to him as a political scientist examining the Israeli political spectrum of the seventies, and he does not discuss the "Canaanites," although he does deal with Uri Avneri (pp. 55–71). My concern in this book is with a critique of Zionism's first

principles and a priori assumptions rooted in a secular nativist perspective.

Isaac's scheme of conceptualization is different from Schnall's. In it all the anti-Zionist leftist groups that Schnall discusses (e.g., Rakah, Matzpen, Moked) are seen as responses to the challenge of Arab nationalism and are subsumed within it (see Isaac, *Party and Politics*, p. 173). Thus within her scheme there are only three major critiques of Zionism: those derived from Jewish religion (Neturei Karta), those related to Arab nationalism (the leftist parties), and the "Canaanites." This is why she can say that "the Canaanites . . . provided the only ideological alternative to the . . . established conceptions of the Jewish state. . . ." I accept this conceptual framework and contend that "Canaanism" is worth studying precisely because the nativist critique it offers is as challenging and as profound as the other two, as its staying power, discussed below, indicates.

16. Emile Marmorstein writes: "The frequency with which their names are hurled as abusive epithets during heated exchanges between religious and secular representatives of the legislature would suggest that the Guardians of the City (Neturei Karta) and the Canaanites are the shock-troops of religious and secular opinion respectively, the opposite poles that attract the particles floating between them" (*Heaven at Bay: The Jewish Kulturkampf in the Holy Land* [London: Oxford University Press, 1969], p. 125).

17. Ibid., p. 104. Marmorstein understands the wound to be the revulsion secular Israelis of the older generation felt at seeing their offspring complete the process of secularization by "displaying a readiness to sacrifice their secular heritage for the favor of acceptance in the Middle East. [This] was too reminiscent for comfort of the speed with which the traditional heritage had been jettisoned in the dawn of emancipation in the equally passionate hope of 'belonging.'" But I think "the wound" is even deeper than this, as I hope shall become clear from the following chapters.

18. I heard this metaphor from the poet Hayim Guri (personal interview, Jan. 6, 1984). Guri speaks of a "manifest Canaanism," which he says has passed from the scene, and a "latent Canaanism," which he feels is very much present. I maintain this distinction throughout this book.

19. "The Nature and Origins of the Young Hebrews (Canaanite) Movement," *Lu'ah Ha'arets* 5713 (1952–53, Hebrew): 107–29. This is reprinted in Kurzweil's *Our New Literature: Continuity or Revolt?*, 3d enlarged ed. (Tel Aviv & Jerusalem: Schocken Publishing Co., 1971, Hebrew), pp. 270–300. A condensed English translation is in *Judaism* 2:1 (Jan. 1953): 2–15.

20. This point is made by Hayim Guri in "The Canaanite Hour," *Ma'ariv*, Sept. 24, 1980, Hebrew.

21. Ya'akov Shavit, *From Hebrew to Canaanite* (Jerusalem: Domino Press, in cooperation with the Rosenberg School of Jewish Studies at Tel Aviv University, 1984, Hebrew). Henceforth this work will be abbreviated as "Shavit."

22. "The Event—and its Academic Reflection," *Yedi'ot Aharonot*, March 2, 1984, Hebrew. This is a review of Shavit's book.

23. The term "Hebrew" (*'ivri*) was widely used in contradistinction to "Jew" (*yehudi*) both before Ratosh adapted it to his own ideological needs and afterwards. See Shavit's full discussion of this point (pp. 30–42) as well as Stanley Nash, *In Search of Hebraism: Shai Hurwitz and His Polemics in the Hebrew Press*, Studies in Judaism in Modern Times, ed. Jacob Neusner, vol. 3 (Leiden: E. J. Brill, 1980).

II: The Contradictions of Zionism: Paradox, Dialectic, or Syncretism?

1. David Vital, "The History of Zionism and the History of Judaism," *Hatsiyonut* 7 (1981, Hebrew): 7f. Vital notes that the Zionist archives contain

112 meters of shelves of documents of the World Zionist Congress and the political section of the Jewish Agency (1948–1981) alone, 27 meters [of shelves] of Sokolov's private documents, 10 [meters of shelves] for Herzl's documents, 7 of Zangwill's, 11 of Yitshak Greenbaum's, 640 of documents of the Mapai party, and so on. . . . Only 2 volumes of Herzl's letters have come out (for the years 1895–1899), although additional volumes are in the stages of active preparation. No similar project is planned—much less begun—with respect to Nordau, Ussishkin, Motzkin, Sokolov, Jabotinsky, Greenbaum, or even for Lilienblum or Pinsker, most of whose documents do not exist. Actually, of the major figures of Zionism's formative years [the only good source material] available . . . is for Weizmann . . . and Ahad Ha'am.

2. Rael Jean Isaac, *Party and Politics in Israel: Three Visions of a Jewish State* (New York & London: Longmans, 1981), p. 46.

3. Vital, "The History of Zionism and the History of Judaism," p. 9. Another example, noted by Isaac, is the way the Revisionists and the underground are handled in accounts written from a Labor perspective (*Party and Politics*, p. 46). Shlomo Avineri's treatment of Jabotinsky in his *The Making of Modern Zionism: The Intellectual Origins of the Jewish State* (New York: Basic Books, 1981), pp. 159–86, comes to mind.

4. Vital, "The History of Zionism and the History of Judaism," p. 10.

5. Ibid.

6. Yosef Oren, "And to Its Source Shall It Return," *M'oznayim* 42:3 (Feb. 1976, Hebrew): 201.

7. Arthur Hertzberg, introduction to *The Zionist Idea: A Historical Analysis and Reader* (New York & Philadelphia: Meridian Books and Jewish Publication Society, 1960), p. 15.

8. Thus David Vital in his introduction to *The Origins of Zionism* (Oxford: Clarendon Press, 1975), p. viii, writes: "Of course, the whole vast scene of Jewish life at the end of the nineteenth century was one of tumult and change and the rise of Zionism was only a particular aspect of it. Accordingly, without some regard for the total scene's complexity, variety, and many paradoxes the roots of Zionism are difficult to lay bare and the inner significance of the movement in the recent history of the Jews remains obscure." Walter Laqueur, when he attempts to sum up the movement whose history he has detailed over several hundred pages, writes: "The origins of Zionism and its subsequent fortunes are full of paradoxes; some of them appear a little less inexplicable in the light of the unique character of Jewish history and the position of the Jews in 19th century European society" (*A History of Zionism* [New York, Chicago & San Francisco: Holt, Rinehart & Winston, 1972], p. 590).

9. Harold Fisch, *The Zionist Revolution: A New Perspective* (New York: St. Martin's Press, 1978), p. 1.

10. Ibid., p. 7.

11. Avineri, *The Making of Modern Zionism*, p. 3.

12. Ibid., p. 10.

13. Vital, "The History of Zionism and the History of Judaism," p. 12.

14. Ibid.

15. Gershom Scholem, interview with Ehud Ben Ezer in *Unease in Zion* (New York: Quadrangle Books, 1974), pp. 273, 275.

16. Note, for example, that Barukh Kurzweil formulates his entire treatment of modern Hebrew literature in terms of this question, as the title of his first collection of essays on the subject makes clear: *Our New Literature: Continuity or Revolt?* (in Hebrew, see below, n. 66). Similarly, Shemu'el Almog bases his presentation of the first decade of the Zionist movement on just this question. He begins his study thus: "This book grew out of the desire to answer the question:

is Zionism a continuity or a rebellion in Jewish history? Zionist thought has been bothered by this question since its beginning and no agreed upon answer has yet been found. The question, which comes up anew from time to time, assuming varying forms, still awaits an answer. . . . We might even go so far as to say that the answer we give in effect shapes our identity" (*Zionism and History* [Jerusalem: Magnes Press of the Hebrew University, 1982, Hebrew], p. 7).

17. English version printed in *Modern Hebrew Literature*, ed. Robert Alter (New York: Behrman House, Inc., 1975), pp. 271–87.

18. There is a certain congruence between the views Yudka (Hazaz) expresses here and those of Ratosh. See below, chapter 4, n. 74.

19. Vital, "The History of Zionism and the History of Judaism," p. 14.

20. Hertzberg, *The Zionist Idea*, p. 18. See also Jacob Neusner, "Zionism and the Jewish Problem," in *Stranger At Home: "The Holocaust," Zionism and American Judaism* (Chicago & London: The University of Chicago Press), pp. 186ff.

21. See Yehiel Halpern, *The Jewish Revolution: Spiritual Struggles in Modern Times* (Tel Aviv: Am Oved Ltd., 1961, Hebrew), 2:617.

22. See David Hartman, "Zion and the Continuity of Judaism," in *Joy and Responsibility: Israel, Modernity and the Renewal of Judaism* (Jerusalem: Ben Zvi-Posner Publishers, 1978), pp. 259–75.

23. Almog, *Zionism and History*, p. 224.

24. Eliezer Schweid, *Israel at the Crossroads*, trans. from the Hebrew by A. Winters (Philadelphia: Jewish Publication Society, 1973), p. 111.

25. In the same way "radicalism" signifies not just a revolutionary tendency but a return to the roots.

26. Almog, *Zionism and History*, p. 15.

27. Ibid., p. 11.

28. Ibid., p. 60.

29. Ibid., pp. 61–129. Almog notes that Ahad Ha'am was not opposed to religion as such, only to Orthodoxy. But it is clear that he handled the tradition in a new and different way.

30. Ibid., pp. 68ff.

31. Ehud Luz, "Zion and Judenstaat: The Significance of the 'Uganda' Controversy," in *Essays in Modern Jewish History: A Tribute to Ben Halpern*, ed. Frances Malino and Phyllis C. Albert (Rutherford: Fairleigh Dickinson University Press, 1982), p. 237.

32. Almog, *Zionism and History*, pp. 174–221. See also Vital's discussion in *Zionism: The Formative Years* (Oxford: The Clarendon Press, 1982), especially pp. 348–64.

33. *Zionism: The Formative Years*, p. 349.

34. Almog, *Zionism and History*, p. 222.

35. David Kena'ani, *The Second Aliyah of Labor and Its Relationship to Religion and Tradition* (Tel Aviv: Sifriyat Po'alim, 1976, Hebrew), p. 15.

36. Kena'ani writes: ". . . what place did religion and tradition hold in the framework of the world [of the Second *Aliyah*]? The question is important in and of itself, and becomes even more so when we take note of the fact that a number of outstanding figures of the Second *Aliyah* were the builders of the State of Israel and their influence is discernible in all aspects of Israel's life: They built the educational system . . . and had a hand in determining the status of religion in the state" (p. 17).

37. Of the young workers who immigrated during the Second *Aliyah*, Ehud Luz writes: "For them the decision in favor of Eretz-Israel was simply an existential-moral act and no more. Rather than being ideological, [it] was an escape from the degenerating . . . reality of the *Golah*. . . . The question of why this

could only take place in Eretz-Israel did not concern them at all, a fact which indicates that their living experience very much outweighed their ideology" ("Zion and Judenstaat," p. 234).

38. Kena'ani, *The Second Aliyah,* pp. 21ff.

39. Ibid., p. 34.

40. Ibid., pp. 32, 42, and 82.

41. Ibid., p. 49.

42. Ibid., p. 68.

43. Ibid., pp. 101ff. The exception to all this was, of course, A. D. Gordon. His attitude toward and practice of the tradition were in relation to the norm of the Second *Aliyah,* more fideistic, idiosyncratic, and without influence upon his contemporaries. See Kena'ani, pp. 56, 64 and 103.

44. Almog, *Zionism and History,* p. 11. Emphasis is mine.

45. This process of the transvaluation of the symbols and myths of the religious tradition led to the development of a Zionist civil religion. For a full treatment of this and the different stages through which it has passed, see Charles S. Liebman and Eliezer Don-Yehiya, *Civil Religion in Israel: Traditional Judaism and Political Culture in the Jewish State* (Berkeley, Los Angeles & London: University of California Press, 1983). For discussion of the Israeli flag, see p. 107 and notes.

46. "In the Press and in Literature (Remarks and Notes)," *Hapo'el hatsa'ir* 4:30 (Nov. 24, 1910, Hebrew). See full discussion in Kena'ani, *The Second Aliyah,* pp. 71–81.

47. *Hapo'el hatsa'ir.*

48. Ibid. See above, chapter 1, n. 23. Eliezer Schweid tries to qualify the extremism of Brenner's vituperativeness by putting it into a specific emotional context. Schweid writes:

> Even those of his contemporaries who debated with him recognized that his words were not to be taken literally. His exaggerated criticism was merely the fruit of an injured love. [In Brenner's] sensation of revolt . . . reverberated an incomparable proclamation of faith. . . . In his hatred of Judaism, Brenner hated himself. This is his justification, but it is also his tragedy. He was unable to affirm his existence consciously. (*Israel at the Crossroads,* p. 114.)

49. Quoted from the periodical *Ha'ahdut,* no. 27 (Iyar 1914) in Kena'ani, *The Second Aliyah,* p. 70. Kena'ani also cites this from Cheshin: "We absolutely must not cease from secularization, the process of [making] a total separation between religion and the culture we initiated at the beginning of the Zionist movement. This is even more necessary here in Palestine, a necessary condition for our entire efforts to build a settlement and a culture."

50. A similar outlook seems to have been held by Avshalom Feinberg, a central figure in the Nili espionage group. Feinberg was not of the Second *Aliyah* but from a farming family of the First *Aliyah.* In his detailed discussion of Feinberg, Aharon Amir notes that at the time of his [Feinberg's] Bar Mitzvah, "the family especially remembered his absolute refusal to put on tefillin. In an argument with his father he held past to this position" ("A Monographic Profile," introduction to *Avshalom Feinberg: Papers and Letters,* ed. Aharon Amir [Haifa: Shikmona Publishing Co., 1971, Hebrew], p. 17). In general the farmers descended from the First *Aliyah* were more traditional than the workers of the Second *Aliyah,* and the two elements looked askance at each other in economic as well as religious matters. See Livneh, Nedavah, and Efrati, *Nili: The History of a Political Audacity,* 2d rev. ed. (Jerusalem & Tel Aviv: Schocken Publishing Co., 1980, Hebrew), p. 46. These two elements of the populace of the *Yishuv* at the

turn of the century can be seen as archetypes of the right and left of the political spectrum that would later develop in Palestine. On Feinberg as a paradigm of secular nativism for Ratosh, see below, chapter 4, section IV.

51. See his essay "Revolution and Tradition," in Hertzberg, *The Zionist Idea,* p. 390.

52. Almog, *Zionism and History,* pp. 224f.

53. Jacob Neusner writes: "For the costs of Zionism . . . are to be balanced against the gains. . . . Against such gains, it is hard to find weighty the costs of paradox, contradiction, and alas, recognition of one's self-deception and inner contradiction nearing hypocrisy" (*Strangers at Home,* p. 170).

54. Interview with Ehud Ben Ezer, *Unease in Zion,* pp. 273–75 passim. For an articulate development of this argument, see Hillel Halkin, *Letters to an American Jewish Friend: A Zionist's Polemic* (Philadelphia: The Jewish Publication Society, 1977), pp. 153–200.

55. Fisch, *The Zionist Revolution,* p. 80. In the Hebrew version: *The Zionism of Zion* (Tel Aviv: Zemorah Biton, 1982), p. 12.

56. Ibid.

57. Ibid., pp. 81f. Shavit utilizes the same explicative method near the end of his book when he notes how the term "Hebrew settlement" *(hayishuv ha'ivri)* is used but is subsumed within the term "Jewish people" *(ha'am hayehudi).* Shavit, like Fisch, also sees this as an "intentional synthesis of opposing concepts" (p. 163).

58. Later on Zev Jabotinsky did the same thing. Eri Jabotinsky emphasizes that, in his opinion, his father was thoroughly secular and the alliance he made with the Orthodox, like the one he made with Ben Gurion, was strictly for pragmatic political reasons. See *My Father, Zev Jabotinsky,* ed. Y. Shavit and A. Amir (Jerusalem: Steimatzky Publishing Co., 1980, Hebrew), p. 101.

59. Laqueur, *A History of Zionism,* p. 380.

60. See Fisch, *The Zionist Revolution,* pp. 17–23. Neusner writes in similar terms when he concludes his essay "Zionism and the Jewish Problem" thus: "The astonishing achievements of Zionism are the result of the capacity of Zionism to reintegrate the tradition with contemporary reality. . . . Zionism speaks in terms of Judaic myth, indeed so profoundly that myth and reality coincide" (*Stranger at Home,* pp. 202f). Of course, everything depends on how one interprets what the myth and the Covenant imply; non-Zionists and anti-Zionists can both base their analyses on their understanding of these concepts.

61. See Fisch's discussion of Rav Kook, *The Zionist Revolution,* pp. 59–66. Fisch sees the limitations of Kook's thought, but I think his own position reduces itself to something quite similar, without the Kabbalistic accouterments.

62. Schweid, *Israel at the Crossroads,* p. 113.

63. Ibid., p. 111.

64. Two other senses are also given: "the fusion of inflectional forms" and "the developmental process of historical growth within a religion." These are more specialized meanings, although the latter would be pointed to by normative Zionists as the one that accurately and nonpejoratively describes the Zionist synthesis of past and present as a syncretism.

65. See my study *Barukh Kurzweil and Modern Hebrew Literature,* Brown Judaic Studies Series (Chico, California: Scholars Press, 1983), pp. 27–41. A key influence in shaping Kurzweil's approach to Zionism was Yitshak Breuer, the founder of Agudat Yisra'el.

66. B. Kurzweil, *Our New Literature: Continuity or Revolt?* 3d enlarged ed. (Jerusalem & Tel Aviv: Schocken Publishing Co., 1971, Hebrew) pp. 294f.

67. A similar, but not identical, critique animates the views of Isaiah Leibowitz, who, though he is an Orthodox Jew, denies any religious meaning to

the State of Israel. See his *Judaism, the Jewish People and the State of Israel* (Jerusalem & Tel Aviv: Schocken Publishing Co., 1976, Hebrew), especially pp. 235–42. This essay has been translated into English in *Diaspora: Exile and the Jewish Condition,* ed. Etan Levine (New York & London: Jason Aronson, 1983), pp. 93–100. Leibowitz holds that:

> You cannot put a halo of holiness around such a political-historical event as that of the establishment of the State of Israel. . . . Religious institutions established by the secular state; the religious seal affixed to secular functions; . . . and a religion which enjoys the help granted by secular power—all these things are travesties of reality, perversions of social and religious truth, and the sources of intellectual and spiritual corruption. The state and secular society must speak their piece without hiding behind the skirt of religion. . . . And religion must say its piece without hiding behind administrative skirts. . . . (Pp. 98 ff.)

For a discussion of more normative Orthodox approaches to Zionism, see Liebman and Don-Yehiya, *Civil Religion in Israel,* pp. 185–213.

68. Isaac, *Party and Politics,* p. 62.

69. This is precisely the adjective Shavit uses in describing how the "Canaanites" view Israeli society (p. 170).

70. In an interview with Hillel Barzel, Ratosh reports that "Kurzweil tried to come to an agreement with him [Ratosh]." See Barzel, *Essays on Modern Hebrew Poets* (Tel Aviv: Yahdav Publication Co., 1983, Hebrew), p. 239, n. 14.

71. Interview with Ehud Ben Ezer in *Unease in Zion,* p. 230.

III: Yonatan Ratosh: The Transformation of Uriel Halpern

1. Aharon Amir holds this view in "Yonatan Ratosh: The Poetic and the Political," *Davar,* Jan. 9, 1981, Hebrew.

2. See, for example, Dan Miron, *Four Faces of Hebrew Literature,* 2d ed. (Jerusalem & Tel Aviv: Schocken Publishing Co., 1975, Hebrew), pp. 195ff., and Hillel Barzel, *Essays on Modern Hebrew Poets* (Tel Aviv: Yahdav Publication Co., 1983, Hebrew), pp. 216f. Barzel writes: "Ideology and poetry are intrinsically different and, at most, one can find a link of common creative aspects between them" (p. 217). See also: Barzel's discussion of Ratosh in *Poets in their Greatness,* Hebrew, pp. 262–96, especially pp. 288ff.; Ya'akov Shavit, "The Relationships Between Idea and Poetics in the Poetry of Yonatan Ratosh," *Hasifrut* 17 (Sept. 1974, Hebrew): 66–91; Dan La'or, "On the Question of the Reception of Ratosh's Poetry," *Yedi'ot Aharonot,* Jan. 30, 1981, Hebrew; and Hayim Pesah, "Ideology and Poetry: Between Ratosh and Pound," *M'oznayim* 54:3–4 (Feb.–Mar. 1982, Hebrew): 9–14.

3. Another reason it would make no sense to include a consideration of Ratosh's poetry even in this context in English is the nature of his poetic language. The important early poems are so highly stylized and replete with archaisms, that they cannot, in my opinion, be meaningfully discussed in translation.

4. Interview with Shin Shifra, *Davar,* Aug. 27, 1971, Hebrew.

5. See the interview with Z. Stavi, *Yedi'ot Aharonot,* Feb. 27, 1981, Hebrew. Ratosh observes: "From an early age I have had inclinations toward scholarly research. Research is a very complex . . . matter. To the extent that it yields insights, the insight is a matter of moments. But the work takes months, even years."

6. So Hillel Barzel in a private communication with me. Hayim Guri, Boaz Evron, Amos Kenan, and many others all testify to Ratosh's indefatigable willingness to sit for hours in intense discussion of the big questions about Israel and Zionism.

7. This is what Miron means when he calls Ratosh's poetry "manneristic." See *Four Faces*, pp. 196ff. and 246f.

8. Boaz Evron, "A Paean to Yonatan," *Yedi'ot Aharonot*, Jan. 30, 1981, Hebrew.

9. Many of the sources of Ratosh's ideas and some aspects of their development have been identified and analyzed by Shavit. One of the problems with his discussion, however, is that it does not present Ratosh's life coherently; the details are sliced up and scattered throughout chapters 3, 5, and 8. The two major autobiographical sources from which the following is drawn are the uncompleted memoir Ratosh wrote a year before his death, published as the introduction to RH, pp. 7–31, and the second of the three interviews with Z. Stavi in *Yedi'ot Aharonot*, Feb. 20, 1981, Hebrew. These two sources are very similar in places and lead me to wonder whether Ratosh repeated parts of his written memoir in the interview.

What I have not been able to utilize is the collection of Ratosh's letters that appeared just as this volume was going to press (Yonatan Ratosh, *Letters: 1937–1980*, ed. Y. Amrami [Tel Aviv: Hadar Publishing Co., 1986, Hebrew]). Included here, among many others, are letters Ratosh wrote to his parents, to Stern, to fellow "Canaanites," and to Gila Dotan, his mistress for several years. In fact, the letters to Dotan take up half the book. There is no question that the Ratosh who emerges from this correspondence is a much tenderer, more romantic, humorous, and multidimensional person than the one I depict. Further, many letters would shed fuller light on some of the issues and relationships I will discuss.

10. So Getsel Kressel, *Lexicon of Hebrew Literature* 2, p. 854. The Hebrew year was 5669 and several other sources give the year of birth as 1908.

The change of name to Ratosh did not take place until 1937 (see below, n. 62). I write about "Ratosh" and not "Halpern" because that is the name under which he chose to exist. Ratosh had other pseudonyms, such as Uriel Shelah and A. L. Haran, all of which testify to an ongoing struggle for identity that I shall presently note. Ratosh never explained the sources for his pseudonyms. Shavit sees the etymology of "Ratosh" in either the verb *ltsh* "to transform" or *ntsh* "to abandon" (p. 215), although I do not see why it cannot be related to the obvious verb *rtsh* "to split open." "Shelah" carries several meanings. It denotes a sword-like weapon (as in Nehemiah 4:11); the sword is one of Ratosh's favorite symbols and metaphors. Perhaps more significantly, Shelah was the father of 'Ever, whom the Anchor Bible describes as "the eponymous ancestor of the Hebrews" (see Genesis 10:24 and 11:14, and also Aharon Amir, "The Poetic and the Political").

11. A. B. Yaffe, "Between Natan Altermann and Yonatan Ratosh," *'Al hamishmar*, April 3, 1981, Hebrew.

12. Ratosh's two brothers became no less deeply involved with the Hebrew language. Uzi Ornan is Professor of Hebrew Language at the Hebrew University and has written extensively on Hebrew grammar. Tsvi Rin is Professor Emeritus of Semitics at the University of Pennsylvania.

13. In the interview with Stavi, Ratosh says, "On Yom Kippur the table would not be set but each one would eat alone according to how hungry he was. That was about the extent of tradition [in the home]" (*Yedi'ot Aharonot*, Feb. 6, 1981).

14. Ibid.

15. Ibid. In another place Ratosh notes that Hebrew was the only language he used until high school. In the polyglot culture of the *Yishuv* this was unusual. His only sources of linguistic inspiration were classical (i.e., biblical and pre-biblical) Hebrew and the developing secular Hebrew. See "My First Book," in *Jewish Literature in the Hebrew Language*, ed. Shin Shifra (Tel Aviv: Hadar Publishing Co., 1982, Hebrew), p. 207.

16. RH, p. 9. On "negative identity," see below, chapter 4, section VI.

17. RH, p. 7.

18. Interview with Stavi, *Yedi'ot Aharonot*, Feb. 20, 1981. See also RH, p. 8.

19. RH, p. 20; interview with Stavi, Feb. 20, 1981.

20. On Ahime'ir, see Walter Laqueur, *A History of Zionism* (New York: Holt, Rinehart & Winston, 1972), pp. 361–65; Ya'akov Shavit, "I Am in the East and My Heart is in the West: On the Zionist 'Monism' of Abba Ahime'ir," *Keshet* 57 (Fall 5732 [1971], Hebrew): 149–59; and Shavit, *From Hebrew to Canaanite*, pp. 43f. Two portrayals of Ahime'ir, the first positive, the second negative, are: Eri Jabotinsky, *My Father, Zev Jabotinsky* (Jerusalem: Steimatzky Publishing Co., 1980, Hebrew), pp. 117–21; and Shabtai Tevet, *The Murder of Arlosoroff* (Jerusalem & Tel Aviv: Schocken Publishing Co., 1982, Hebrew), pp. 17–22.

21. Abba Ahime'ir in a lecture given in April 1962, just before his death. Cited in *We Are Sicarii: Testimonies and Documents on the Berit Habiryonim*, ed. Y. Ahime'ir and S. Shatsky (n.p.: Nitsanim Publishing Co., 1978, Hebrew), p. 28. The late date of this source does not invalidate it as a reflection of Ahime'ir's earlier thought.

22. Interview with Stavi, Feb. 20, 1981. See also RH, p. 20.

23. See Ahime'ir and Shatsky, *We Are Sicarii*, p. 24. The term *Judenrat* occurs only in the 1962 lecture; it could not have been used in the early thirties. See also Tevet, *Murder of Arlosoroff*, pp. 41ff. Tevet believes that Ahime'ir is complicitous in the murder of Arlosoroff if only because of the rhetorical violence and the hate campaign he waged against Mapai.

24. Tevet, *Murder of Arlosoroff*, p. 49. Shavit holds that Greenberg is as crucial an influence on Ratosh's political thought as Ahime'ir (pp. 42–44).

25. Quoted in Ahime'ir and Shatsky, *We Are Sicarii*, p. 19.

26. Rael Jean Isaac, *Party and Politics in Israel: Three Visions of a Jewish State* (New York & London: Longmans, 1981), pp. 135ff.

27. Shavit describes this influence as not only political but "historiosophic." The notion that "the return to *erets yisra'el* is . . . a return to the source of vitality, [is] a necessary condition for turning Judaism . . . into a secular-territorial, politically sovereign nation" (p. 44). But Shavit makes no reference to the key term *malkhut yisra'el* and its leitmotif-like development, which I shall examine.

28. RH, p. 20.

29. Shavit notes that while Jabotinsky personally admired Ahime'ir, he saw no future within his party for the revolutionary activity that maximalism entailed. "The tension between Jabotinsky and Ahime'ir anticipated the split within the ranks of the Irgun in 1940 and no less the withdrawal of the Irgun after 1937 from the . . . New Zionist Party" ("On the Zionist 'Monism' of Abba Ahime'ir," pp. 156f). Eri Jabotinsky is laconic and evasive in his brief account of his father's relationship with Ahime'ir (see *My Father, Zev Jabotinsky*, p. 118).

30. For a short account of this program, see Laqueur, *A History of Zionism*, pp. 369–74. For a full account of its background, see Ya'akov Shavit, *From Majority to State: The Revisionist Movement—The Plan for a Colonizatory Regime and Social Ideas 1925–1935* (Tel Aviv: Hadar Publishing Co., 1978, Hebrew).

31. RH, pp. 21–25. In 1937 Stern, in opposition to Jabotinsky, advocated approaching Italy (which had designs on the Mediterranean basin) as an ally in the struggle against the British. Ratosh drafted the document. (Related by Aharon Amir, personal interview, December 12, 1983). Of Stern's poetry, Aryeh Kotser writes: "He knew many languages. In Hebrew he sought out the archaic, . . . anything that sounded more ancient . . . attracted him. I assume that in this matter the acquaintance and influence of Ratosh had an effect" (*Red Carpet: My Path With Ya'ir* [Tel Aviv: Makada Publishing Co., n.d., Hebrew], p. 181).

32. Interview with Stavi, Feb. 20, 1981.

33. The speech to the council, the five articles, and an undated "Speech to the Coterie" were published together early in 1938 with an enthusiastic note of endorsement by Prof. Joseph Klausner in a pamphlet entitled *Looking Towards Sovereignty: The Front for Tomorrow of the Liberation Movement* (Tel Aviv: Z. Schiff Publishing Co., [1938], Hebrew). Three of the *Hayarden* articles are reprinted in RH, pp. 42–59.

34. Speech to the Palestine Revisionist Council, *Looking Towards Sovereignty*, p. 12. See RH, pp. 42f. for a restatement of this argument.

35. *Looking Towards Sovereignty*, pp. 32f.; RH, p. 53.

36. *Looking Towards Sovereignty*, p. 45.

37. Ibid., p. 47.

38. Ibid., p. 50. Shavit notes the emphasis here on "Hebrew" power in contradistinction to "Jewish" life in the Diaspora (p. 62).

39. The "Speech to the Coterie" at the end of the pamphlet appears to be a talk Ratosh gave to an Irgun cell. An underground atmosphere is clearly in evidence. "The strength of a liberation movement is not in a large and mobile mass but in a faithful, tested and bold band of men, a group within a group. The work must be done on a one-to-one basis, mouth to ear. The elite must be selected out . . . and they must go out to the people and spread among them the demand for sovereignty, . . . the ironclad aspiration for the incipient *malkhut yisra'el*" (pp. 58, 61). The secretive form Ratosh's future political efforts would take is thus visible here; only the content would change.

40. RH, p. 18.

41. Ibid. This was the second meeting Ratosh had with Jabotinsky. The first had taken place six months earlier in Alexandria. Ratosh's recollection is of a cursory, fruitless conversation "with a man whose world was totally and fundamentally different from mine, from ours. From the other side he must have seen things the same way; in his view I was only a weed growing at the side of his public life, essentially a nuisance" (pp. 17f).

42. Ibid., pp. 18f.

43. Ibid., p. 19.

44. The pamphlet was received much more positively in Poland, where it was translated and published in a Warsaw periodical founded by Stern to disseminate Irgun ideas (interview with Stavi, Feb. 20, 1981). See also Shavit, *From Majority to State*, p. 44, n. 40.

45. Interview with Stavi, Feb. 20, 1981. Shavit suggests that "the sense of a personal mission that burned within him . . . and which later found expression in his poetry precipitated his disappointment and the search for a new purpose" (p. 63).

46. The Revisionists had gone there from Prague in order to unify the three wings of their movement: the New Zionist party, Betar, and the Irgun (see Shavit, "The Unknown Pseudonym," *M'oznayim* 54:3–4 [Feb.–Mar. 1982, Hebrew]: 6).

47. In the introduction to RH, Ratosh writes: "A second kind of hassle [occurred] . . . when I was in my twenties and travelled to France. Again the question 'who am I?' 'who are we?' came up. . . . It was explained to me that to define myself as a 'Hebrew' in French would be like someone introducing himself as a 'Sanskrit', [i.e.,] named after the sacred language of Jewish antiquity. . . . I therefore chose to identify myself as a Palestinian . . ." (p. 9). It is unclear from the text which Paris visit Ratosh is referring to; my assumption is that it is the first one.

48. The name sounds like a phonetic Hebraization of Uriel Halpern. See Shavit's full discussion of this phase of Ratosh's life (pp. 63–74) and the earlier "The Unknown Pseudonym." Ratosh evidently utilized his father's assistance in

getting these essays published; see three letters he wrote to his father at this time in *Jewish Literature in the Hebrew Language,* ed. Shin Shifra, pp. 209–13.

49. Shavit understands the etymology to be from Horo, the son of Isis and Osiris (see pp. 54–59, 63–66). Eri Jabotinsky's valuable discussion of Horon is in *My Father, Zev Jabotinsky,* pp. 127–39. See also Uri Avneri, *The War of the Seventh Day* (Jerusalem: Daf Hadash, 1969, Hebrew), pp. 147ff., and "The Truth About the Canaanites," *Ha'olam Hazeh,* no. 766 (reprinted in *Prozah* [Aug.–Sept. 1977, Hebrew], pp. 26f.). Ratosh's description of his meeting with Horon is in RH, pp. 12–15, and in the interview with Stavi, Feb. 20, 1981.

50. Shavit, p. 55. The request to Horon to prepare this pamphlet came from Dr. Binyamin Lubotsky-Eliav, who now was secretary-general of Betar.

51. RH, p. 14.

52. Interview with Stavi, Feb. 20, 1981. It is interesting that Ratosh here uses the same term to describe what attracted him to Horon as what he was disappointed to find lacking in Ahime'ir—"mishnah sedurah" (a systematic approach) (RH, p. 20).

53. Later in life Horon aspired to treat the entire subject of Hebrew antiquity in a book, but he never did this. The outlines of this work, however, are available and were published by Ratosh after Horon's death (N, pp. 207–60). This extended essay, therefore, is the fullest source for examining Horon's mature thinking.

54. Laqueur, *A History of Zionism,* p. 365.

55. Eri Jabotinsky, p. 132.

56. Ibid.

57. Interview with Stavi, Feb. 20, 1981.

58. Shavit, p. 117.

59. In the interview with Stavi (Feb. 20, 1981) Ratosh says it was he who broadened the vision from "the Land of the Hebrews" that Horon spoke about to "the Land of the Euphrates."

60. Shavit, pp. 118ff.

61. RH, pp. 10, 11, 12 passim. It is interesting that in undergoing this intellectual metamorphosis Ratosh inadvertently contradicted his own view that to be a Hebrew one had to be born in "the Land of the Euphrates." Instead he corroborated Horon's opinion that one could become a Hebrew by an act of consciousness. This disagreement between them is reported in Avneri, *The War of the Seventh Day,* p. 149.

62. In January 1938 he sent a group of poems he had written in the thirties under this name to Avraham Shlonsky in Tel Aviv for publication. He feared, apparently, that his real name would betray his Irgun leanings and reduce his chances of getting published. But poems under the name Ratosh had appeared in *Hayarden* in 1937. See Shavit, p. 94. Many, if not all, of the poems in question would appear in 1941 as his first and most celebrated collection, *Huppah shehorah* (Black canopy).

63. Shavit, p. 8.

64. Yoram Bronovsky, "Yonatan Ratosh: A Poet Nevertheless," *Ha'arets,* Feb. 3, 1984, Hebrew.

65. Aharon Amir, "The Poetic and the Political," *Davar,* Jan. 9, 1981, Hebrew.

66. Eri Jabotinsky writes that "it was interesting that . . . Gourevitch knew how to energize a small circle of disciples but he could never get beyond [this] . . . to the stage of real, independent political activity" (p. 136). In time the same judgment would be true of Ratosh.

In Paris Horon and his group began to put out *Shem: Revue D'Action Hébraïque.* Shavit notes that the name was borrowed from the *Action Française* founded by Charles Mauras as a part of the general influence of right-wing French "integral nationalism" upon Horon and Ratosh (pp. 90f.). The first issue of *Shem* came out in June 1939 and contains an article by A. Gour, "Hébreux et Juifs" (probably a reworking of "Canaan et les Hébreux"). Ratosh says he had a small role in the publication, but it is unclear just what this was (interview with Stavi, Feb. 20, 1981). Eri Jabotinsky says that six more issues of *Shem* were published by Horon's cohorts after the war broke out and Horon had gone to the United States. In New York Horon was active with Hillel Kook (Peter Bergson) and Eri Jabotinsky in setting up the *Va'ad Leshihrur Ha'umah* (The Committee for the Liberation of the Nation), a political arm of the Irgun. See Eri Jabotinsky, p. 136; Uri Avneri, "The Truth About the Canaanites," in *Prozah*, p. 26; and Shavit, pp. 103–105.

67. RH, p. 29. Ratosh and Horon's relationship hardly ended here. The two corresponded over the years and, while there were disagreements, they became good friends, especially after Horon moved to Israel in 1959. Horon died in 1972 (interview with Stavi, Feb. 20, 1981).

68. Uri Avneri's account of Ratosh's activity at this time is at variance with all other sources. According to Avneri, Ratosh, upon his return to Tel Aviv, tried once more with the Revisionist party, sending them a memorandum outlining the need for turning it into a Hebrew liberation movement. This communication never got a hearing, for its submission coincided exactly with the split of the Irgun. "In the uproar Uri Shelah and his memorandum were forgotten. At the end of 1940 Shelah left the New Zionist party and set up his own independent group . . ." ("The Truth About the Canaanites," *Prozah*, p. 26). While this is possible, it seems clear that Ratosh had already given up on the New Zionist party; his experience in Paris would not have been likely to result in his seeking a rapprochement with it. Also, the formation of his own group did not take place that early.

69. Stern's biographer, Ya'akov Weinshal, notes that Stern was captivated by religion. In his Irgun days it enchanted him to see his colleague David Razi'el as tied to his *tallit* and *tefillin* as he was to his pistol. "When we marry" he told his fiancée, "the first condition for our happiness is for everything to be in accordance with the tradition" (*The Blood on the Threshold*, 2d enlarged ed. [Tel Aviv: Ya'ir Publications, 1978, Hebrew], pp. 68, 73).

70. Shavit, p. 98. In spite of all this, it is possible to see the influence of Ratosh in the formulation of some of the eighteen principles. For example, there is the emphasis on conquering the land from "foreigners" (#10, #14) and the centrality of the Hebrew language in the national revival (#17). The "Principles" are in Weinshal, *Blood on the Threshold*, p. 161. Aharon Amir, who is not neutral in this matter, feels that Stern chose his ideological path out of a more pragmatic motive: it was risky enough for him to operate on the extreme of something already established; to cross over to something that marked a brand new ideological beginning could only jeopardize and was not necessary for his purposes (author's interview, December 12, 1983).

71. See Y. S. Brenner, "The 'Stern Gang,'" *Middle Eastern Studies* 2:1 (Oct. 1965): 2–20. Stern's splinter group was originally called the *Irgun Tsva'i Le'umi biYisra'el* (as opposed to Razi'el's *Irgun Tsva'i Le'umi*), but now there was the desire to dissociate it completely from the Irgun. It was the Lehi that maintained the emphasis on *malkhut yisra'el*, and very soon the Irgun and the Herut party under Begin chose to differentiate themselves from the Lehi by de-emphasizing the motif of territorial maximalism. See Isaac, *Party and Politics*, p. 136. It is important to note here that the Lehi was by no means ideologically monolithic; it had a left wing as much as it had a right wing, and after Stern was killed his "18 Principles" were honored in the breach. This point was emphasized by an ex-member of the Lehi, Boaz Evron, in a personal interview (December 12. 1983).

72. These qualities of Palestinian youth became the object of concern to Jewish intellectuals who had come from Europe. Dov Weinryb in 1939 notes the

drift of the young into the underground and writes: "At a time of transition, when the foundations have collapsed; at a time when phony verbal vestiges of days gone by cover over the inner crisis of everyday life in society and in culture, the youth, who do not make peace with the tide of counterfeit [existence], arise and rebel. . . ." He compares all this to the European phenomenon of "Young Italy" and "Young Germany" (*M'oznayim* 8 [Tishri–Adar 5699 (1938–39), Hebrew]: 16–21, 217–20). See also Barukh Kurzweil, "The School and the Youth Movement," written in the autumn of 1943 (reprinted in *Facing the Spiritual Perplexity of Our Time,* ed. Moshe Schwarcz [Ramat Gan: Bar-Ilan University, 1976, Hebrew], pp. 165–76).

73. A good description of this early phase of the "Canaanite" movement is in Aharon Amir's memoir "The Sword and the Lyre," in his collection of essays and stories *Prose* (Tel Aviv: Yariv Publications & Hadar Publishing Co., 1978, Hebrew), pp. 55–62 and 63f.

74. In RH, pp. 32–37 passim. In 1901 Nachman Syrkin wrote "A Call to the Jewish Youth," in which, in the name of secular socialist nationalism, he vigorously identified Jewish religion as the enemy and attacked it as regressive superstition. See David Kena'ani, *The Second Aliyah of Labor and Its Relationship to Religion and Tradition* (Tel Aviv: Sifriyat Po'alim, 1976, Hebrew), pp. 42f.

75. Cited in Amir, *Prose,* p. 84.

76. This letter was published by the committee together with the "Open Letter to the Hebrew Youth" in 1943 (no date, place, or publisher given). The "Epistle to the Lehi" has never been reprinted.

77. Natan Yellin-Mor, *Fighters for the Freedom of Israel: People, Ideas, Episodes* (Jerusalem: Shikmona, 1975, Hebrew), pp. 146f. Bet-Tsuri was one of the two assassins of Lord Moyne, the British minister of state in the Middle East, in Cairo in November 1944. A full account of his life is in Gerold Frank, *The Deed* (New York: Simon & Schuster, 1963). See especially pp. 96ff., where Bet-Tsuri's relationship to Ratosh and his friendship with Uzi Ornan are described. (Ornan's name is disguised here as Adi Landau; in the Hebrew version, *Hama'as,* it is not.) At his trial in Cairo Bet-Tsuri tried to justify the killing in distinctly "Canaanite" terms: "We do not recognize England's right to give us Palestine or take it away from us. Let me make clear to the court: My ideas are not Zionist ideas. We don't fight to uphold the Balfour Declaration. We don't fight for the sake of the National Home. We fight for our freedom. In our country a foreign power rules" (Frank, *The Deed,* p. 262). See also Y. S. Brenner's discussion of the effects of this speech on the Lehi and on Egyptian nationalism ("The 'Stern Gang'," pp. 12f). Another good presentation of Bet-Tsuri's relationship to the "Canaanites" is in Amir's "The Sword and the Lyre," the impetus for the writing of which was the reburial of the bodies of Bet-Tsuri and the other assassin, Eliahu Hakim, at a state funeral in Jerusalem in the autumn of 1975.

78. *The War of the Seventh Day,* p. 149.

79. Amos Kenan, interview with Dan Omer in *Prozah* (Aug.–Sept. 1977), p. 4, Hebrew.

80. Uri Avneri, *The War of the Seventh Day,* pp. 152f. See also p. 166.

81. See RH, p. 28.

82. The group was originally called *Tse'irei Yisra'el* (Young Israel) but was more commonly known by the name of its publication, *Bama'avak* (In the struggle). *Bama'avak* abandoned the term "Hebrew" in favor of "Semitic"; in place of "the Land of the Euphrates" it put forth its idea of "the Semitic Region" (*Merhav Hashemi*). Its main goal was to achieve political power through the Haganah, "in order to put the War of Independence on an organized, mass basis," and thus, in concert with the Arabs, drive out the British. See Avneri, "The Truth About the

Canaanites," in *Prozah*, p. 27. Avneri never denied his intellectual debt to Ratosh but displays an ambivalent attitude toward him (see *The War of the Seventh Day*, pp. 169–73). Ratosh, for his part, always regarded Avneri as a demagogic upstart. For further discussion of Avneri and his relationship to "Canaanism," see below, chapter 5, section IV.

83. Aharon Amir, "In the Wake of 'The Sword and the Lyre,'" in *Prose*, p. 103.

84. This is Ratosh's metaphor (RH, p. 28). A balanced assessment of the role of the underground in expediting the departure of the British is a task that still awaits historians of the period.

85. Ratosh's initial thought in August 1947 was to put out a literary journal, *Mahbarot latarbut hamoledet* (Notebooks of national culture), which would reflect Hebrew thought and culture, but British suppression and imprisonment of some of the possible backers of this project foiled it. Amir believes the project did come to fruition in 1958, when the periodical *Keshet*, which he edited until 1976, began. See "In the Wake of 'The Sword and the Lyre.'" *Prose*, p. 106. See further discussion below, chapter 6, section III.

86. Author's interview with Aharon Amir, December 12, 1983.

87. For further discussion of this point, see below, chapter 4, section V.

88. The two most articulate members of the generation are Amos Kenan and Boaz Evron. It is worth recalling Amir's observation that "among the sparse ranks of the 'Canaanites' there was always a high [degree] of mobility" (*Prose*, p. 67). Binyamin Tammuz, for example, who was one of the first to follow Ratosh in the early forties, had by this time left the movement.

89. Shavit, p. 101.

90. See above, chapter 1, n. 8.

91. *Alef*, no. 11 (Nov. 1951).

92. Aharon Amir says he opposed this step at the time. He felt the center would have needed at least five more years in order to be ready to do something like that (author's interview).

93. That Kurzweil's critique of "Canaanism," which went a long way toward endowing it with intellectual respectability, came out when it did (autumn 1952) seems to verify the notion that a cultural phenomenon attracts most attention and is taken most seriously after it has already peaked.

94. Aharon Amir notes that it is likely that at certain times the Israeli Secret Service (*Shin Bet*) monitored the group's activities and possibly even infiltrated it on occasion (author's interview).

95. Shavit, p. 102.

96. See E.

97. "The Event—and Its Academic Reflection," *Yedi'ot Aharonot*, March 2, 1984, Hebrew.

98. From 1964 to 1967 a "Forum for Hebrew Thought" (*Mo'adon leMahashavah 'Ivrit*) existed. This was a small fellowship for discussion and lectures (Shavit, p. 102). Shavit himself was evidently a participant in this group, although he does not say so in his book (see Aharon Amir's review of it, "From Rome—To 'Ever and Canaan," *Ha'arets*, April 6, 1984, Hebrew).

99. The prewar issue of *Alef*, written June 4, 1967, and published June 5, the day the war broke out, predicts an Israeli victory. An English translation in mimeo was also put out. *Alef* came out from time to time from 1968 to 1972.

100. Tel Aviv: Hadar Publishing Co., 1967, Hebrew.

101. *1967 and What Next?* pp. 12f. The fascistic overtones here as well as Ratosh's views on democracy will be discussed below, chapter 4, end of section V.

102. The Jewish and religious name of this war is significant. Aharon Amir

takes exception to it and to the nomenclature of all of Israel's wars. "These are very banal names. They evade . . . [consideration] of their significance. I think that this running away from ideas is in large measure what brought us to the situation we are in today. . . . The matter of defining wars, like defining concepts and terms in our collective reality in general, is a higher priority than anything else, more [important]–than determining [the causes of] military or political failures" (spoken at a symposium, "To the Root of Things," following the war, in February 1974; reprinted in *Keshet* 62 [Winter 1974, Hebrew]: 6).

103. See N.

104. N, pp. 9f.

105. N, pp. 27f.

106. Author's interview with Boaz Evron. Ratosh admired Sharon, and it is not hard to understand why. It was Sharon whom he held up as the possible "strongman" or "chancellor" he called for. See N, pp. 195, 205.

107. A few months earlier in 1980, Haifa University's art gallery held an exhibition on "The Myth of Canaan: The Influence of the Ancient Middle East on Modern Israeli Art." While Ratosh himself was not involved in this, a recognition of the influence of his thought was implicit in the whole project. See further discussion below, chapter 6, section I.

108. In addition to the one with Stavi, printed in three parts, there was one with the poet Natan Zach published in *Monitin*, April 1981, p. 66, and May 1981, p. 81, Hebrew.

109. Interview with Stavi, Feb. 6, 1981.

110. "My First Book," in *Jewish Literature in the Hebrew Language*, ed. Shin Shifra, p. 208. See below, chapter 5, n. 45.

IV: Yonatan Ratosh and the Deconstruction of Zionism

1. Shemu'el Almog, *Zionism and History* (Jerusalem: The Magnes Press of the Hebrew University, 1982, Hebrew), pp. 93f. Almog notes that Nietzsche's influence was hardly confined to Berditchevsky but rather was "common currency" among cultural Zionists (p. 92). Compare, for example, Berditchevsky's and Ahad Ha'am's essays of the same title, "Shinui 'arakhin" (The transvaluation of values). Shavit finds Berditchevsky's thought an important conceptual link in the development of the term *'ivri* (Hebrew) as an antonym to *yehudi* (Jew) (pp. 28ff.), and see also Almog, p. 88.

2. Cited in David Vital, *Zionism: The Formative Years* (Oxford: Clarendon Press, 1982), p. 191. See his entire discussion, pp. 189–98, and Almog, pp. 65ff.

3. Vital, *The Formative Years*, pp. 195, 196, 197 passim.

4. Uri Avneri, *The War of the Seventh Day* (Jerusalem: Daf Hadash Publication Co., 1969, Hebrew), p. 156. I would add here that MP is the prose counterpart of Ratosh's argumentative poem "Haholkhi bahoshekh" (The walker in the darkness), which he wrote between 1942 and 1964.

5. MP, p. 169.

6. Ibid., p. 180.

7. Ibid., pp. 186f.

8. Ibid., pp. 188ff.

9. Ibid., p. 199.

10. Rael Jean Isaac says that "Ratosh had what can only be called anti-Semitic attitudes" (*Party and Politics in Israel: Three Visions of a Jewish State* [New York & London: Longmans, 1981], p. 183, n. 11). For a conjectural discussion of the psychological processes at work here, see Jay Y. Gonen, *A Psychohistory of Zionism* (New York: Mason/Charter, 1975), pp. 295–313. Gonen holds that Ratosh and

the "Canaanites" had "negative identity." He writes: "People who were once one thing and have successfully become another do not need to lash out with venom at what they no longer are. But the poisonous anti-Jewish declarations of the Young Hebrews . . . clearly indicate that the Canaanites do have such a need. . . . It is a fair speculation that had the general public not been able to sense this malaise of self-hatred and self-abnegation, the Canaanites would have had greater following" (p. 311).

11. Gonen, pp. 311, 313.

12. See Yehezkel Kaufmann's vigorous attack on the concept and the rhetoric it generated in his essay of 1934, "Hurban hanefesh" (Ruination of the soul). This essay originally appeared in *M'oznayim* (Tevet 5694) and is reprinted in the anthology of Kaufmann's essays *Behevlei hazeman* (In the pangs of time) (Tel Aviv: Dvir, 1936, Hebrew), pp. 257–74. A translation appears in *Zionism Reconsidered: The Rejection of Jewish Normalcy,* ed. Michael Selzer (New York: Macmillan Co., 1970), pp. 117–29. Kaufmann writes: "The vocabulary of abuse contained in Hebrew literature (in which Jews can speak to one another without fear or exaggeration) is paralleled only in overtly anti-Semitic literature of the worst kind." He cites the terminology that the likes of Frischmann, Berditchevsky, Brenner, and A. D. Gordon used to describe Diaspora Jews and their life: "a dog's life," "not human," "filthy dogs," "parasites" (see Selzer, p. 121).

13. MP, p. 150.

14. Ibid.

15. Ibid., p. 174.

16. Ibid., p. 196.

17. Ibid., p. 178.

18. Ibid., pp. 176f.

19. Ibid., pp. 178ff.

20. Peter Berger, Brigitte Berger, and Hansfried Kellner, *The Homeless Mind* (New York: Random House, 1973), p. 167.

21. Shlomo Avineri understands Zionism primarily as a response to the secular nationalism that resulted from the French Revolution. See his introduction to *The Making of Modern Zionism: The Intellectual Origins of the Jewish State* (New York: Basic Books, Inc., 1981), pp. 3–13.

22. The one-dimensional analysis of "Canaanism" primarily as "Geschichtskonstruktion" is a major weakness of Shavit's study. As if Zionism evinces no "deep internal contradiction between 'archaism' and 'modernity' " and creates no "fictive world" or "mytho-poetic non-historical past, even when it makes a strenuous attempt to prove its 'historicity'"! (see pp. 133 and 138). Shavit seems unaware that Zionism, too, is founded on myth and a discrete historiography, nor does he explain why these are necessarily more relevant to Israeli society than the ones "Canaanism" proposed. He simply assumes it. For a brief discussion of Zionist historiography, see Almog, *Zionism and History*, pp. 33–36.

23. This passage is quoted from Shemu'el Yavni'eli, *The Period of Hibat Tsiyon* (1942–44, Hebrew), in Yig'al Elam, *An Alternative Introduction to Zionist History* (Tel Aviv: Lewin-Epstein Publishing Co., [1972], Hebrew), p. 18.

24. See above, chapter 2, section V.

25. Quoted in Elam, *An Alternative Introduction*, p. 21.

26. Ibid., p. 177.

27. See, for example, Brenner's *Bahoref* (In winter).

28. See interview with Amos Kenan in *Prozah* (Aug.–Sept. 1977, Hebrew) p. 6, and see below, chapter 5, section I.

29. See David Kena'ani, *The Second Aliyah of Labor and Its Relationship to Religion and Tradition* (Tel Aviv: Sifriyat Po'alim, 1976, Hebrew), pp. 36–46.

30. See "Haholkhi bahoshekh" (The walker in the darkness), lines 230–33, 283ff., 320–84, 533–38. This work is found in Ratosh's *Shirim* (Poems) (Tel Aviv: Hadar Publishing Co., 1977).

31. See Zev Hanun (Tsvi Rin), "In the Prison of the Sacred," *Alef*, no. 2 (May 1950, Hebrew), and "Jews, To Your Tents," *Alef*, no. 7 (Jan. 1951, Hebrew). More negative descriptions of traditional Judaism would be hard to find. Hanun's fiercest attack is on the ritual of circumcision, which he says he finds barbarous. The indication is that Ratosh and his closest followers either did not have their sons circumcised or had this done by a doctor. Uzi Ornan argues that in preserving circumcision as a religious rite it is Judaism that uncritically retains the primitive; "Canaanism," he says, is more selective in its appropriation of the archaic past; see "Continuity or Beginning?" in *Alef*, no. 18 (Feb. 1953, Hebrew). It is interesting to note that Nimrod the Hunter as depicted in Yitshak Danziger's statue (1939) is uncircumcised. The statue became something of a symbol of the "Canaanite" movement, mostly for its evocation of the "Hebrew" as hunter. But the implications of his uncircumcised status seem clear. Theologically we may say that the "Canaanite" movement represents the antithesis to the whole idea of the Jewish people in Covenant with God. See below, chapter 5, section III, for a discussion of Ornan's involvement with the League for the Abolishment of Religious Coercion.

32. For an excellent study of this important and hitherto neglected topic, see W. D. Davies, *The Territorial Dimension of Judaism* (Berkeley, Los Angeles & London: The University of California Press, 1982).

33. Letter to the editor of *Hashahar* (1880), quoted in Arthur Hertzberg, *The Zionist Idea: A Historical Analysis and Reader* (New York & Philadelphia: Meridian Books & Jewish Publication Society, 1960), p. 165. It is not surprising that Ratosh regards Ben-Yehudah as one of his heroes; see interview with Z. Stavi, *Yedi'ot Aharonot*, Feb. 27, 1981, Hebrew.

34. MP, pp. 152f. This biological or geographical determinism was softened in the pages of *Alef*. There it is stated that in an immigrant society that is still in formation one can "consciously choose" to understand himself as part of a new nation and not as a member of a faith-community (*Alef*, no. 4 [Aug. 1950]: 16). This principle is what allowed Ratosh, Amir, and others who were born in Europe to call themselves "Hebrews."

Ratosh successfully entreated the Ministry of the Interior to allow his nationality to be listed on his identity card as "Hebrew" and not "Jewish." Years later he misplaced this card and was, apparently, forced to list his nationality as "Jewish" on the new one. In 1969 he sent a personal petition to the Knesset requesting that his Hebrew status be restored. The text of this petition provides a good summary of Ratosh's personal views on Jewish religion and peoplehood. It is found in N, pp. 122–26.

35. See *Avshalom Feinberg: Papers and Letters*, ed. Aharon Amir (Haifa: Shikmona Publishing Co., 1971, Hebrew) and Amir's monographic introduction. Ratosh's paean to Feinberg is "Our Eternally Young Ancestor," reprinted in N, pp. 291–94. On Feinberg, see also Livneh, Nedavah, and Efrati, *Nili: The History of a Political Audacity*, 2d rev. ed. (Tel Aviv & Jerusalem: Schocken Publishing Co., 1980, Hebrew).

36. Shavit speaks of the Feinberg myth pejoratively (p. 42). He evinces no understanding of myth as the belief-system and the assumptions a culture or a society must have if it is to develop. His four definitions of myth (p. 130) seem restrictive and inadequate.

37. When his father and his uncle urged him to consider going to Turkey, Feinberg refused, writing: "to get up and travel to a people that is ugly in my

eyes, whose language is foreign to me and whose interests are opposed to mine? No. . . . I am a Jew" (*Papers and Letters*, p. 17).

38. MP, pp. 184, 183.

39. Ibid., p. 161.

40. Ibid., p. 185.

41. Ibid., pp. 186f.

42. See E.

43. MP, p. 172.

44. In S. Y. Agnon's novel *Shirah*, Manfred Herbst, one of the main characters, says: "Were I to write a book about the character of nations, I would not hesitate to write of the character of Judaism that the Jews do not seek a state and a political Jewish life but simply to worship God and make a decent living" (quoted in Amos Oz, *In the Land of Israel*, trans. Maurie Goldberg-Bartura [San Diego: Harcourt Brace Jovanovich, 1983], p. 121).

45. Shavit holds that since "Canaanism" was such a fringe ideology even before the state was founded, it was not overwhelmed by anything after 1948 (pp. 160f). In his review of Shavit's book, Boaz Evron takes sharp exception to this. He says that this "denigration of the value of vanguard elites calls into question his [Shavit's] analytical abilities and understanding as a historian" ("The Event—and its Academic Reflection," in *Yedi'ot Aharonot*, March 2, 1984, Hebrew).

46. *Alef*, no. 1 (Spring 1950).

47. *Alef*, no. 10 (Sept. 1951, Hebrew). See also E, p. 214.

48. *Alef*, no. 10 (Sept. 1951, Hebrew).

49. Platform of the Center for Young Hebrews in *Alef*, no. 11 (Nov. 1951). This document is reprinted in Shavit, pp. 182–86.

50. Ibid.

51. Ibid.

52. See Walter Laqueur, *A History of Zionism* (New York: Holt, Rinehart & Winston, 1972), p. 362.

53. Interview with Natan Zach in *Monitin* (May 1981, Hebrew). Ratosh says that "there was, to my regret, no real chance that a government and a Knesset of parties would ever accept this idea, but in actuality things did develop in this direction. In a dramatic meeting with the Prime Minister [before the war's outbreak] the generals threatened to resign. . . . The government was threatened with the possibility that the army would initiate hostilities . . . and the leadership of the people would actually pass over to the General Staff."

54. Ibid.

55. Ratosh saw Gen. Ariel Sharon as a suitable head for such a presidential council (N, p. 205). It is true that this article was originally published in *Ma'ariv* in 1972, when Sharon was perhaps a different quantity. But the longing for a "strong man" must qualify any understanding of Ratosh's professed democratic principles.

56. See Shavit, p. 238, n. 11.

57. Ibid., p. 134.

58. One of the main points that emerges from Dan Miron's consideration of Ratosh's poetry is that underneath the archaisms and studied mannerism that are apparent on its surface is a distinctly modern view of the human situation and an existentialist-like "code" of how reality is perceived. See *Four Faces of Hebrew Literature*, 2d ed. (Jerusalem & Tel Aviv; Schocken Publishing Co., 1975, Hebrew), pp. 209–44.

59. Hayim Pesah, "Ideology and Poetics: Between Ratosh and Pound," *M'oznayim* 54:3–4 (Feb.–Mar. 1982, Hebrew): 14.

60. Miron, *Four Faces of Hebrew Literature*, p. 254.

61. MP, p. 177.

62. These are only a few examples of the hyperbolic statements and the tone that pervade the "Open Letter to the Hebrew Youth" and MP.

63. Interview with Shin Shifra, *Davar*, August 27, 1971, Hebrew. Ratosh similarly fulminates against Zionist appropriation of the word *'ivriyut* (Hebraism) as another attempt to paper over the irrevocable difference he sees between Jews and Hebrews. See MP, pp. 200–202, and the essay "A Term of Deceit," reprinted in RH, pp. 60–62.

64. Gonen, *A Psychohistory of Zionism*, p. 309. But I think that Zionism itself and some of its protagonists are not exempt from this same psychological syndrome; witness the "we/they" posture often taken when the subject of Diaspora Jewry comes up.

65. See Yoram Bronovsky, "Yonatan Ratosh: A Poet Nevertheless," in *Ha'arets*, February 3, 1984, Hebrew.

66. Ya'akov Rotem, "Yonatan Ratosh from Up Close," in *'Al hamishmar*, April 3, 1981, Hebrew.

67. Initially, he says, his application for membership was rejected because of his views; later in life he was accepted, but he refused to pay dues to an organization that was receiving funds from other sources (interview with Z. Stavi, *Yedi'ot Aharonot*, February 6, 1981, Hebrew).

68. Ibid.

69. Boaz Evron, "A Paean to Yonatan," in *Yedi'ot Aharonot*, January 30, 1981, Hebrew.

70. The expression is that of Gerson Cohen, which he once used in reference to Abraham Joshua Heschel.

71. Binyamin Tammuz, "Farewell to Yonatan Ratosh," in *Ha'arets*, April 10, 1981, Hebrew.

72. See Daniel J. Elazar, *Community and Polity: The Organizational Dynamics of American Jewry* (Philadelphia: The Jewish Publication Society, 1976), pp. 79–83 and 334f.

73. MP, p. 179.

74. Hayim Hazaz makes the same point in his short story "Haderashah" (The sermon). Indeed, the arguments in this oft-cited work are remarkably similar to those of Ratosh. The date of the publication of "The Sermon" (autumn 1942) is suspiciously close to the first "Canaanite" writings of Ratosh, although I can find no evidence of any influence either way. In his review of Hazaz's play *Bekets hayamim* (At the end of days), Amir scores Hazaz for not having the courage of his convictions. While Amir does not say so outright, he insinuates that if Hazaz were serious about what he had put forth in "The Sermon," he would be with the Young Hebrews. According to Amir, Hazaz lost his nerve, for "The Sermon" was originally supposed to have had a continuation, "but nevertheless there was no continuation. Why? Because it made too many waves. Because Hazaz found out how much the rejections and denial in his story matched the natural feelings of the masses of Hebrew youth. . . . Because he found out about the intense arguments his sermon provoked within the various youth groups. Because he found out how much the youth accepted his words at face value, as 'sanctioning from on high' their feelings of distinctiveness and their alienation from Judaism. He heard this—and retreated." Amir thus sees the setting of the subsequent play, "At the End of Days," in the time of the Sabbatian heresy, as a regression on Hazaz's part and a substitute for bringing "The Sermon" to its logical, "Canaanite" conclusion (see "From Yudka to Yuzpah," *Alef*, no. 3 [June–July 1950, Hebrew]: 8).

75. See A. B. Yehoshua, "The Golah: The Neurotic Solution," in *Between*

Right and Right (New York: Doubleday, 1981), pp. 21–74. A condensed version of this piece appears in *Diaspora: Exile and the Jewish Condition,* ed. Etan Levine (New York & London: Jason Aronson, 1983), pp. 15–35. See also in that volume Hillel Halkin, "The Ba'al Shem Tov and the Flaming Sword," pp. 37–42.

76. MP, p. 177.

77. Vincent B. Leitch, *Deconstructive Criticism: An Advanced Introduction* (New York: Columbia University Press, 1983), p. ix.

78. Quoted from Paul de Man in Christopher Norris, *Deconstruction: Theory and Practice* (London: Methuen, 1982), p. xii. See especially chapter 5, "Between Marx and Nietzsche: the Politics of Deconstruction." This discussion substantiates the Nietzschean nature of Ratosh's thought and work. The difficulties Marxism has with Nietzsche are comparable to, and in some ways anticipate, those Zionism as a system has with Ratosh.

V: "Canaanism and Israeli Polity and Policy

1. Amos Kenan, Interview with Dan Omer, *Prozah* (Aug.–Sept. 1977, Hebrew), p. 4.

2. I do not, however, wish to suggest that "Canaanism" was spawned exclusively by the contradictions of Zionism. There was also a contextual factor that needs to be mentioned: a kind of cultural irredentism that pervaded many countries of the Middle East. See Shavit's discussion of some of the small, parallel "Canaanite"-type movements that existed in Egypt, Lebanon, Syria, and Turkey (pp. 46–53). See also Mikha'el Assaf, "Pharaohnites, Canaanites 'A' and Canaanites 'B,' " *Davar,* October 3, 1952, Hebrew.

3. See Yosef Oren, "And to Its Source It Returns," M'oznayim 42:3 (Feb. 1976, Hebrew): 203f.

4. J. L. Teller, "The Spartan Youth of Israel: A Generation Searches for its Soul," *Commentary* 10:1 (July, 1950), p. 7. This article was translated into Hebrew and published in *Alef,* no. 5 (Oct. 1950).

5. Ibid., p. 11.

6. Ya'akov Aschman, "To Die—But For What?" reprinted in *Prozah* (Aug.–Sept. 1977, Hebrew), pp. 28f. See also the short story "The Battle for the Williams Fortress," by Etan Notav (Shraga Gafni), pp. 20f.; a more explicit expression of the disassociation of the fighters from Zionism would be hard to imagine.

7. Of the story "The Battle for the Williams Fortress," Amos Kenan says, "it caught exactly my feeling as it was then: that we, the generation that fought [the war of] 1948 are continuing some children's mythology that was grafted onto us. . . . Already in 1949 I felt that this story . . . described correctly the inner world of those who fought." Kenan cites the observation of Barukh Nadel that "the Palmah was created by two men—Yitshak Sadeh and Gary Cooper" (interview with Dan Omer). See also S. Yizhar's celebrated novel *Yemei tsiklag* (1958) as an important indicator that this alienated outlook was not an isolated phenomenon.

8. Amos Kenan, interview with Dan Omer, p. 6.

9. Rael Jean Isaac, *Party and Politics in Israel: Three Visions of a Jewish State* (New York: Longmans, 1981), p. 222.

10. Aharon Amir, "The Younger Generation Is Dead—Long Live the Younger Generation!" *Alef,* no. 5 (Oct. 1950, Hebrew), p. 5. Emphasis is Amir's.

11. Boaz Evron, "The Event—and Its Academic Reflection," *Yedi'ot Aharonot,* March 2, 1984, Hebrew. Emphasis is Evron's. For a philosophical amplification of this, see Ernst Simon's important essay "Are We Israelis Still Jews?" in *Luah*

Ha'arets 5712 [1951–52], pp. 97–129, Hebrew. This is reprinted in *Perakim bayahadut,* ed. E. Spicehandler and J. Petuchowski (Jerusalem & Cincinnati: M. Newman Publishing Co. & Hebrew Union College Press, n.d.), pp. 250–78, Hebrew.

12. Shavit, p. 152.
13. Interview with Dan Omer, p. 6.
14. Ibid.
15. Author's interview with Boaz Evron, December 12, 1983.
16. Amos Kenan, interview with Dan Omer, p. 6.
17. Georges Friedmann, *The End of the Jewish People?* trans. from the French by Eric Mosbacher (Garden City, N.Y.: Doubleday & Co., 1967), pp. 239–42. See also an earlier study that comes to a similar conclusion: Melford Spiro, *Children of the Kibbutz* (Cambridge, Mass.: Harvard University Press, 1958).
18. Simon N. Herman, *Israelis and Jews: The Continuity of an Identity* (New York: Random House, 1970), p. 199.
19. Charles S. Liebman and Eliezer Don-Yehiya, *Civil Religion in Israel: Traditional Judaism and Political Culture in the Jewish State* (Berkeley, Los Angeles & London: University of California Press, 1983), p. 5.
20. Ibid., p. 245, n. 40.
21. See Avner Cohen, "Jewish Identity as Paradox: Marginal Notes on an Old-New Motif," *Davar,* Sept. 10, 1980, Hebrew.
22. See Herman, *Israelis and Jews,* pp. 202f. Hayim Guri tells of an interesting exercise that he saw performed in the Israeli army. A new group of recruits is put into a classroom. On the blackboard are written three words: "Israeli," "Jew," and "human being." The recruits are asked to go up individually to the board, point to the word that best approximates their own self-understanding and explain their selection. Guri says in all the many times he saw this exercise played out, the results were quite similar: a small percentage chooses "human being," mostly, he says, as a safe option that could be easily defended. The rest more or less split on the two remaining options (author's interview with Hayim Guri, Jan. 6, 1984).
23. Dan V. Segre, *A Crisis of Identity: Israel and Zionism* (Oxford: Oxford University Press, 1980), pp. 30–32 passim.
24. For a good assessment of the "Jewish consciousness" program, see Liebman and Don-Yehiya, *Civil Religion,* pp. 170–77 and also pp. 123f.
25. This locution is attributed by Segre to the French writer Paul Giniewski (p. 1).
26. Shalom Rosenberg, "Identity and Ideology in Contemporary Jewish Thought: An Essay in Meta-Language," *Bitefutsot hagolah* 18 (77–78) [Summer 1976, Hebrew]: 14.
27. For an attempt to reassert the secular foundation of Israeli identity, see Amnon Rubinstein, *The Zionist Dream Revisited: From Herzl to Gush Emunim and Back* (New York: Schocken Books, 1984). Rubinstein's argument seems confused. It stands on a contradiction: on the one hand, he admits and demonstrates that secular Zionism was inadequate to the challenges of Jewish nationhood, yet on the other hand that is what he ultimately calls for. Further, his intellectual debt to "Canaanism" is much greater than he is willing to admit. The result is an argument that seems to be a kind of ideological salad of disparate and conflicting elements, which is described best in Rubinstein's own words: "a concoction combining a bit of Herzlian Zionism, spiced by messianic religiosity, with a smattering of neo-Canaanite thinking." This is precisely what Rubinstein himself disavows: "an exercise in intellectual dishonesty" (p. 169). But as I shall note in the excursus, his argument does point in what I consider the right direction. For further discussion of the limitations of secular Zionism, see Avner Cohen, "Jew-

ish Identity as Paradox," and the second part of that essay, "The Trap of 'Sane Zionism,'" in *Davar*, Sept. 19, 1980, Hebrew.

28. "To the Roots of Things," *Keshet* 62 (Winter 1974, Hebrew): 23f. The symposium took place in Tel Aviv on Feb. 1, 1974. This candid, substantial, and passionate discussion is a superb source for understanding the crisis of contemporary Zionism and deserves translation into English.

29. Ibid. and also p. 31. Guri's many essays on the problems of Israeli identity include a serious engagement with "Canaanism." See, for example: "The Canaanite Hour," *Ma'ariv* Sept. 24, 1980; "The Grandson and the Melody," *Ma'ariv*, Oct. 31, 1980; and "The Duality and the Chasm," *Ma'ariv*, n.d., 1980 (all in Hebrew). While he clearly rejects it, Guri eloquently acknowledges the value of Ratosh's thought. "This is not an abstract argument about something that will arise in the future but a discussion about the State of Israel after a generation of independence and five wars" ("The Duality and the Chasm"). See also Guri's "Chapters from a Confession at Midnight," *Ma'ariv*, Dec. 26, 1975; "The Call to the Hebrews," *Davar*, n.d., 1983; and "We the Homeborn," *Davar*, July 13, 1984 (all in Hebrew). An English translation of this last essay by Stanley F. Chyet is in *Moment* 10:7 (July–August 1985): 13–16.

30. *Keshet* symposium, p. 30. See also pp. 41f.

31. Author's interview with Boaz Evron. Binyamin Tammuz, who was one of Ratosh's earliest followers but later abandoned "Canaanism" without ever formally disavowing it, has symbolically depicted many of the dilemmas of Israeli identity discussed here and later in this chapter in his excellent novel *Hapardes* (1971, Hebrew; trans. Richard Flantz, under the title *The Orchard* [Providence: Copper Beech Press, 1984]). In its deepest sense the whole complex of issues in the Israeli identity reaches back to the larger crisis of Jewish identity in the modern world precipitated by the Emancipation. A discussion that wide in perspective and that theoretical in nature is beyond the scope of this one.

32. See "The Conflict over the Constitution," in Norman L. Zucker, *The Coming Crisis in Israel: Private Faith and Public Policy* (Cambridge & London: The MIT Press, 1973), pp. 62–72, and S. Zalman Abramov, *Perpetual Dilemma: Jewish Religion in the Jewish State* (Rutherford: Fairleigh Dickinson University Press, 1976), pp. 135–46. Elazar holds that Israel's Scroll of Independence "is in itself of constitutional significance in the traditional way, that is to say, as a founding covenant that sets forth the guidelines within which a constitution can be developed and a regime established, without specifying either" (*Kinship and Consent: The Jewish Political Tradition and Its Contemporary Uses*, ed. Daniel J. Elazar [Washington, D.C.: University Press of America, 1983], p. 36, and see n. 32).

33. Zucker, *The Coming Crisis*, p. 2.

34. Ibid., pp. 210ff.

35. Abramov, *Perpetual Dilemma*, p. 18.

36. Ibid., p. 321.

37. Moshe Samet, *Religion and State in Israel: The Conflict over the Institutionalization of Jewish Values in the State of Israel* (Jerusalem: Papers in Sociology, Hebrew University, 1979, Hebrew), pp. 19, 2.

38. Ibid., p. 78. See also Oscar Kraines, *Impossible Dilemma: Who Is a Jew in the State of Israel?* (New York: Bloch Publishing Co., 1976).

39. Zucker, *The Coming Crisis*, pp. 178f. Zucker points out that this definition, in that it excludes Jewish apostates, actually goes beyond *halakhah* in order to prevent individuals like Brother Daniel from claiming Israeli citizenship under the Law of Return. It thus squares not only with *halakhah* but with the demands of Israeli nationalism. Further, the stipulation that conversion to Judaism be "in accordance with the *halakhah*" was designed to delegitimize the conversions

performed under the auspices of Conservative and Reform rabbis. This is an issue that continues to be challenged and debated.

40. Samet, *Religion and State*, p. 79.

41. Ibid., p. 24,

42. See Amnon Rubinstein, *To Be a Free People* (Jerusalem & Tel Aviv: Schocken Publishing Co., 1977, Hebrew), pp. 183–86.

43. See Zucker, *The Coming Crisis*, pp. 154–58 and 188–90, and Kraines, *Impossible Dilemma*, pp. 34ff.

The SS *Shalom* was a luxury liner that Zim Lines, a shipping company sponsored by the Israeli government, sought to operate with two kitchens, one kosher and one nonkosher. The rabbinate and the NRP both opposed this arrangement and applied pressure in the form of threats to withdraw kosher certification from all Zim carriers and to bring down the government. The league strenuously campaigned against what it saw as an infringement of freedom of conscience.

Rina Eitani was the daughter of a Gentile mother and a Jewish father who, after the latter's death, had come to Israel in 1947, been registered as a Jew, and granted Israeli citizenship in 1952. Later she became active in local politics in Nazareth and her political rivals in the NRP challenged her citizenship. After much controversy her citizenship was upheld.

44. *Kol ha'ir*, Dec. 30, 1983, Hebrew, pp. 45. 47.

45. In the tradition of his brother Ratosh, but with much less rhetorical bombast, Ornan continues his lonely personal campaign with occasional articles and letters to the editor. See, for example, "The True Roots," in the Hebrew University student newspaper *Pi ha'aton*, no. 8 (Feb. 1980, Hebrew) in which Ornan outlines briefly the main principles of a secularist world-view.

This entire complex of issues was played out in a most concrete way in October 1985, when seven Israelis vacationing in the southern Sinai were murdered by an Egyptian border policeman. Among them were Ratosh's eldest son, Haiman, his wife, and daughter. Inasmuch as they held themselves not to be Jews, Ornan insisted, on their behalf, that there be no Jewish religious funeral, and he resisted all attempts by the Jerusalem Burial Society to prepare the bodies as is required for interment in a public cemetery in Israel. The family was buried in the private cemetery of the secular kibbutz Nahshon in the Jerusalem corridor. The incident served as a dramatic reminder of the distance between Israeli public policy and the "Canaanite" perspective.

46. Theodore Herzl, *The Jewish State* (New York: American Zionist Emergency Council, 1946), p. 146.

47. Gershon Weiler, *Jewish Theocracy* (Tel Aviv: Am Oved Publishers, 1976, Hebrew).

48. See Weiler, chapter 6: "Spinoza's Critique of Religious Authority," especially pp. 97ff. and 103–106. In his introduction Weiler writes: "This whole book of mine is nothing more than a footnote to Spinoza and its only distinctive feature is that it is written now. If we want to maintain a sovereign state, we are going to have to pay attention to these issues much more than we have in the past" (p. 11). Eliezer Schweid, however, working out of a normative Zionist approach, is critical of Spinoza's analysis and, therefore, more optimistic about the possibility of Israel's overcoming the dangers of theocracy; see "The Attitude Toward the State in Modern Jewish Thought Before Zionism," in *Kinship and Consent*, ed. Elazar, pp. 127–47, especially pp. 145ff.

49. Ibid., p. 296. I would add that those who were more philosophically inclined and, more important, who considered the implications and the agenda of the Enlightenment to be still unfinished did see this connection. This group included Ahad Ha'am and the *Demokratische Fraktion*, but it really goes back to

Y. L. Gordon. Gordon had written: "So long as the Rabbis have the upper hand and the religion, which they imposed on us, remains intact, the people of Israel will never be able to establish self-government" (cited in Ehud Luz, "Zion and Judenstaat: The Significance of the Uganda Controversy," in *Essays in Modern Jewish History: A Tribute to Ben Halpern,* ed. Frances Malino and Phyllis C. Albert [Rutherford: Fairleigh Dickinson University Press, 1982], p. 219).

50. Ibid., p. 296. The fact is that in his time Rav Kook as chief rabbi pushed the secular Zionist authorities for the same concessions to theopolitics that his less-admired successors have sought, such as *kashrut* in public institutions and no public transportation on the Sabbath—and he got them. See Samet, *Religion and State,* p. 83. Rav Kook's legitimation of secular Zionism is not a halakhic one but rather is rooted in his mystical outlook.

51. Weiler, *Jewish Theocracy,* pp. 297–309. See also Segre, *A Crisis of Identity,* pp. 137–45, and Liebman and Don-Yehiya, *Civil Religion,* pp. 128–31.

52. See Weiler's review of N, "One Truth and Many Fallacies Versus One Fallacy and Many Truths," *Davar,* Feb. 11, 1977, Hebrew.

53. Boaz Evron, "Israel After Zionism," *The Nation* 273:19 (Dec. 5, 1981), p. 597.

54. It is significant that two of the most readable popular books about Israel both conclude with a discussion of this problem. See Amos Elon, *The Israelis: Founders and Sons* (New York, Chicago & San Francisco: Holt, Rinehart, & Winston, 1971), pp. 327–34, and Lawrence Meyer, *Israel Now: Portrait of a Troubled Land* (New York: Delacorte Press, 1982), pp. 346ff.

55. Uzi Ornan, "And What Next?" *Yedi'ot Aharonot,* July 3, 1981, Hebrew.

56. *Keshet* symposium, p. 29.

57. Uri Avneri, *The War of the Seventh Day* (Jerusalem: Daf Hadash Publication Co., 1969, Hebrew), p. 174. See also Shavit, pp. 145–54. Ratosh took exception to some articles Avneri had published in *Hahevrah* and a meeting between the two was arranged. See Avneri, *The War of the Seventh Day,* p. 146.

58. Avneri, *The War of the Seventh Day,* p. 166; see also p. 153.

59. Uri Avneri, *Israel Without Zionists: A Plea for Peace in the Middle East* (New York & London: The Macmillan Co., 1968), p. 12. Shavit observes that this position had already been developed by the Berit Shalom group in the thirties (p. 150).

60. Avneri, *The War of the Seventh Day,* pp. 173, 180; *Israel Without Zionists,* p. 13.

61. *War or Peace in the Semitic World* (Tel Aviv: the Political Department of the Young Palestine Association, Oct. 1947, Hebrew). See also Avneri, *The War of the Seventh Day,* p. 13.

62. Shavit, p. 153.

63. When Avneri began publishing his weekly magazine *Ha'olam hazeh,* he was apparently identified in the established Israeli press as a member of the Young Hebrews and the *Alef* group. For a vigorous disclaimer of this connection by the latter see *Alef,* no. 10 (Sept. 1951), p. 12. For a discussion of Avneri's total political outlook (but one that does not trace its sources in "Canaanism"), see David J. Schnall, *Radical Dissent in Contemporary Israeli Politics: Cracks in the Wall* (New York: Praeger Special Studies, 1979), pp. 55–71. As a member of the Knesset, Avneri presented a bill proposing the separation of religion from state (Schnall, p. 70, n. 6).

64. In a semi-serious analogy Amir, borrowing from Jewish symbolism, says that if Ratosh is the "Moses" of "Canaanism," he sees himself not as its "Aaron" (as his name and his accommodating disposition indicate) but as its "Joshua," who would seek to implement the vision (author's interview with Aharon Amir, Dec.

12, 1983). See also Amir's *Prose* (Tel Aviv: Hadar Publishing Co., 1978, Hebrew), pp. 101 and 106.

65. Interview with Rael Jean Isaac, Jan. 28, 1970, cited in her *Israel Divided: Ideological Politics in the Jewish State* (Baltimore & London: The Johns Hopkins University Press, 1976), p. 52.

66. Ibid., p. 54. See also Avneri, *The War of the Seventh Day*, p. 170.

67. Isaac notes that the Action Staff for the Retention of the Territories was much more demonstrative than the Greater Land of Israel Movement. It was a fear of this activism that was one reason for the Laborites' opposition. "It was not without irony that one of the first activities of the anti-Jewish Canaanites was an effort on behalf of the . . . settlers (all religious) of the Etzion bloc and the circulation of propaganda for the establishment of *yeshivot* . . . in Hebron" (*Israel Divided*, p. 184, n. 23).

68. See I Kings 9 for the account of the ties between Solomon and Hiram of Tyre.

69. *Lebanon: A Land, A People, A War* (Tel Aviv: Hadar Publishing Co., 1979, Hebrew). See p. 202.

70. The following material was related to me by Amir in my interview with him.

71. Amir says he deduced the reason why Weizman must have been opposed to the project from a book Weizman subsequently wrote. He is no doubt referring to Weizman's *The Battle for Peace* (New York & London: Bantam Books, 1981), where in assessing Operation Litani he writes:

> I did my utmost to assist the Lebanese Christian minority. Nevertheless, I differ with many Israelis in my belief that our future depends on links with the Muslim world whose hundreds of millions of believers surround us on all sides. It would be an error for Israel to rely overmuch on ties with other Middle East minorities just because we, too, are a minority in the region, with supposed interests in common. Our exceptional attitude toward the Lebanese Christians is for humanitarian reasons; being a minority ourselves, we cannot bear to see the . . . suffering of another minority. As a Jew and as a member of the human race, I found it hard to hear half a million Lebanese Christians begging for help . . . while the Christian world— including the Vatican—remained silent. (P. 280)

72. For a full presentation of this issue with respect to Israeli Arabs, see Ian Lustick, *Arabs in the Jewish State: Israel's Control of a National Minority*, Modern Middle East Series, no. 6, sponsored by the Center for Middle Eastern Studies, University of Texas at Austin (Austin & London: University of Texas Press, 1980).

73. Aharon Amir observes that the Camp David agreement with Egypt was tragic in one respect: it turned the Sinai into a buffer and a barrier between the two countries when the region could have been disposed of more imaginatively as an area cooperatively shared and developed (author's interview).

74. See MP, p. 171. In this respect Ratosh and the anti-Zionist religionists of Neturei Karta are in substantial agreement.

75. E, p. 207.

76. Eliezer Schweid, "A Question of Identity," in *Yedi'ot Aharonot*, October 22, 1976. In another place Schweid notes that the values his own definition implies are upheld more in the breach than in actuality; see "Identification with the Jewish People in Israeli Education" (Jerusalem: the Institute of Contemporary Jewry, the Hebrew University, 1973, Hebrew). This paper (presented to the study circle on Diaspora Jewry at the home of the then President of Israel, Zalman Shazar), plus the introduction by Moshe Davis and the excerpts from the discussion that followed, are valuable testimony to the pervasiveness of a latent

"Canaanite" attitude toward the Diaspora within Israeli society in spite of the Zionist educational system and its "Jewish consciousness" program.

77. "The Interests of American Jewry," *Alef*, 1967. The quotation is from the mimeographed English translation of the Hebrew original that was published on June 5, 1967. The author is one E. Hadad, which may be a pseudonym for either Ratosh or Ornan.

78. This citation as well as those in subsequent paragraphs are drawn from my interview with Aharon Amir.

79. The lead editorial of *Alef*, no. 15 (Sept. 1952), called for a "Second Revolution." It notes that the first revolution succeeded in ousting the British and was fought without any formulated ideology for the simple purpose of gaining a state. Now this second revolution needs to transpire with clear goals: to fight the drift toward exclusiveness, theocracy, and *"shnorrerism"* in the new state. This piece was written against the background of the Naguib revolution in Egypt, which must have encouraged the "Canaanites" to think that the Zionist regime they saw as corrupt could also be overthrown. See also *Alef*, no. 16 (Oct.–Nov. 1952) and no. 19 (April 1953). Uri Avneri, writing in 1969, says that his *"Bama'avak* group sought to precipitate a revolution in Israel, but "today it is clear that this revolution will continue at least a whole generation, and Israel's fate hinges on its success. This revolution is inevitable, the necessary outcome of the new reality created in Israel in the wake of the Zionist revolution . . ." (*The War of the Seventh Day*, p. 180).

80. Shin Shifra in the *Keshet* symposium.

81. Ezra Zohar, *In the Vise of the Regime: Why Has No One Risen Up?* 3d ed. (Jerusalem: Shikmona, 1975, Hebrew), p. 173. Emphasis is Zohar's.

82. In the elections for the eleventh Knesset in 1984, Zohar headed a one-man ticket that ran on the platform of abolishing the income tax. Like many other single-issue candidates, he got less than 1.2 percent of the vote and thus failed to qualify for a seat.

83. See the last interviews with Z. Stavi, *Yedi'ot Aharonot*, Feb. 27, 1981, and with Natan Zach, *Monitin*, May 1981, p. 85. Both are in Hebrew.

84. These details were related to me by Aharon Amir in my interview with him.

85. Amos Kenan, interview with Dan Omer, p. 11.

VI: "Canaanism" and the Israeli Artistic Imagination

1. Ratosh never really differentiated the agendas his thought implies into political and cultural facets. The distinction is mine, made strictly as a heuristic device. I am persuaded, though, that Ratosh's thought is preponderantly directed at sociopolitical and not esthetic issues. Of the 24-point program of the Center for Young Hebrews, only the last item speaks to the cultural issue explicitly. Further, Ratosh's utterances on "Hebrew" literature were formulated at the outset of statehood and, unlike some of the sociopolitical issues, did not take root in later years in Hebrew cultural or literary theory. There is thus less "Canaanite" material to present on cultural issues than on the ones described in preceding chapters.

2. Gid'on Efrat Friedlander, "Canaanites Without Canaan," *Davar*, Sept. 17, 1982, Hebrew.

3. See Ami Shin'ar, "And The Canaanite Was in the Land—Then and Now," *Ha'arets*, July 18, 1980, Hebrew.

4. See *Our New Literature: Continuity Or Revolt?* 3d enlarged ed. (Jerusalem & Tel Aviv: Schocken Publishing Co., 1959, 1971, Hebrew), p. 274. Shavit overlooks Tammuz's *The Orchard* and points only to his "Holot hazahav" (The golden

sands). As another example he identifies the work of Medad Schiff (see p. 156 and also p. 244 n. 28).

5. Ramat Gan: Sifriat Makor, Agudat Hasoferim, & Massada Publishing Co., 1969, Hebrew. This is the first part of a planned trilogy. Nun is the quintessential Hebrew hero. Note the symbolism of his name: Nun was Joshua's father. Amir draws on autobiographical memories of the 1936 Arab riots in Jaffa but he objectifies his protagonist somewhat by making him a few years older than himself. The second part, entitled *Nun '48*, appeared in 1985. Amir's two other novels, both in Hebrew, are less obviously related to "Canaanism": *And Death Shall Have No Dominion* (1955) and *A Better World* (1979).

6. There probably are other minor poets who sought to imitate Ratosh. Yisra'el Eliraz names Eitan Eitan and Varda Ginossar as examples; see "'Canaanism' in the Israeli Theater," *Yedi'ot Aharonot*, Aug. 1, 1980, Hebrew.

7. This is, however, not the whole story. A theater of protest has flourished in Israel (e.g., the *te'atron hazirah* [The Circle Theater] in the fifties). Eliraz correctly notes the resurgence of this tendency in the wake of the uncertainty about Zionism that has prevailed since the 1973 war. The work of such dramatists as Hanokh Levin, Hillel Mittelpunkt, and Yehoshua Sobol, while not "Canaanite" in the strict sense of the term, can and should be seen as the expression in drama of the phenomenon of individuals from the left moving to a critique of Zionism similar to that of Ratosh. Sobol's play *Nefesh yehudi* (The soul of a Jew: The last night of Otto Weininger, 1982), in its linkage of Zionism and Judaism, seems to me to be particularly close to Ratosh's arguments.

8. Eliraz, "'Canaanism' in the Israeli Theater."

9. Nili Neumann, "Questions of the Relationships of Art and Locale," *Kav* 4/5 (Nov. 1982, Hebrew): 3. See also Gid'on Efrat (Friedlander), *Here: On a Different Localism in Israeli Art* (Jerusalem: Amanut Yisrael Publishing Co., 1984, Hebrew).

10. See the opening editorial statement in the very first issue of *Alef* (1948). This is reprinted in *Prozah* (Aug–Sept. 1977, Hebrew). See also Aharon Amir, "Basic Assumptions in the Building of a Hebrew Culture," *Alef*, no. 17 (Dec. 1952, Hebrew): 8–10, and the youthful attempts by Sha'ul Eshba'al [Sha'ul Migron] to define the content of "Canaanite" culture in *Alef*, no. 18 (Feb. 1953) and no. 19 (April 1953).

11. See Binyamin Tammuz's vignette about his apprenticeship as a sculptor with Danziger in "Between Eden and Ophir," in *Alef* (Spring 1948, Hebrew), reprinted in *Prozah* (Aug–Sept. 1977): 30. Also note M. Jana, "Let There Be Sculpture," *Alef*, no. 4 (Aug. 1950, Hebrew): 12. In his introduction to *Art in Israel* (n.p., Massada, 1963) Tammuz says the effect of the prohibition in the second commandment in stifling the plastic arts among Jews should not be overstated. It is rather the objective historical experience of Diaspora that has vitiated a deep relationship to the spatial and to the material (p. 7). For a good discussion of the relationship of "Canaanism" to Israeli sculpture, see Yig'al Tsalmonah, "The Past Is the Present—The Canaanites," *Kav* 4/5 (Nov. 1982, Hebrew): 50–57.

12. Amos Kenan, interview with Dan Omer, *Prozah* (Aug.–Sept. 1977, Hebrew): 7. Kenan believes that the ultimate significance of *Alef* was linguistic: the fledgling writers who tried their literary wings within its pages wrote a Hebrew that made the language of Oz and Yehoshua possible. "I repeat: colloquial Hebrew was first written in '48 and not one day before that, and not one day before it was written in *Alef*." For an indication that Ratosh and Amir were aware of their roles as catalysts of a linguistic revolution see "Who Are The People? Linguistic Observations," *Alef*, no. 7 (Jan. 1951, Hebrew): 10.

13. "Israeli Literature or a Trans-Jewish Literature?" in *Jewish Literature in the Hebrew Language,* ed. Shin Shifra (Tel Aviv: Hadar Publishing Co., 1982, Hebrew), pp. 46f.

14. In making its polyglot character an aspect of a "Jewish" literary norm, Ratosh anticipates Cynthia Ozick's ideas worked out in her essay "Toward a New Yiddish," in *Art and Ardor* (New York: Knopf, 1983), pp. 154–77. Where the two part company is in their estimation of this norm. What to Ratosh is provincial is to Ozick the epitome of universalism.

15. The tension between the spatial and the temporal may underlie the sensibility of uprootedness (the *"talush"* figure) that is so pervasive in Hebrew fiction of the early twentieth century, when the "negation of Diaspora" motif was at its height.

16. Ratosh, "Israeli Literature or a Trans-Jewish Literature?" p. 47.

17. "Jewish Literature in the Hebrew Language," in Shifra, *Jewish Literature in the Hebrew Language,* p. 40. This essay originally appeared in *Alef* of January, 1950.

18. Ibid.

19. Ratosh's proposal was explained to me in these terms by Boaz Evron. See also Ratosh's third interview with Z. Stavi in *Yedi'ot Aharonot,* Feb. 27, 1981, Hebrew. One would think that Ratosh would cling to the "Assyrian" script because of its historical connection to the prebiblical past. That he does not is further evidence that the "Hebrew" past is not a decisive factor in his thought. Perhaps the "Assyrian" script was too identified with the particularism of Jewish religion to connote the kind of distinctiveness Ratosh had in mind, and so he would drop it in favor of the universal Latin characters.

20. Less successful and accepted was the turgid Hebrew terminology that resulted from Ratosh's translation of Wellek and Warren's *Theory of Literature.* Here what Ratosh thought was universal was actually very particular.

21. See interview with Z. Stavi. Ratosh notes there that he would regularly check editions of *Ha'arets* for examples of this encroachment and claims to have found 300 foreign words in it on any given day. He is willing to use a foreign word if it is readily assimilable into Hebrew grammatical forms. Years later Amir initiated a protest against the reliance on English textbooks in Israeli universities and encouraged students to demand course material only in Hebrew (see *Ma'ariv,* Nov. 13, 1979).

22. Interview with Shin Shifra, *Davar,* Aug. 27, 1971, Hebrew.

23. Ibid. See also "Jewish Literature in the Hebrew Language," p. 40.

24. "Israeli Literature or a Trans-Jewish Literature?" p. 47.

25. See Peninah Meislish's interview with Amir, "Why I Am Closing Down *Keshet,*" *Yedi'ot Aharonot,* Nov. 26, 1976, Hebrew. In my interview with him, Amir notes that he helped fund *Keshet* in part from his own money. It was only in *Keshet*'s latter years that he agreed to accept money from the government's cultural budget for a portion of the review's support revenue.

26. Ratosh, "Jewish Literature in the Hebrew Language," p. 39.

27. See, for example, *Our New Literature: Continuity or Revolt?* 3d rev. ed. (Jerusalem & Tel Aviv: Schocken Publishing Co., 1971, Hebrew), pp. 11–146.

28. See discussion in James S. Diamond, *Barukh Kurzweil and Modern Hebrew Literature,* Brown Judaic Studies Series (Chico, California: Scholars Press, 1983), pp. 105–10.

29. Interview with Z. Stavi, *Yedi'ot Aharonot,* Feb. 27, 1981, Hebrew. See also Diamond, *Barukh Kurzweil,* pp. 101ff.

30. See Shin Shifra's introduction to *Jewish Literature in the Hebrew Language,* pp. 7–17.

31. See Dov Sadan, "On Our Literature," in *Testing Stones: On Our Literature, Its Basis and Currents* (Tel Aviv: Ha-Kibbutz Ha-Me'uhad, 1962, Hebrew), pp. 9–66.

32. Dan Miron, "Modern Hebrew Literature: Zionist Perspectives and Israeli Realities," *Prooftexts* 4:1 (Jan. 1984): 64.

33. Ibid.

34. B. Kurzweil, "The Nature and Origins of the 'Young Hebrews' (Canaanite) Movement," in *Our New Literature: Continuity or Revolt?* pp. 276f.

35. Interview with Dan Omer, *Prozah*, p. 8.

36. Author's interview with Hayim Guri, January 6, 1984. Guri describes himself culturally as a "millionaire."

37. Miron, in *Prooftexts*, p. 49.

38. Amos Kenan, interview with Dan Omer, *Prozah*, pp. 11f.

39. For an adumbration of this posture, see Ya'akov Shabtai, "On The Sabra and Sensitivity," in *M'oznayim* 57:5–6 (Oct.–Nov. 1983, Hebrew): 17f., and the dramatic works mentioned above, note 7. See also my discussion "The Israeli Writer as Moral Resource," in *The Reconstructionist* 49:1 (Oct. 1983): 15–18.

VII: Conclusions

1. See Charles S. Liebman & Eliezer Don-Yehiya, *Civil Religion in Israel: Traditional Judaism and Political Culture in the Jewish State* (Berkeley, Los Angeles & London: University of California Press, 1983), pp. 214–17.

2. Ibid., p. 215.

3. See Eliezer Schweid, "A Question of Identity," *Yedi'ot Aharonot*, October 22, 1976, Hebrew.

4. Ibid.

5. P. 171.

6. The essence of a footnote is precisely its relevance to the text.

7. Shemu'el Almog, *Zionism and History* (Jerusalem: The Magnes Press of the Hebrew University, 1982, Hebrew), p. 79.

8. It is possible to argue that in Judaism the distinction between the secular and the religious is arbitrary and illusory, and therefore one should avoid drawing any conclusions based upon it. It seems to me that this argument is itself a circular one, for it can only be made from religious premises. In the *havdalah* ceremony, which marks the transition from the sacred time of the Sabbath day to the six secular days *(hol)*, it is affirmed that it is God who makes the distinction, not man. To the religionist nothing is intrinsically secular, but to the secularist the sacred is unverifiable and possibly an illusion. The problem at bottom, then, is one not of philosophy and policy but of epistemology.

9. In that essay Scholem writes: ". . . behind the extravaganzas of the so-called 'Canaanites' who demand to be heard among us, one finds the genuine problem of which I have previously spoken [in the two metaphors]. The question to which that problem can be reduced, and which we encounter everywhere, is . . . : what are we first and foremost, Jews or Israelis? It is evident that this question is of decisive significance for the relationship between Israel and the Diaspora. It leads to a parting of minds" ("Israel and the Diaspora," in *On Jews and Judaism in Crisis: Selected Essays*, ed. Werner J. Dannhauser [New York: Schocken Books, 1976], p. 257).

10. F. Nietzsche, *On the Advantage and Disadvantage of History for Life*, trans. Peter Preuss (Indianapolis & Cambridge: Hackett Publishing Co., 1980), pp. 11ff. See also Paul de Man, "Literary History and Literary Modernity," in *In Search of Literary Theory*, ed. Morton W. Bloomfield (Ithaca & London: Cornell University Press, 1972), pp. 243ff.

11. Uri Tsvi Greenberg, *Rehovot hanahar* (The streets of the river) (Jerusalem & Tel Aviv: Schocken Publishing Co., 1951, Hebrew), p. 37. See James S. Diamond, *Barukh Kurzweil and Modern Hebrew Literature*, Brown Judaic Studies Series (Chico, California: Scholars Press, 1983), pp. 31–36.

12. See Diamond, p. 120, and also Yosef Hayim Yerushalmi, *Zakhor: Jewish History and Jewish Memory* (Seattle & London: University of Washington Press, 1982).

13. Amos Oz, *In the Land of Israel*, trans. Maurie Goldberg-Bartura (San Diego, New York & London: Harcourt Brace Jovanovich, 1983), p. 9.

14. Ibid., p. 19.

15. E, pp. 218f. For a recent description of the details of the "psychology of dependence" and its relation to the perpetual crisis in the Israeli economy, see Lawrence Meyer, *Israel Now: Portrait of a Troubled Land* (New York: Delacorte Press, 1982), pp. 96–151, especially pp. 133ff.

16. In 1984 a small group organized under the "Canaanite" name and symbol in, of all places, Kiryat Shemonah. Its announced aim was to work for a secular democratic Israeli society. The group held a public program observing the third anniversary of Ratosh's death and attempted to call attention to the problems raised by the interpenetration of religion and state in Israel (related to me by Dr. Uzi Ornan). At the present time this occurrence cannot be regarded as anything more than a historical curiosity.

Excursus: "Canaanism" and the Reconstruction of Zionism: The Case for a Secular Israel

1. My argument here derives from my own interpretation of "Canaanism." As such it has some general affinities to what is advanced in two works by Israeli writers. The first is Yosef Agassi's *Between Religion and Nation: Toward an Israeli National Identity* (Tel Aviv: Papyrus Press, Tel Aviv University, 1984, Hebrew). Agassi bases his views on the "Canaanism" of Hillel Kook (Peter Bergson). The second is Amnon Rubinstein's *The Zionist Dream Revisited: From Herzl to Gush Emunim and Back* (New York: Schocken Books, 1984). See above, chapter 5, n. 27. Compare also Isaiah Leibowitz, who likewise propounds the necessity of a secular Israel but from directly opposing premises. See above, chapter 2, n. 67.

2. Author's interview with Aharon Amir, Dec. 12, 1983.

3. Author's interview with Dr. Uzi Ornan, Dec. 21, 1983.

4. See Daniel Gavron, *Israel after Begin* (Boston: Houghton Mifflin Co., 1984), pp. 181–99.

5. Quoted in David J. Schnall, *Radical Dissent in Contemporary Israeli Politics: Cracks in the Wall*, Praeger Special Studies (New York: Praeger, 1979), p. 65.

6. Lawrence Meyer, *Israel Now: Portrait of a Troubled Land* (New York: Delacorte Press, 1982), p. 387.

7. Noted in Dan V. Segre, *A Crisis of Identity: Israel and Zionism* (Oxford: Oxford University Press, 1980), p. 133.

8. To be sure, the removal of "Zion" as a religious-eschatological ideal from the ideology renders the term "Zionism" an absurdity. But I think the name is too entrenched. In any case the issue here is not nomenclature.

9. Amos Oz, *In the Land of Israel*, trans. Maurie Goldberg-Bartura (San Diego, New York & London: Harcourt Brace Jovanovich, 1983), pp. 17f.

10. Author's interview with Dr. Uzi Ornan.

11. This is one of Eliezer Schweid's arguments against "Canaanism." See "A Question of Identity," *Yedi'ot Aharonot*, October 22, 1976, Hebrew.

12. An example of this potential repression is the "archaeology law" that the Agudat Yisra'el faction has been seeking to introduce in the Knesset. If passed it

would severely impair the freedom of archaeologists to excavate anything in Israel for fear of disturbing Jewish graves. I have no doubt that the implementation of this law would, in time, lead to other restrictions of other kinds of scientific inquiry and eventually of artistic expression as well.

13. For a fictive projection of what Israel as a theocracy might look like, see Binyamin Tammuz's recent anti-utopian novel, *Jeremiah's Inn* (Jerusalem: Keter Publishing Co., 1984, Hebrew). This is set in the middle of the twenty-first century, when Jerusalem is under the rule of a reestablished Sanhedrin and secularists are a persecuted minority.

14. Various models for such a text-centered Diaspora life existed in Europe. Within Orthodoxy we can look back to the great yeshivot of Eastern and Central Europe. Within non-Orthodoxy the efforts of Franz Rosenzweig and Martin Buber in Germany between the two world wars are the most suggestive. See Rosenzweig's *On Jewish Learning*, ed. N. Glatzer (New York: Schocken Books, 1955). In North America the yeshivah endures as a viable institution for the nourishment of Jewish text study out of the canons of Orthodoxy. For a superior presentation of non-Orthodox approaches to the Jewish literary tradition, see *Back to the Sources: Reading the Classic Jewish Texts*, ed. Barry W. Holtz (New York: Summit Books, 1984).

15. For an exposition of this idea, see Michael Selzer, *The Wineskin and the Wizard* (New York: Macmillan, 1970), and for a forceful pressing of the underlying theological issues, see Steven S. Schwarzschild, "On the Theology of Jewish Survival," *CCAR Journal* 15:4 (October 1968): 2–21. See also Arthur Hertzberg, "The Lessons of Emancipation," in *Diaspora: Exile and the Jewish Condition*, ed. Etan Levine (New York & London: Jason Aronson, 1983), pp. 85–92. Hertzberg writes:

> There still remains the question . . . of . . . why desire survival as a discrete people? In the name of what? Two centuries of intellectual modernity in all its varieties prove one simple conclusion: universalist ideas such as democracy and socialism have not provided those Jews who have been their proponents with any long-range reason for remaining within a distinctly Jewish community. Ultimately, even if disguised as secular rhetoric, the reason for continuing a distinctly Jewish community has been religious. I suspect that many more Jews believe in the God who chose them than are willing to affirm that He also commanded them to be obedient to every stricture of the *Halakhah*. Jewish disbelief is not of the variety that asserts "let us be like all the other nations." It wants to assert the divinely ordained mystery of Jewish existence without quite knowing what to do with the inherited law. The true watershed in Jewish life in the modern age is between those who share in awe at this otherness and those who would abandon it or forget it. It is only to the degree to which such a conviction is alive that Jewish existence continues. (P. 91).

16. See Charles S. Liebman & Eliezer Don-Yehiya, *Civil Religion in Israel: Traditional Judaism and Political Culture in the Jewish State* (Berkeley, Los Angeles & London: University of California Press, 1983), pp. 10–12. See also Ian Lustick, *Arabs in the Jewish State: Israel's Control of a National Minority* (Austin & London: University of Texas Press, 1980), pp. 266–71. Lustick concludes his study thus:

> In the absence of a political base for a Jewish leadership committed to changing the fundamental terms of the relationship between Jews and Arabs in Israel, the guided transformation of Israel toward a consociational or pluralist society will not take place. However, if control over the minority breaks down, accompanied either by the crystallization of a mass-based Arab political organization with electoral and economic bargaining power or by widespread violent protest, a radical reassessment of the position of Arabs in Israel will be required. Under such circumstances

pluralist or consociational futures could become relevant; on the other hand, so might the possibility, now discussed publicly only in ultranationalist circles, of eliminating the problem through mass expulsions. (P. 271)

17. Oz, *In the Land of Israel,* p. 18.
18. Ibid., p. 226. Emphasis is mine.
19. Ibid., pp. 239f.
20. *1967—And What Next?* (Tel Aviv: Hadar Publishing Co., 1967, Hebrew), p. 84.

GLOSSARY

Agudat Yisra'el—Lit. Association of Israel. An ultra-Orthodox religious party. Originally contained both anti-Zionist and non-Zionist elements, today largely non-Zionist.

Aliyah—Lit. ascent. Immigration to Israel or a specific wave of immigration.

Berit Shalom—Lit. Covenant of Peace. A Jewish organization in Palestine in the late twenties and early thirties that advocated Jewish-Arab cooperation in Palestine in a manner that would lead to a binational state.

Betar—Abb. of Berit Trumpeldor. Zionist youth movement in Eastern Europe. Formed in 1923 and flourished in the thirties. Its ideology was modeled on the thought of Jabotinsky and the personal example of Joseph Trumpeldor. Closely allied with Revisionist party.

Biluim—Acronym for "Bet ya'akov lekhu venelkhah" ("O House of Jacob, let us go forth," *Isaiah* 2:5). Russian Jews who settled in Palestine in the 1880s.

Diaspora—Jewish life and communities outside the land and State of Israel.

Golah—Lit. Exile. Refers to same thing as "Diaspora" but in a pejorative sense.

Gush Emunim—Lit. Bloc of the Faithful. Jewish settlement effort begun in 1970s aimed at populating the West Bank and thus returning Jews to biblically mandated areas.

Haganah—Lit. defense. The Jewish defense corps founded in 1921. Later became the backbone of the Israeli Defense Forces.

Halakhah—Jewish religious law.

Hazon Ish—Rabbi Avraham Yeshayahu Karelitz (1878–1953). Eminent European Talmudic scholar and rabbinic figure. Settled in Palestine in 1933 and was consulted by David Ben Gurion on many halakhic matters.

Herut—Lit. freedom. The political party of Revisionist Zionism.

Histadrut—Abb. of Histadrut ha'ovdim be'erets yisra'el (Israeli Workers Federation).

Kashrut—The Jewish dietary laws.

Knesset—Lit. assembly. Israel's legislative parliament of 120 elected members.

Mapai—Acronym for Mifleget po'alei erets yisra'el (Israeli Workers Party). A socialist Labor Zionist party dominant until 1977.

Mapam—Acronym for Mifleget po'alim me'uhedet (United Workers Party). A Marxist Labor Zionist party.

Mizrachi—Acronym for Merkaz ruhani (Spiritual Center). An Orthodox religious Zionist party.

Musar school—A nineteenth-century movement in Lithuanian yeshivot that sought to promote inwardness and spiritual and ethical growth in the individual.

Neturei Karta—Lit. Guardians of the City (Aramaic). Ultra-Orthodox Jews who regard Zionism as a Jewish heresy and the secular State of Israel as illegitimate. Originally part of Agudat Yisra'el.

Palmah—Acronym for Pelugot mahats (Strike Forces). An elite unit of the Haganah founded in 1941, it played a key role in the 1948 War for Israeli Independence. After 1948 it became part of the Israel Defense Forces.

Rabbi Meir Ba'al Haness—Lit. Rabbi Meir the miracle worker. A figure of uncertain historical background around whose grave in Tiberias grew legends about miracles. It has long been considered meritorious to contribute to the fund established for the grave's upkeep as a protection against illness and misfortune. A coin box for this fund was common in traditional Jewish homes as a symbol of the tie to the Land of Israel.

Rebbe—A Hasidic rabbi and/or master.

Schnorrer—Beggar (Yiddish).

Shalom 'Akhshav—Lit. Peace Now. The Israeli peace movement.

Shin Bet—Abb. for Sherut bitahon (Security Service). The Israeli security and counterintelligence agency.

Shinui—Lit. change. An Israeli political party begun by Amnon Rubinstein after 1973 war. Advocates secular democratic ideals. United with Yig'al Yadin's Democratic Party to form the Movement for Democratic Change.

Shtreimel—A round fur hat worn by Hasidic Jewish men on Sabbath and holy days.

Tanakh—The Hebrew Bible. Acronym for "Torah, Nevi'im, Ketuvim" (the Pentateuch, the Prophetic books, and the Writings).

Yeridah—Lit. descent. Emigration from Israel.

Yeshivah—An academy for rabbinical studies. Plural: yeshivot.

Yiddishkeit—Yiddishism for Judaism, Jewish life and/or values.

Yishuv—Lit. settlement. The Jewish community in Palestine before Israeli statehood. The term "old Yishuv" is commonly used to refer to the Jewish community of the nineteenth-century, before the advent of the Zionist movement; the term "new Yishuv" is used to denote the community and society that resulted from Zionist activity and immigration in the twentieth century.

SELECTED BIBLIOGRAPHY

Abramov, S. Zalman. *Perpetual Dilemma: Jewish Religion in the Jewish State.* Rutherford, Madison & Teaneck, N.J.: Fairleigh Dickinson University Press, 1976.

Agassi, Yosef. *Bein dat vile'om: likr'at zehut le'umit yisra'elit* (Between religion and nation: Toward an Israeli national identity). Tel Aviv: Papyrus Press, Tel Aviv University, 1984.

Ahime'ir, Yosef, and Shemu'el Shatsky, eds. *Hinenu sikrikim: 'eduyot umismakhim 'al berit habiryonim* (We are Sicarii: Testimonies and documents on the Berit Habiryonim). [Tel Aviv]: Nitsanim Publishing Co., 1978.

Alef. Four unnumbered issues: April 1948, November 1948, October 1949, January 1950; 1 (Spring 1950), 2 (May 1950), 3 (June–July 1950), 4 (August 1950), 5 (October 1950), 6 (November–December 1950), 7 (January 1951), 8 (May 1951), 9 (June 1951), 10 (September 1951), 11 (November 1951), 12 (January 1952), 13 (March 1952), 14 (July 1952), 15 (September 1952), 16 (October–November 1952), 17 (December 1952), 18 (February 1953), 19 (April 1953); special issue: June 5, 1967.

Almog, Shemu'el. *Tsiyonut vehistoriah* (Zionism and history). Jerusalem: The Magnes Press, Hebrew University, 1982.

Amir, Aharon. *Ahavah: sippurim* (Love: Stories). Tel Aviv: Mahbarot Lesifrut Publishing Co., 5712 [1952].

———. *Velo tehi lemavet memshalah* (And death shall have no dominion). Tel Aviv: Tsohar Publishing Co., 1955.

———. "B'ati likebor et hasimposiyon" (I have come to bury the symposium. Remarks at Anglo-Jewish-Israeli writers' conference). *M'oznayim* 23 (Elul 5726–Tishri 5727) [September–October 1966]: 377–78.

———. *Nun: o do'h 'al tsir'ah ke'ish tsa'ir* (Nun: Or report on a wasp as a young man). Ramat Gan: Sifriat Makor, Agudat Hasoferim Publishing Co., & Massadah Publishing Co., 1969.

———. *Prozah* (Prose). Tel Aviv: Yariv Publications & Hadar Publishing Co., 1978.

———. *'Olam shekulo tov: roman* (A better world: A novel). [Tel Aviv]: Massadah Publishing Co., 1979.

———. "Yonatan Ratosh: hapiyuti vehapoliti" (Yonatan Ratosh: The poetic and the political). *Davar,* January 9, 1981.

———. "Purah darakhti levadi" (I trod out a vineyard alone. On Ratosh's death). *Ha'arets,* April 3, 1981.

———. "MeRomi—le'Ever veliKena'an" (From Rome—to 'Ever and Canaan. Review of Shavit's book). *Ha'arets,* April 6, 1984.

———, ed. *Avshalom: ketavim umikhtavim* (Avshalom Feinberg: Papers and letters. With monographic introduction by editor). Haifa: Shikmona Publishing Co., 1971.

———, ed. *Levanon: erets, 'am, milhamah* (Lebanon: A land, a people, a war. A reader). Tel Aviv: Hadar Publishing Co., 1979.

Ammi-Horon [Adolphe Gourevitch?]. "Perspectives du Mouvement National Hebreu." *Shem: Revue d'Action Hebraique* 1 (June 1939): 60–77.

Aschman, Ya'akov. "Lamut—aval ba'ad mah?" (To die—but for what?). *Alef* [Spring 1949]. Reprinted in *Prozah* (August–September 1977): 28–29.

Atar, Moshe. "Halomam hamatok shel ha'kena'anim'" (The sweet dream of the "Canaanites." Review of N). *Ha'arets,* November 12, 1976.

Avineri, Shlomo. *The Making of Modern Zionism: The Intellectual Origins of the Jewish State.* New York: Basic Books, 1981.

Avneri, Uri. *Milhamah o shalom bamerhav hashemi* (War or peace in the Semitic world). Tel Aviv: Political Department of the Young Palestine Association, October 1947.

———. *Israel Without Zionists: A Plea for Peace in the Middle East.* New York & London: The Macmillan Co. & Collier Macmillan Ltd., 1968.

———. *Milhemet hayom hashevi'i* (The war of the seventh day. Hebrew version of the preceding volume). Jerusalem: Daf Hadash Publishing Co., 1969.

———. "Ha'emet 'al ha'kena'anim'" (The truth about the "Canaanites"). *Ha'olam hazeh,* no. 766. Reprinted in *Prozah* (August–September 1977): 26–27.

Barzel, Hillel. *Meshorerei besorah* (Essays on modern Hebrew poets). Yahdav Publication Co., 1983.

Ben Ezer, Ehud, ed. *Unease in Zion.* New York: Quadrangle/N.Y. Times Book Co., 1974.

Brenner, Y. S. "The 'Stern Gang' 1940–48." *Middle Eastern Studies* 2:1 (October 1965): 2–30.

Brenner, Yosef Hayim. *See* Yosef Haver.

Bronovsky, Yoram. "Yonatan Ratosh: uvekhol z'ot meruah hashirah" (Yonatan Ratosh: A poet nevertheless). *Ha'arets,* February 3, 1984.

Cohen, Avner. "Hazehut hayehudit keparadoks: he'arot beshulei motiv yashan-hadash" (Jewish identity as paradox: Marginal notes on an old-new motif). *Davar,* September 10, 1980.

———. "Hazehut hayehudit keparadoks: milkud 'hatsiyonut hashefuyah'" (Jewish identity as paradox: The trap of 'sane Zionism'). *Davar,* September 19, 1980.

Cohen, Yisra'el. "Teshuvah leAmir" (A response to Amir. At Anglo-Jewish-Israeli writers conference). *M'oznayim* 23 (Elul 5726–Tishri 5727) [September–October 1966]: 378–79.

Davies, W. D. *The Territorial Dimension of Judaism.* Berkeley, Los Angeles & London: The University of California Press, 1982.

Diamond, James S. *Barukh Kurzweil and Modern Hebrew Literature.* Brown Judaic Studies Series. Chico, California: Scholars Press, 1983.

———. "The Israeli Writer as Moral Resource." *Reconstructionist* 49:1 (October 1983): 15–18.

Efrat [Friedlander], Gid'on. "Kena'anim beli kena'an" (Canaanites without Canaan). *Davar,* September 17, 1982.

———. *K'an: 'al mekomiyut aheret be'amanut yisra'el* (Here: On a different localism in Israeli art). Jerusalem: Amanut Yisra'el Publishing Co., 1984.

"El shoreshei hadevarim" (To the roots of things. Symposium after the 1973 War). *Keshet* 62 (Winter 1974): 5–48.

Elam, Yig'al. *Mav'o lehistoriah aheret* (An alternative introduction to Zionist history). Tel Aviv: Lewin-Epstein Publishing Co., [1972].

Elazar, Daniel J., ed. *Kinship and Consent: The Jewish Political Tradition and Its Contemporary Uses.* Washington, D.C.: University Press of America & The Center for Jewish Community Studies, 1983.

Eliraz, Yisra'el. "Ha'kena'aniyut' bete'atron hayisra'eli" ("Canaanism" in the Israeli theater). *Yedi'ot Aharonot,* August 1, 1980.

Evron, Boaz. "Mizmor liyonatan" (A paean to Yonatan. On the 40th anniversary of the publication of *Huppah shehorah*). *Yedi'ot Aharonot,* January 30, 1981.

————. "Israel After Zionism." *The Nation* 273:19 (December 5, 1981): 597–601.

————. "Hama'aseh—ubavu'ato ha'akademit: (The event—and its academic reflection. Review of Shavit's book). *Yedi'ot Aharonot*, March 2, 1984.

Fisch, Harold. *The Zionist Revolution: A New Perspective*. New York: St. Martin's Press, 1978.

Fish, Har'el [Harold Fisch]. *Tsiyonut shel tsiyon* (The Zionism of Zion. Hebrew version of the preceding volume). Tel Aviv: Zemorah Biton Publishing Co., 1982.

Frank, Gerald. *The Deed*. New York: Simon & Schuster, 1963.

Friedmann, Georges. *The End of the Jewish People?* Translated from French by Eric Mosbacher. Garden City, N.Y.: Doubleday, 1967.

Gavron, Daniel. *Israel after Begin*. Boston: Houghton Mifflin Co., 1984.

Gonen, Jay Y. *A Psychohistory of Zionism*. New York: Mason/Charter, 1975.

Gour, A. [Adolphe Gourevitch]. "Hébreux et Juifs." *Shem: Revue d'Action Hébra ïque* 1 (June 1939): 7–28.

Grodzensky, Shlomo. *Tesumet-lev: ma'amrim ureshimot be'inyanei hevrah* (Considerations: Political and social essays). Tel Aviv: Hakibbutz Hame'uhad, 1975.

Guri, Hayim. "Perakim mividui hatsot" (Chapters from a confession at midnight). *Ma'ariv*, December 26, 1975.

————. "Hasha'ah hakena'anit" (The Canaanite hour). *Ma'ariv*, September 24, 1980.

————. "Hanekhed vehamanginah" (The grandson and the melody). *Ma'ariv*, October 31, 1980.

————. "Hakefel vehaker'a" (The duality and the chasm). *Ma'ariv*, n.d., 1980.

————. "Hakeri'ah el ha'ivriyim" (The call to the Hebrews). *Davar*, n.d., 1983.

————. "Anahnu hamekomiyim" (We the homeborn). *Davar*, July 13, 1984. English translation by Stanley F. Chyet in *Moment* 10:7 (July–August 1985): 13–16.

Halkin, Hillel. *Letters to an American Jewish Friend: A Zionist's Polemic*. Philadelphia: The Jewish Publication Society, 1977.

Halpern, Ben. *The Idea of a Jewish State*. 2d ed. Cambridge, Mass.: Harvard University Press, 1969.

Halpern, Uriel (*see also* Yonatan Ratosh). *Lakever Yishma'el* (To the grave of Ishma'el). Tel Aviv: "Ov" Publications, 1932.

Hartman, David. *Joy and Responsibility: Israel, Modernity and the Renewal of Judaism*. Jerusalem: Ben-Zvi-Posner Publishers & The Shalom Hartman Institute, 1978.

Haver, Yosef [Yosef Hayim Brenner]. "Ba'itonut uvasifrut" (In the press and in literature). *Hapo'el hatsa'ir* 4:3 (November 24, 1910).

Herman, Simon N. *Israelis and Jews: The Continuity of an Identity*. New York: Random House, 1970.

Hertzberg, Arthur, ed. *The Zionist Idea: A Historical Analysis and Reader*. New York & Philadelphia: Meridian Books & Jewish Publication Society, 1960.

Hochman, Baruch. "Cna'anim—A Study in Reaction." *Jerusalem Post*, February 13, 1953.

Hurvitz, Shai Ish. "Lish'elat kiyum hayahadut (hegiyonot vehirhurim)" (On the Question of Jewish Survival [Thoughts and Reflections]). *Hashiloah* 13(73–78) [January–June 1904]: 287–303.

Isaac, Rael Jean. *Israel Divided: Ideological Politics in the Jewish State*. Baltimore & London: The Johns Hopkins University Press, 1976.

————. *Party and Politics in Israel: Three Visions of a Jewish State*. New York & London: Longmans, 1981.

Jabotinsky, Eri. *Avi, Z'ev Jabotinsky* (My father, Z'ev Jabotinsky). Edited by Ya'akov

Shavit & Aharon Amir. Jerusalem, Tel Aviv & Haifa: Steimatzky Publishing Co., 1980.

Jabotinsky, Z'ev. "Yisra'el veKartago" (Israel and Carthage). *Hazit ha'am* 2 (February 2, 1932).

Kena'ani, David. *Ha'aliyah hasheniyah ha'ovedet veyahasah ledat velamasoret* (The Second Aliyah of labor and its relationship to religion and tradition). Institute for the Research of Labor and Society of Tel Aviv University, No. 4. Tel Aviv: Sifriyat Po'alim, 1976.

Kenan, Amos. Interview with Dan Omer. *Prozah* (August–September 1977): 4–13.

Kotser, Aryeh. *Marvad adom: darki 'im Ya'ir* (Red carpet: My path with Ya'ir). Tel Aviv: Makada Publishing Co., n.d.

Kraines, Oscar. *Impossible Dilemma: Who is a Jew in the Sate of Israel?* New York: Bloch Publishing Co., 1976.

Kurzweil, Barukh. "Mahutah umekorotehah shel tenu'at ha'ivriyim hatse'irim (Kena'anim)" (The nature and origins of the Young Hebrews [Canaanite] Movement). In *Lu'ah Ha'arets* 5713 [1952], pp. 107–29. Reprinted in Kurzweil, *Sifrutenu hahadashah* (see below), pp. 270–300. Condensed version in English translation by Theodore Friedman in *Judaism* 2:1 (January 1953): 2–15.

———. "Ha'uvdah habilti efsharit ('al ha'ivriyim hatse'irim)" (The impossible fact [on the Young Hebrews]). *Ha'arets,* October 24, 1952.

———. *Sifrutenu hahadashah: hemshekh o mahapekhah?* (Our new literature: Continuity or revolt?). 3d enlarged ed. Jerusalem & Tel Aviv: Schocken Publishing Co., 1971.

———. *Lenokhah hamevukhah haruhanit shel dorenu: pirkei hagut uvikoret* (Facing the spiritual perplexity of our time). Edited with an introduction by Moshe Schwarcz. Ramat Gan: Bar Ilan University & The Barukh Kurzweil Memorial Foundation, 1976.

La'or, Dan. "Lish'elat hahitkablut shel shirat Ratosh" (On the question of the reception of Ratosh's poetry). *Yedi'ot Aharonot,* January 30, 1981.

Laqueur, Walter. *A History of Zionism.* New York, Chicago & San Francisco: Holt, Rinehart & Winston, 1972.

Leibowitz, Isaiah. *Yahadut, 'am yehudi umedinat yisra'el* (Judaism, the Jewish people and the State of Israel). Jerusalem & Tel Aviv: Schocken Publishing Co., 1976.

Levine, Etan, ed. *Diaspora: Exile and the Jewish Condition.* New York & London: Jason Aronson, 1983.

Liebman, Charles S., and Eliezer Don-Yehiya. *Civil Religion in Israel: Traditional Judaism and Political Culture in the Jewish State.* Berkeley, Los Angeles & London: The University of California Press, 1983.

———. *Religion and Politics in Israel.* Bloomington: Indiana University Press, 1984.

Livneh, Eliezer, Yosef Nedavah, and Yoram Efrati. *Nili: toledoteha shel he'azah medinit* (Nili: The history of a political audacity). 2d rev. ed. Jerusalem & Tel Aviv: Schocken Publishing Co., 1980.

Lustick, Ian. *Arabs in the Jewish State: Israel's Control of a National Minority.* Modern Middle East Series, no. 6, sponsored by the Center for Middle Eastern Studies, the University of Texas at Austin. Austin & London: University of Texas Press, 1980.

Luz, Ehud. "Zion and Judenstaat: The Significance of the 'Uganda' Controversy." In *Essays in Modern Jewish History: A Tribute to Ben Halpern,* edited by Frances Malino & Phyllis Albert, pp. 217–37. Rutherford, Madison, & Teaneck, N.J.: Fairleigh Dickinson University Press, 1982.

Marmorstein, Emile. *Heaven at Bay: The Jewish Kulturkampf in the Holy Land.* London: Oxford University Press, 1969.

Meyer, Lawrence. *Israel Now: Portrait of a Troubled Land.* New York: Delacorte Press, 1982.

Miron, Dan. *Arb'a panim basifrut ha'ivrit* (Four faces of Hebrew literature). 2d ed. Jerusalem & Tel Aviv: Schocken Publishing Co., 1975.

―――. "Modern Hebrew Literature: Zionist Perspectives and Israeli Realities." *Prooftexts* 4:1 (January 1984): 49–69.

Nash, Stanley. *In Search of Hebraism: Shai Hurwitz and His Polemics in the Hebrew Press.* Studies in Judaism in Modern Times, edited by Jacob Neusner, vol. 3. Leiden: E. J. Brill, 1980.

Nedavah, Yosef, ed. *Yosef Lishansky ish Nili: ketavim, mikhtavim, divrei zikhronot* (Joseph Lishansky: Papers and letters). Tel Aviv: Hadar Publishing Co., 1977.

Neumann, Nili. "Sh'elot 'al yahasei amanut umakom" (Questions of the relationship of art and locale). *Kav* 4/5 (November 1982): 3–5.

Neusner, Jacob. *Stranger at Home: "The Holocaust," Zionism and American Judaism.* Chicago & London: The University of Chicago Press, 1981.

Nietzsche, Friedrich. *On the Advantage and Disadvantage of History for Life.* Translated with introduction by Peter Preuss. Indianapolis & Cambridge: Hackett Publishing Co., 1980.

Notav, Eitan [Shraga Gafni]. "Hakerav 'al mivtsar viliams" (The battle for the Williams Fortress). *Alef,* no. 1 (Spring 1950). Reprinted in *Prozah* (August–September 1977): 20–21.

Oren, Yosef. "V'el motsa'ah tashuv" (And to its source shall it return). *M'oznayim* 42:3 (Shevat 5736) [February 1976]: 201–204.

Oz, Amos. *In the Land of Israel.* Translated from Hebrew by Maurie Goldberg-Bartura. San Diego, New York & London: Harcourt Brace Jovanovich Publishers, 1983.

Pesah, Hayim. "Idi'ologiah upo'etikah: bein Ratosh LePound" (Ideology and poetics: Between Ratosh and Pound). *M'oznayim* 54:3–4 [February–March 1982]: 9–14.

Ratosh, Yonatan [Uriel Halpern]. *'Eineinu nesu'ot el hashilton: hazit hamahar shel tenu'at hashihrur* (Looking towards sovereignty: The front for tomorrow of the liberation movement). Foreword by Prof. Joseph Klausner. Tel Aviv: Z. Schiff Publishing Co., [1938].

―――. *Mas'a hapetihah: bamoshav hava'ad 'im shelihei hata'im (moshav rish'on)* (The opening discourse: In executive session with the agents of the cells [First Meeting]). [Tel Aviv]: Hava'ad legibbush hano'ar ha'ivri, Summer 1944.

―――. *1967 umah hal'ah? shalom 'ivri* (1967 and what next? A Hebrew peace). Tel Aviv: Hadar Publishing Co., 1967.

―――. *Shirim* (Poems). Tel Aviv: Hadar Publishing Co., 1977.

―――. *R'eshit hayamim: petihot 'ivriyot* (The first days: Hebrew overtures). Tel Aviv: Hadar Publishing Co., 1982.

―――. *Sifrut yehudit bileshon ha'ivrit: petihot bevikkoret ubeva'ayot halashon* (Jewish literature in the Hebrew language: Introductory studies in critical and linguistic problems). Edited with an introduction by Shin Shifra. Vol. 1. Tel Aviv: Hadar Publishing Co., 1982.

―――, ed. *Minitsahon lemapolet: me'asef Alef* (From victory to collapse: An *Alef* anthology). Tel Aviv: Hadar Publishing Co., 1976.

Rosenberg, Shalom. "Zehut ve'idi'ologiah bahagut hayehudit bat zemanenu: mas'a bemeta-safah" (Identity and ideology in contemporary Jewish thought: An essay in meta-language). *Bitefutsot hagolah* 18(77–78) (Summer 1976): 5–15.

Rotem, Ya'akov. "Yonatan Ratosh mikarov: tagim lidemuto" (Yonatan Ratosh from up close: Some profile details). *'Al hamishmar,* April 3, 1981.

Rubinstein, Amnon. *Lihiot 'am hofshi* (To be a free people). Jerusalem & Tel Aviv: Schocken Publishing Co., 1977.

———. *The Zionist Dream Revisited: From Herzl to Gush Emunim and Back.* New York: Schocken Books, 1984.

Samet, Moshe. *Hakonflikt odot missud 'erkei hayahadut bimedinat yisra'el* (The conflict over the institutionalization of Jewish values in the State of Israel). Papers in Sociology. Jerusalem: The Eliezer Kaplan School of Economics and Social Sciences of the Hebrew University, 1979.

Samuel, Maurice. *Level Sunlight.* New York: Alfred A. Knopf, 1953.

Schnall, David J. *Radical Dissent in Contemporary Israeli Politics: Cracks in the Wall.* Praeger Special Studies. New York: Praeger Publishers, 1979.

Scholem, Gershom. *On Jews and Judaism in Crisis: Selected Essays.* Edited by Werner J. Dannhauser. New York: Schocken Books, 1976.

Schwarzschild, Steven S. "On the Theology of Jewish Survival." *CCAR Journal* 15:4 (October 1968): 2–21.

Schweid, Eliezer. *Israel at the Crossroads.* Translated from Hebrew by Alton M. Winters. Philadelphia: Jewish Publication Society, 1973.

———. *Hakarat ha'am hayehudi behinukh beyisra'el* (Identification with the Jewish people in Israeli education). Jerusalem: The Institute of Contemporary Jewry—Sprinzak Division, The Hebrew University, 1973.

———. "Sh'elah shel zehut" (A question of identity. Review of N). *Yedi'ot Aharonot,* October 22, 1976.

Segre, Dan V. *A Crisis of Identity: Israel and Zionism.* Oxford: Oxford University Press, 1980.

Selzer, Michael. *The Wineskin and the Wizard.* New York & London: The Macmillan Co., 1970.

———, ed. *Zionism Reconsidered: The Rejection of Jewish Normalcy.* New York: The Macmillan Co., 1970.

Shabtai, Ya'akov. "'Al hatsabar ve'al yefut hanefesh" (On the sabra and sensitivity). *M'oznayim* 57:5–6 (October–November 1983): 17–18.

Shaked, Gershon. "First Person Plural—Literature of the 1948 Generation." *The Jerusalem Quarterly* 22 (Winter 1982): 105–19.

Shavit, Ya'akov. "Ani bamizrah velibi bama'arav: 'al ha'monizm' hatsiyoni shel Ab'a Ahime'ir (I am in the East and my heart is in the West: On the Zionist "monism" of Abba Ahime'ir). *Keshet* 57 (Fall 5732 [1971]): 149–59.

———. "Hayahasim bein idi'ah lepo'etikah beshirato shel Yonatan Ratosh" (The relationships between idea and poetics in the poetry of Yonatan Ratosh). *Hasifrut* 17 (September 1974): 66–91.

———. "Hakena'anim: sikkum helki" (The Canaanites: A partial summary. Review of N). *Bitefutsot hagolah* 18(79–80) (Winter 5736 [1976]): 179–83.

———. *Merov limedinah: hatenu'ah haRevizionistit—hatokhnit hahityashvutit ve-hara'ayon hahevrati 1925–1935* (From majority to state: The Revisionist movement—The plan for a colonizatory regime and social ideas 1925–1935). Tel Aviv: Yariv Publications in cooperation with Hadar Publishing Co., 1978.

———. Meshorer levado yishkon: 'im moto shel Yonatan Ratosh" (A poet who dwells alone: On the death of Yonatan Ratosh). *Ha'arets,* April 3, 1981.

———. "Hapsevdonim habilti yadu'a" (The unknown pseudonym). *M'oznayim* 54:3–4 [February–March 1982]: 6.

———. *Me'ivri 'ad kena'ani* (From Hebrew to Canaanite). Jerusalem: Domino Press in cooperation with the Rosenberg School of Jewish Studies of Tel Aviv University, 1984.

Shifra, Shin. Interview with Yonatan Ratosh. *Davar,* August 27, 1971.

Shin'ar, Ami. "Vehakena'ani az ba'arets—vehayom" (And the Canaanite was in the Land—then and now). *Ha'arets,* July 18, 1980.

Simon, Ernst. "Ha'im 'od yehudim anahnu?" (Are we Israelis still Jews?) In *Lu'ah Ha'arets* 5712 (1951–52], pp. 27–129. Reprinted in *Perakim beyahadut,* edited by E. Spicehandler and J. Petuchowski, pp. 250–78. Jerusalem & Cincinnati: M. Newman Publishing Co., & Hebrew Union College Press, n.d.

Stavi, Z. Interview with Yonatan Ratosh. *Yedi'ot Aharonot,* February 6, February 20, February 27, 1981.

Tammuz, Binyamin. *Hapardes.* Tel Aviv: Hakibbutz Hame'uhad, 1971. Translated by Richard Flantz, under the title *The Orchard.* Providence: Copper Beech Press, 1984.

———. "Bein 'Eden le'Ofir" (Between Eden and Ophir). *Alef* [Spring 1949]. Reprinted in *Prozah* (August–September 1977): 30.

———. "Pereidah miYonatan Ratosh" [Farewell to Yonatan Ratosh]. *Ha'arets,* April 10, 1981.

———. *Pundako shel Yirmiyahu* (Jeremiah's inn). Jerusalem: Keter Publishing Co., 1984.

———, and Max Wykes-Joyce, eds. *Art in Israel.* [Tel Aviv]: Massadah Publishing Co., 1963.

Teller, J. L. "The Spartan Youth of Israel: A Generation Searches for Its Soul." *Commentary* 10:1 (July 1950): 7–14.

Tevet, Shabtai. *Retsah Arlozorov* (The murder of Arlosoroff). Jerusalem & Tel Aviv: Schocken Publishing Co., 1982.

Tsalmonah, Yig'al. "He'avar hu hahoveh—hakena'anim" (The past is the present—the Canaanites). *Kav* 4/5 (November 1982): 50–57.

Vital, David. *The Origins of Zionism.* Oxford: Clarendon Press, 1975.

———. "Divrei yemei hatsiyonim vedivrei yemei hayahadut" (The history of Zionism and the history of Judaism). *Hatsiyonut* 7 (1981): 7–17.

———. *Zionism: The Formative Years.* Oxford: Clarendon Press, 1982.

Weiler, Gershon. *Tei'okratiah yehudit* (Jewish theocracy). Tel Aviv: Am Oved Publishing Co., 1976.

———. "Emet ahat ushekarim harbeh keneged sheker ehad ve'amitot harbeh" (One truth and many fallacies versus one fallacy and many truths. Review of N.) *Davar,* February 11, 1977.

Weinshal, Ya'akov. *Hadam asher basaf: sippur hayav umoto shel Ya'ir-Avraham Shtern* (The blood on the threshold: The life and death of Ya'ir-Abraham Stern). Edited by Tova Elizur-Segalovitch. 2d enlarged ed. Tel Aviv: Ya'ir Publications, 1978.

Yaffe, A. B. "Bein Natan Alterman leYonatan Ratosh" (Between Natan Altermann and Yonatan Ratosh). *'Al hamishmar,* April 3, 1981.

Yellin-Mor, Natan. *Lohamei herut yisra'el: anashim, ra'ayonot, 'alilot* (Fighters for the freedom of Israel: People, ideas, episodes). Jerusalem: Shikmona Publishing Co., 1975.

Zach, Natan. Interview with Yonatan Ratosh. *Monitin,* April 1981 and May 1981.

Zohar, Ezra. *Bitsevat hamishtar: madu'a af ehad lo kam?* (In the vise of the regime: Why has no one risen up?) 3d ed. Jerusalem: Shikmona Publishing Co., 1975.

Zucker, Norman L. *The Coming Crisis in Israel: Private Faith and Public Policy.* Cambridge & London: The MIT Press, 1973.

INDEX

179

JAMES S. DIAMOND teaches in the Jewish and Near Eastern Studies area program and is Executive Director of the B'nai B'rith Hillel Foundation at Washington University, St. Louis. He is the author of *Barukh Kurzweil and Modern Hebrew Literature*.